The Encyclopedia of
Modern Marbles,
Spheres,
& Orbs

Mark P. Block

4880 Lower Valley Road, Atglen, PA 19310 USA

Flyleaf photo:
Figure 1a. Hand painted. Single gather. *"One Man's World"* Multi-color glass, enamel painted scene, clear glass. Harry Besett, Ken Leslie. 5-1/2 in., ca. 1998. Photo: C. Frieburg. *Courtesy of the artists.*

Library of Congress Cataloging-in-Publication Data

Block, Mark P.
  The encyclopedia of modern marbles, spheres, & orbs / Mark P. Block.
       p. cm.
  Includes bibliographical references and index.
  ISBN 0-7643-2294-X (hardcover)
1. Marbles (Game objects)—Collectors and collecting— United States. 2. Art glass—Collectors and collecting— United States. I. Title.

NK6215.B573 2005
796.2—dc22

2005015142

Designed by "Sue"
Cover design by Bruce Waters
Type set in Lydian BT/Dutch801 Rm BT

ISBN: 0-7643-2294-X
Printed in China

Published by Schiffer Publishing Ltd.
4880 Lower Valley Road
Atglen, PA 19310
Phone: (610) 593-1777; Fax: (610) 593-2002
E-mail: Info@schifferbooks.com

For the largest selection of fine reference books on this and related subjects, please visit our web site at
www.schifferbooks.com
We are always looking for people to write books on new and related subjects. If you have an idea for a book please contact us at the above address.

This book may be purchased from the publisher.
Include $3.95 for shipping.
Please try your bookstore first.
You may write for a free catalog.

In Europe, Schiffer books are distributed by
Bushwood Books
6 Marksbury Ave.
Kew Gardens
Surrey TW9 4JF England
Phone: 44 (0) 20 8392-8585; Fax: 44 (0) 20 8392-9876
E-mail: info@bushwoodbooks.co.uk
Free postage in the U.K., Europe; air mail at cost.

Dedication

For the artists and craftsmen of the rapidly growing and evolving Contemporary Marble Movement. Their works excite and entice our sense of sight. They continually succeed in expanding and extending our appreciation of art, while enhancing the four-decades long tradition of the Studio Glass Movement.

Orb sculpture. Single gather. "Single Orb Construction #8." Various color glass, anodized aluminum. Rolf and Genie Wald. 20 cm. x 18 cm., ca. 1990. *Courtesy of the artists.*

Acknowledgments

An encyclopedic volume such as this one involves the input and cooperation of many individuals. I am fortunate there were many committed, talented, and hardworking people who had an extended hand in providing assistance, either through personal conversation, e-mail, postal mail, or their works to ensure this book would be both detailed and comprehensive. No researcher or writer can effectively bring credit to a subject as broad as the studio art movement without such aid, and to all who's input was given I offer a most appreciative thank you for your willingness to step forward and contribute.

I am extremely grateful for the professional assistance provided by Jill Thomas-Clark, Rights and Reproductions Manager, The Corning Museum of Glass, Corning, New York. The Corning Museum was gracious in providing outstanding images from the museum's collection which have been used to illustrate some of the milestones in glass. These include Roman and Islamic glass, early American glass, American Brilliant Period cut glass, pressed glass, and later studio art glass.

A very special thank you to master glass craftsman Jody Fine, one of the early pioneers of the Contemporary Marble Movement for his Foreword to this volume and set up shots of traditional rod- and cane-cut marble making. He and his wife, Jodene, are a real joy to know and work with.

Thanks to Jerry Kelly, a talented artist who was kind enough to agree to assist in this project by providing exclusive set up shots from work at the torch, as well as background information on the fast growing use of borosilicate and the flame- or torchwork method by many younger artists/craftsmen.

My former camp counselor, Bruce Breslow, of the Moon Marble Company in Bonner Springs, Kansas, has my thanks and appreciation for making available a torchwork glass marble set-up from glass glob to finished piece. Who would have known that all those years ago on the camp ground in Connecticut we would meet up again at a marble meet.

My sincerest thanks and great appreciation to Paul Stankard and Pauline Stankard Iacovino for being important resources in accurately assisting me in ensuring the work of this master glass craftsman was available, illustrated properly, and the written text provides a true picture in words of the artists contributions to the advancement of the Contemporary Marble Movement. Paul Stankard has set new standards in the field of torchwork encasement in the spherical form.

Deborah Levin at Josh Simpson Contemporary Glass for her quick response to my request for images of Simpson Planets and studio. The shots she provided show why this artist's work is both well-know internationally and consistently sought out by collectors. Deborah is always a joy to work with as she remains nestled in the Berkshires with Josh and his terrific staff. You have my sincerest thanks.

Jody Fine, Mike Edmundson, Shell Neisler, Gateson Recko, David Salazar, Paul Stankard, Rolf Wald, and many other artists continued through the months to encourage the research and work that make up this volume—thank you.

My brother Robert, the most knowledgeable person I know in totality of the hobby of marbles, not only deserves, but earned, my deepest thanks for supporting me in focusing on the task at hand. He provided valuable information and resource materials to examine the relationship between antique handmade, machine-made, and contemporary marbles, spheres, and orbs. His tremendous assistance in aiding me in categorizing and valuing all styles and types of marbles, spheres, and orbs has made this publication truly comprehensive. He steered me in appropriate directions to enable this volume to be thorough in its treatment of the subject when comparisons were made to those works of earlier eras.

My deep appreciation and thanks to the Marble Collectors Society of America (MCSA) and Stanley Block for making available for illustration numerous historically important contemporary and antique pieces from the MCSA permanent collection and his own personal collection, along with valuations. And to Claire Block for listening and encouraging me to focus on the positives. It went a long way in making the subsequent realities of this publication possible.

The staff at Schiffer Publishing Ltd. cannot be commended enough for their dedication to producing books of the highest quality in the antiques, collectible, and art market. Peter Schiffer is not just my publisher but also my friend. He has always been supportive of my work, through good days and frustrating days, and continues to encourage me to expand my own boundaries in research and writing. Bruce Waters photography and assistance in this project go unmatched. He is a consummate professional, and I enjoyed having the opportunity to work along side him. The process of photographing nearly 900 images was made less tedious and even pleasurable by the assistance of my wife Ann and daughter Emily. They were both patient and meticulous in bagging, tagging, numbering, and cataloging the works—on two occasions. Jeff Snyder, my editor, took me on again—thank you Jeff for taking all of my calls, answering my questions, and not losing your patience. I enjoy the experience more and more with each project. Nancy Schiffer is a source of wonderment. Her ability to articulate my concepts in the writing process, steer me in directions I may not have otherwise considered, and made the "road less traveled" much less lonely. I want to thank you for your kindness, caring, and thoughtful words.

My thanks to the many artists and craftsmen who contributed both their works, words, encouragement, and belief that bridging the span from ancient, antique handmade and machine-made marbles to today's contemporary glass art was both noble and laudable. I offer you my sincerest thank you for your commitment to quality in each and every piece your produce.

Most importantly, as this book project was being prepared to be "put to bed," a serious family health crisis began for my wife, one that continues. As she faces each day with optimism and vigor she has enabled me to continue to face my own ongoing illness and occasional darkened days. Along with the wonderfully infectious nature of our beautiful young daughter as a family we have faced a "road that's rougher, lonelier, and tougher..." and come to enjoy the beauty as seen from the highest mountains, this after being enveloped by the quiet and stillness of the deepest valley. Where there is life there is hope, and because of the support, encouragement, and prayers of so many we keep hope alive. Thank you!

Contents

Foreword by Jody Fine 9
    My Love Affair with Marbles

Introduction 14

On the Cover 17

Author's Note 19

Chapter One: Concise History of Glass...20
    American Studio Glass Movement 25

Chapter Two: Contemporary Marbles and the Studio Glass Movement 29
    The Expanding World of Contemporary Marbles 31

Chapter Three: More About Marbles 34
    Ancient and Antique Handmade Marbles...34
    American Machine-Made and Foreign Manufactured Marbles 35

Chapter Four: Collecting Contemporary Marbles, Spheres, and Orbs 37
    Building Your Collection..37
    Caring For Your Collection...39

Chapter Five: Edition Types 40
    What Contemporary Works to Collect 41
    Regular Stock or Open Edition Production Stock 41
    Prototype's 42
    Limited Editions 43
    Experimental Works 44

Chapter Six: The Artist's Mark 45
    Trademark and Copyright Use 46

Chapter Seven: Crafting Contemporary Marbles, Spheres, and Orbs....................47
    Studio Glass Works..47
    Decorative Glass House Works 47
    Artist's/Craftsman's Work 49
    The Crafting Process 49

Chapter Eight: Grading 54
    Valuating 55

Chapter Nine: More About Marbles, Spheres, and Orbs.......................................56
    Ancient, Mineral and Handmade Non-Glass Marbles, Spheres, and Orbs 57
    Handmade Glass Marbles, Spheres, and Orbs 78
    Swirls..78
    End-of-Day 112
    Lutz or Aventurine Glass 123

American Machine-Made and Foreign Manufactured Glass Marbles
And Contemporary Works 125

Chapter Ten: Mimics, Reproductions and Repairs 148

Chapter Eleven: "Novel and Inventive" Contemporary Marbles,
Spheres, and Orbs 151
Millefiori and Murrini 151

Conclusion: In Their Own Words 229
Artist's/Craftsmen of the Contemporary Marble Movement 229

Glossary of Terms 233

Associated Value Guide 239

Select Bibliography 252

Index 255

Enamel painted stylized
face, black glass base.
Douglas Sweet. 2 3/4 in.,
ca. 1991. *Courtesy of
Robert Block.*

Foreword

My Love Affair with Marbles

Jody Fine

Talk to anyone long enough and they'll have a story to tell about marbles. People are always telling me about their playing days, about their collections, or about how much they love their spheres. They reminisce about a great champion from their neighborhood, a marble treasure found while gardening, or an old jar filled with marbles of all colors and patterns that Grandpa stashed in the attic. It seems to me that marbles are universally cherished as objects of joy, youth, and innocence. People always have a smile when they see a bag of marbles. I see those smiles and think, "This is a mind on marbles." [Figure 1]

When I was in the 4th grade, our schoolyard was demolished so it could be made bigger and better for us kids. Well, of course, with no playground in which to kick a ball around on, our attention naturally turned to playing marbles—and we played for keeps! We played hard, we played smart (sometimes), and we always found ourselves yearning to win that mythological mib. Our teacher, Mr. Santell, ruled over our sport. He was not only our instructor and judge, he was our champion. Many, many marbles changed hands that year and most of them wound up in Mr. Santell's. I'll bet he still has an aggie or two of mine. I can still recall finding the biggest Bennington marble I'd ever seen. I gave it to a girl I liked. Though I've long forgotten who she was, I do remember that Bennington—now that was a beauty! [Figure 2]

Figure 1. Jody Fine at work in the studio. *Photo: John Heisch. Courtesy of Jody Fine.*

CANYON SCHOOL   SANTA MONICA, CALIFORNIA   A6 CLASS OF JANUARY 1964

Figure 2. Jody Fine (*top row, second boy from right*). Mr. Santell (*far left*). Sixth Grade. Canyon School, Santa Monica, California. January 1964. *Courtesy of Jody Fine.*

Long after those days in the schoolyard, I found myself surrounded by marbles every day. Not old collectables from Germany or contemporary machine-made marbles, but those of my own making. During the 1970s I had the good fortune of working with Richard (Dick) Marquis in Berkeley, California. [Figure 3]

Figure 3. Jody Fine working marble stock in the Berkeley, California studio. Mid-1970s. *Courtesy of Jody Fine.*

Contemporary handmade marbles became a bread and butter item for us. We were having such a good time, we asked Jack Wax, another early studio glass artist, to come play and create with us. Our marbles, mostly 7/8" swirls, were sold under the name of H.O.T.M.I.R.E., "Hippies Out To Make It Rich, Enterprises," and I became known as "Captain Marble." The actual details of how I became the Captain are shrouded in mystery. Let's just say that it was a full moon, and chanting may have been involved. Despite the viscous rumors, no tattooing occurred. [Figure 4]

Figure 4. Jody Fine at lecture and demonstration, University of California, Los Angeles (UCLA). Richard Marquis, the professor, during the H.O.T.M.I.R.E. years. *Courtesy of Jody Fine.*

In those early days of contemporary marble making, the marble crafting community consisted of Dick Marquis, Jack Wax, Ro Purser, and myself. At the time, sales were made primarily through arts and craft galleries, marbles were a perfect "peoples" item. They sparkled like magic and possessed a craftsman's quality equal to anything else in the exploding contemporary glass movement. Best of all, they were affordable for nearly everyone, allowing all to own a piece of contemporary glass art. [Figure 5]

Figure 5. Marquis Deluxe Studios; original postcard. Reverse reads: "Handmade Glass Marbles and Non-Functional Murrini Glass Teapots from Marquis Deluxe Studios, 1800 Fourth Street, Berkeley, California 94710." *Photo: Charles Frizzell. Courtesy of Jody Fine.*

I suppose you could say we had stumbled onto something, because soon other talented glass blowers began making handmade contemporary marbles. One of the first glass artists to seriously approach marble crafting was Josh Simpson. Josh let me know he was beginning to produce marbles. Anyone who knows Josh Simpson understands he is an extremely respectful and courteous man. He kindly acknowledged my contribution to the craft and assured me that his work would be distinct and unique. Indeed it was. I believe Josh's "Planet" marbles opened the door to "marble-as-legitimate-art-form," thus spawning a wave of new ideas for the sphere.

While marbles had always been just one part of my studio work, new glass blowers began to specialize in marble making. Geoffrey Beetem, Harry Besett, James Holmes, Mark Matthews, David Salazar, Douglas Sweet, and Rolf and Genie Wald were but a few among the first wave of dedicated "sphere-ologists." [Figure 6]

Numerous others throughout the 1980s and 1990s, mostly working in the cane- and rod cut method, then followed them. From the later 1990s through today we have seen the invasion of the home and studio flame-working borosilicate craftsmen. These men and women are changing the way we think about marbles. Now, as I survey all the variety of creative styles and methods of marble-making today, I find myself amazed and a little envious. That this "scene" has grown so quickly and so creatively makes me proud to have been at the forefront of the contemporary movement.

Even before the beginning of contemporary marble making, there were marble collectors. The growth of both contemporary marble making and the resurgence of marble collecting are due largely to the dedication and deep commitments of longtime collectors. With the early support of the Marble

Figure 6. Jim Holmes, later of Chatham Glass; Jody Fine "hard at work." Holmes was the first employee of J. Fine Glass. The original "kid marble." *Courtesy of Jody Fine.*

Collectors Society of America (MCSA), contemporary marble makers were introduced to a world beyond the craft and art market. The Block family, Stanley, founder and chairman of the MCSA in 1975, Claire, Robert, and Mark, have worked tirelessly to document, authenticate, and bring marble collecting into the mainstream of collectible hobbies. Bert Cohen busily traversed the country promoting marbles and marble meets, making sure he included me and many other contemporary marble makers. And, of course, there are the hundreds of collectors who by virtue of their undying enthusiasm have spread the fever of marble collecting throughout the land.

After twenty-eight years of living with marbles every day, the little orbs continue to bring me a sense of wonder and joy. Though, I still don't know all that much about them. I really *should* know the difference between an Onionskin and an End of Day marble. Gazing at the myriad of marble creations made by human hands and modern machines, we may be reminded of long-forgotten memories. Perhaps we'll recall the beauty of those marbles found in the yard, or maybe even be moved to climb the attic stairs and fetch Grandpa's jar. I might even remember the girl who got that big Bennington back in 1962. If Mr. Santell, my schoolyard marble king, should see this book he'll be able to identify all of the marbles he took off us hapless children. I just hope he still has them. I've got mine.

Everybody read this book. Then go find a marble. You won't regret it.

Knuckle down and shoot 'em straight!

Captain Marble
AKA Jody Fine, BTU
Austin, Texas [Figure 7]

Figure 7. Assorted glass rods and swirls. ca. 1990s. Jody Fine. *Courtesy of the Artist.*

Introduction

Collecting contemporary marbles, spheres, and orbs can be both a wildly exciting undertaking and at times a truly confusing hobby. What are we to make of these round ornamental and decorative objects? Are they the work of serious artists and craftsmen or the whimsies of glass workers whose instinctive attention is devoted to the more long recognized and accepted forms of studio glass, including platters, bowls, and goblets, functional vases and perfumes, paperweights and other items of use and ornamentation?

Since the publication of *Contemporary Marbles and Related Art Glass* [Schiffer Publishing 2001] there has been an overwhelmingly positive response to what I came to term the Contemporary Marble Movement, from serious and neophyte contemporary marble collectors and a continuously growing number of glass art collectors. And possibly more important, the world of contemporary marbles, spheres, and orbs continues to expand unabated. The growing number of artists/craftsmen who maintain it is important as they continue to push the boundaries of this movement through the works they produce.

In part, as a result of conversations with nationally recognized glass art curators and prominent collectors, a consensus has developed around the genesis that the foundation of contemporary marble collecting is based on the toy or "child's playthings" of earlier generations. To bridge time and generations, or at the very least contribute to the written and visual historical analysis of antique handmade and later machine-made marbles and their contemporary handmade studio art "cousins" it became increasingly important to go back to the beginning. By doing so, time allowed for the important research necessary to compare, contrast, and illustrate both old and new works, thus providing an opportunity to explain and reveal the close relationship these "child's playthings" and today's studio art have with each other; all while simultaneously exhibiting the divergent path the handmade studio artist's work has achieved. This has occurred in both technical and stylistic ability.

In studying the field of contemporary marbles, spheres, and orbs and viewing a seemingly endless number of works by hundreds of artists/craftsmen I kept coming back to the original research questions I posed in my outline for this book:

> *Is there a definitive difference in the design, type, and style of contemporary handmade marbles, spheres, and orbs, one that is fundamentally different from the children's marbles of earlier generations? If so, are these works ones that can be considered true glass art, or merely extensions of what has previously been crafted?*

After months of research, writing, photographing, classifying, and studying the works and those who created them I found the answers to the questions posed both intriguing and somewhat different than those I had gone into the process with when this project first began. As you read this book and view the nearly nine hundred images in it you will have the opportunity to answer these questions for yourself. Will there be fundamental differences in the way collectors and glass art experts view and interpret the works of today's contemporary marble, sphere, and orb studio artist? Will all agree that many of the works have a readily recognized antique or machine-made look? While others placed in specific categories might then rightfully be described as "Novel and Inventive" contemporary marbles, spheres, and orbs? And as such, can agreement on all of the categories and placement of works within them in this volume be likely? As a researcher, for now the finality to these questions for me remain unanswered. However, the more important function of this book is to expose the reader to the extensive variety of works being crafted today, as they are compared and contrasted to earlier "child's playthings" of other generations. As the Contemporary Marble Movement grows it is likely we will continue to see shifting opinions on what I have come to term "novel and inventive contemporary" or "true contemporary" marbles, spheres, and orbs.

The field of art, any art, is an ever-changing one. A landscape in our world filled with colorful characters, both interesting and intriguing works, and intensely personal pieces. Whether the artist works as a sculptor, painter, jewelry maker, glass artist or in any of the other mediums used to express themselves, their work is inherently subjective. In this book I offer you my assessment of the Contemporary Marble Movement as it exists in the earliest years of the twenty-first century.

In researching I have found the best way to look at the hobby of collecting contemporary marbles, spheres, and orbs is to gaze beyond the artists' works themselves to the long history marbles have played in use as children's toys and games. By doing so, you will see that the advent and growth of the contemporary work is a natural outgrowth of those child's toys that came before them. These include the antique German handmade marbles of the late nineteenth and early twentieth century, followed by the millions of machine-made marbles produced by glass factories in the United States and later Japan, Mexico, and elsewhere around the globe.

While all things have a beginning, these spherical objects of both interest and beauty are collected by many, appreciated by more, and have a unique and documented history. Rarely does anything in the arts and crafts movement begin in a vacuum without benefit of predecessors to pave the way for more refined or accepted forms of art. Contemporary marbles, spheres, and orbs have earned a rightful place next to their paperweight cousins and other forms of glass art as an exciting addition to the studio glass movement. A movement begun in the mid-1970s has rolled into a serious full-fledged artistic tide on its own merits. All with the widely accepted notion that while marbles are simply "child's playthings" the works of the artists and craftsmen of the Contemporary Marble Movement are done strictly for ornamental and decorative purposes.

As you will see throughout the pages of this book, in both color illustration and text, the preconceived notions you might have had as to what a contemporary marble, sphere or orb is may be quite different from what is actually being crafted today. All by some very talented individuals and studios.

It is important to note early in this text, the purpose of this book is **NOT** to provide a litany of artists or biographical book of craftsmen. This was first accomplished in the earlier volume, *Contemporary Marbles and Related Art Glass*, and will be addressed again in detail in future books. Rather, the overriding goal of this book is the significance of comparing and contrasting the works being crafted today with those that provided the inspiration and impetus for the glass and china, mineral and other works available today. Additionally, this book will focus important attention on works that have no apparent relationship to others done at an earlier time in history. Both unique and beautiful, these pieces dazzle the eye and entice the imagination of the viewer to wonder aloud "How did they do that"? While it is unlikely that question will be answered satisfactorily for everyone, it is hoped you will close this book and feel a sense of wonderment, curiosity, and interest.

Whether you are a first time collector, a serious aficionado of contemporary marbles, spheres, and orbs, or one who simply but gratefully receives one as a gift, the works of the talented artists and craftsmen who are illustrated within the chapters of this book will hopefully give you a moment to pause and reflect on the tremendous achievement that has been made in taking the art of the sphere and expanding the confined boundaries well beyond anything that could have been expected a few short years ago.

You will find with each illustration a detailed caption identifying the piece or pieces. The size, year crafted, and artist/craftsmen will be identified whenever possible. This is primarily done so you can begin to compartmentalize the styles you most like for your own collection and the artists who craft them. After all, in collecting, the hunt for the most beautiful works is at least half the fun of the hobby. You'll also be encouraged by the illustrated works to expand your own boundaries in the manner which you display your collection and how you have others view the pieces you enjoy most.

As with any guide, the accompanying valuations assigned to the works in this book are only as accurate as the market at the time of writing. Price fluctuations occurring with glass art are not uncommon, and therefore, those utilized in this publication should be viewed only as a guide at the time of publication. No warranty is made by the author, either expressed or implied, in assuming any loss or gain as a result of any valuation published. What is known is the value of contemporary marbles, spheres, and orbs continues to increase in many instances. While this does not necessarily occur proportionate to each other, as a general trend it is clearly taking place.

Though with any collectible as you have no doubt read or heard, the most important value is the one you place on the piece yourself. The enjoyment you will receive from your collection cannot be quantified in dollars, pounds, euros or any other monetary form. Rather, it is a value of enjoyment and appreciation for excellence in crafting as well as the uniqueness of the art form itself.

My hope is that you will gain both knowledge and appreciation as you go through the pages of this book. The effort to continue documenting the history of the Contemporary Marble Movement begun with *Contemporary Marbles and Related Art Glass* is a necessary one as the art form expands and openly welcomes new collectors. Therefore, let me offer my own personal welcome to the wonderful world of contemporary marbles, spheres, and orbs, and most importantly—Enjoy Glass™!

Mark Block
Trumbull, Connecticut

On the Cover

Recognized as a pioneer in the studio glass movement for promoting flame working techniques through demonstrations and teaching, Paul J. Stankard has achieved the highest respect and status within the glass art world.

Stankard has earned an international following for his Floral Glass Paperweights and Botanical Glass Sculpture. The hallmark of Stankard's career has been his ability to invigorate his glass art with originality and content, evidenced by his recent Botanical Orbs series.

The Orb series has set new standards for botanical themes in glass. In the artist's hands, the flame working process gives the glass delicacy and detail, referred to by Stankard as organic credibility. The Honeycomb Bouquet Swarm, a commissioned piece illustrated on the cover of this book, is among Stankard's most ambitious work to date.

Paul Stankard, considered among the top flame working artists in the field, has been discovered by the marble enthusiasts vaulting him to the top of the Contemporary Marble Movement, placing his work in the center of a rapidly evolving American glass art form. Influenced by a love of poetry, especially the words of Walt Whitman, Stankard demonstrates an uncanny ability to "freeze nature in glass."

Stankard's work is in the permanent collections of over forty museums internationally and is one of the most respected glass artists in the world. He has integrated personal symbols into his glass art through the use of *pate de vere* masks, sculpted figures, word canes, and insects. His techniques have elevated the glass flowers to a three dimensional view, evidenced by the development of the Orb series. Stankard invites the viewer to experience the work from a 360-degree perspective, which highlights the *trompe l'oeil* illusions achieved by flame worked glass.

The perfection of design, clarity of crystal, originality of his vision, and the high level of risk invested into each piece is clearly visible. Stankard's glass art celebrates a new standard for artists and craftspeople to be challenged by. [Figure 8-13]

Figure 8. Lilac Honeycomb Bouquet Swarm Orb. Flamework. Multi-flora, berries, honeycomb, honeybees. *Commission.* Paul J. Stankard. 5-5/8 in., ca. 2004. *Courtesy of the author.*

Figure 9. Lilac Honeycomb Bouquet Swarm Orb. Flamework. Multi-flora, berries, honeycomb, honeybees. *Commission.* (*close-up*) Paul J. Stankard. 5-5/8 in., ca. 2004. *Courtesy of the author.*

Figure 10. Lilac Honeycomb Bouquet Swarm Orb. Flamework. Multi-flora, berries, honeycomb, honeybees. *Commission.* (*close-up*) Paul J. Stankard. 5-5/8 in., ca. 2004. *Courtesy of the author.*

Figure 11. Honeycomb Bouquet Swarm Orb. Handwritten notes, sketches. *Commission.* Paul J. Stankard. 8 1/2 x 11 in. ca. 2004. *Courtesy of Paul Stankard.*

Figure 12. Paul Stankard working at the torch on component for Honeycomb Bouquet Swarm Orb. *Commission.* (*close-up*) ca. 2004. *Courtesy of Paul Stankard.*

Figure 13. Paul Stankard working at the torch on Honeycomb Bouquet Swarm Orb. *Commission.* ca. 2004. *Courtesy of Paul Stankard.*

Author's Note

The author has compiled the information contained in this book from what are recognized and believed to be authoritative sources, and believes that it is both accurate and factual as of the date printed. All written information and illustrations are offered only as a guide to the reader concerning the subjects mentioned. The author makes no representations regarding the interpretation that may be obtained by the reader. It shall be the responsibility of the reader to determine the suitability of any information mentioned. Because industry agreement does not universally exist on the use of the terms "torchwork" and "flamework," the author uses them interchangeably within the text. Additionally, whenever appropriate the author uses the terms "piece(s)," and "work(s)," to discuss contemporary handmade marbles, spheres, and orbs. This is done most often when the item discussed is not an antique German handmade or machine-made marble as generally recognized by collectors and experts in the field.

In a number of instances throughout the body of this book works have been illustrated and captioned that were crafted by unidentified artists and craftsmen. In these cases the pieces are noted as being "Unsigned. Unidentified." Efforts have been made to ensure that wherever possible, primarily through the artist's mark works have been correctly attributed to their maker(s). With over 900 objects illustrated and more not used in this volume, on occasion a piece has been included without artist/craftsman provenance. This has been done only when a specific work or piece could not be positively identified by the author or other contributors to this book. The artist's mark is discussed in more detail in chapter six.

All copyright and trademark works and names illustrated and discussed in this book are the properties of the artists, craftsmen and studios, and companies that own them. No attempt to infringe on any copyrights and trademarks has been made in this book. The research for this book is solely the work of the author. This book is presented for the education and entertainment of the readership.

Chapter 1
Concise History of Glass

Figure 14. The Morgan Cup. Roman Empire, first half of the first century A.D. Translucent deep blue and opaque white glass; blown, case, carved, cut. H. 6.2 cm. 52.1.93. *Courtesy of The Corning Museum of Glass, gift of Arthur A. Houghton.*

In order to know where you are going in collecting contemporary marbles, spheres, and orbs, it is both helpful and important to put into context this relatively new collectible within the history of glass as an artistic medium. As has been said, only when you know where you have been can you begin to know where you can venture forth to. Therefore, this succinct history of glass will provide you with a brief overview of the centuries old tradition of glass making. From this overview you can almost place yourself in the position of one who approaches glass as a medium for creativity, a sense of the importance history plays in an artist/craftsman's life, and the necessity to appreciate the trial and error that is a continuing part of the glass makers process in creating works of both functional and decorative art.

The origin of glass is not completely known, though discoveries appear to suggest the first pieces of glass were created nearly twenty-five hundred years Before the Common Era (B.C.E.). Most likely discovered accidentally by firing clay pots so hot they turned to glass. Beginning to become prominent in regions of the eastern Mediterranean around 50-100 B.C.E., what is apparent is that glass gained in importance during the Roman Empire where it was a highly regarded commodity made available to the wealthy. As glassmaking and glass blowing developed over the centuries it became more accessible to those who were not of the wealthiest class. [Figure 14]

While glass making is a science that requires precise recipes and artists today can spend years perfecting their own formulas, glass is essentially a composite of sand, soda, potash, and lime—and most importantly—heat.

With the decline of the Roman Empire glassmaking fell out of favor until the rise of the Islamic world and its culture of beautifully colored, decorated, and delicately shaped glass. [Figure 15]

Figure 15. The Corning Ewer. Western Asia or Egypt, ca. app. 1000. Colorless and transparent light green glass; blown, cased, cut. H. 16.0 cm. 85.1.1. *Courtesy of The Corning Museum of Glass, Corning, New York, United States, Clara S. Peck Endowment.*

And while glass continued to entice and entrance, it would rise and fall with the various powers of the world until the Italian Renaissance. The glass of Venice and the island of Murano, then the centers of world glassmaking, are rich in their beauty and elegance. [Figure 16]

Figure 16. Covered goblet with filigree decoration. Italy, probably Venice, ca. app. 1575-1625. Colorless and opaque white glass; vetro. H. 34.9 cm. 64.3.9. *Courtesy of The Corning Museum of Glass, Corning, New York, United States.*

While used for practical purposes, this glass was made with an eye toward the importance of design and style. Long have collectors admired the sinuous beauty and linear quality of Italian glass. Using only a few simple tools, the glassmakers of these times and those that came later in the great cities of Europe endured working with tremendous heat and fire to create beautiful forms. Always working to increase their knowledge and skills, glassmakers would often compete with each other to produce the most uniform or precise piece possible, all while maintaining a sense of individuality. Though we know this individuality was confined within the necessity to produce pieces that would be accepted, whether by kings and queens, nobles or commoners.

It is believed that there were nearly a half dozen glassblowers who came to Jamestown in what is today's Virginia from Great Britain, thereby expanding the sphere of influence to the New World itself. Generations of glassmakers and blowers toiled long hours to support their families. Many of these workers dying at an early age from the inhaling of glass dust in the

Figure 17. Bowl and Pitcher. Saratoga (Mountain) Glass Works, Mount Pleasant, New York, United States, ca. app. 1844-1865. Transparent aquamarine glass; blown, applied, tooled. H. 21.8 cm. (pitcher) 50.4.447 *Courtesy of The Corning Museum of Glass.*

Figure 18. Book. United States, Corning, New York, United States. J. Hoare & Co., app. 1900. Colorless glass; cut, engraved. H. 10.4 cm. 74.4.187. *Courtesy of The Corning Museum of Glass, Corning, New York, gift of W.E. Doherty Jr.;* Cordial, goblet and wine glass. United States, Corning, New York, Steuben Division, Corning Glass Works, designed by Frederick Carder, probably engraved by Henry Keller, 1920s. Colorless and transparent purple glass; blown, cased, engraved. H. (tallest) 25.3 cm. 69.4.174; 69.4.172; 69.4.173. *Courtesy of The Corning Museum of Glass, Corning, New York, gift of Mr. and Mrs. Samuel B. Feld;* Fingerbowl and plate, *Russian* pattern. United States, 1881-1900. Colorless; blown, cut. D. (plate) 34.0 cm. 57.4.9. *Courtesy of The Corning Museum of Glass, Corning, New York, gift of Miss F. Ethel Wickham;* Plate, *Russian* pattern. United States, Corning, New York, T.G. Hawkes & Co., app. 1906. Colorless glass; blown, cut. D. 34.0 cm. 51.4.536. *Courtesy of The Corning Museum of Glass, Corning, New York, gift of T.G. Hawkes;* Champagne and goblet, *Russian* pattern. United States, app. 1882-1900. Colorless; blown, cut. H. (goblet) 15.8 cm. 57.4.9. *Courtesy of The Corning Museum of Glass, Corning, New York, gift of Miss F. Ethel Wickham;* Vase. United States, Corning, New York, Hunt Glass Works, app. 1900. Colorless and transparent turquoise blue glass; blown, cased, cut. H. 31.5 cm. 92.4.155. *Courtesy of The Corning Museum of Glass, Corning, New York, gift of Robert Rockwell III and the Rockwell Museum;* Tray, *Assyrian* pattern. United States, Corning, New York, H.P. Sinclaire & Co., app. 1909-1918. Colorless; blown, cut. L. 30.5 cm. L.193.4.76. *Courtesy of The Corning Museum of Glass, Corning, New York, private collection.*

etching, cutting or engraving processes. And while highly collectible today, the glass of earlier times is most often found in the great museum collections throughout the world. Having survived the years of use and high likelihood of breakage, glass of the ancients, the Europeans, and even early American's was done more as regional cottage industries throughout the world rather than as organized production on a large scale. [Figure 17]

The change from glassmaker to glassworker occurred with the advent of the industrial revolution. Glass could now be mass produced, or at least what was considered mass production at the time in the United States and Europe. Cut glass and later pressed glass became available to nearly everyone. With the cost so low that an entire table could be set with beautiful bowls and compotes, tumblers and dishes, glass was turned out from patterns often designed by the shift supervisor. Companies came and went over the years of the nineteenth and early twentieth century, but the patterns they created endured and are collected today. [Figure 18, 19]

Sadly, artists who had the desire to design for glass had little choice but to work in commercial factories where nearly all glass was made strictly for utilitarian purposes. Rarely, did an artist have an opportunity to craft for aesthetic reasons only. However, the glass houses of Lalique, Orrefors, Steuben, Tiffany, Waterford, and others produced some of the most beautiful pieces of glass. Many of the ornately designed and decorated works were highly sought after by early glass collectors. Change came slow, but when it did a new craft later to become art was born. The year 1962 saw what is considered to be a major turning point in the individual production of glass by artists and craftsmen. [Figure 20]

Figure 19. Pressed Glass. American. c. mid-20th century. *Courtesy of The Corning Musuem of Glass.*

Figure 20. Gazelle Bowl. Clear glass with etched images. Steuben. Sidney Waugh. Corning, New York, United States. ca. 1935. 90.4.244. *Courtesy of The Corning Museum of Glass.*

American Studio Glass Movement

Harvey Littleton, a college professor, held two workshops in early to mid-1962 at the Toledo Museum of Art, Ohio. Littleton had begun experimenting with melting glass a couple of years earlier, and with the aid of a friend, Dominic Labino, who worked in the commercial scientific field, they built a small furnace and began creating rudimentary blown pieces. These workshops set the stage for molten glass to be both workable and available to artists working in private studios for the first time. With eleven students from various fields of the arts, Littleton and Labino had done what no one had previously accomplished, and by doing so changed the manner and effort in which glassblowing could be treated as art.

Not much later, while making a survey of glass educational opportunities in Europe, Littleton met noted glassmaker Erwin Eisch in Germany. Soon after his return to the United States, Littleton began teaching glassblowing at the University of Wisconsin, Madison, Wisconsin. This is the first recorded class in glassblowing to be part of the permanent curriculum of an American university.

A couple of short years later in 1964, Dominic Labino built a furnace to be used in glassblowing demonstrations at Columbia University, New York City, New York, during the World Congress of Craftsmen. Harvey Littleton, his students, Erwin Eisch, and others gave demonstrations in glassblowing.

The late-1960s and 1970s was a time of experimentation. While an emphasis was placed on new technologies and education, artists were free to express themselves, though somewhat confined by their limitations on knowledge and the availability of material. Self-expression became a central element of the creative process and sales took a back seat to the excitement generated by the artist's ability to create primarily hot glass forms. With the medium so new there was limited interest by either galleries or museums and virtually no critics to rank or rate these early studio glass artists.

A revival of techniques used in the earlier Art Nouveau period such as feathering and fuming were both popular and important in establishing the artist as a serious representative of the new glass movement. And because many of the first students of Littleton and Labino were sculptors and ceramicists, the search for form versus technique in crafting a well-executed object was one that often created a tension within the artists work. [Figure 21, 22]

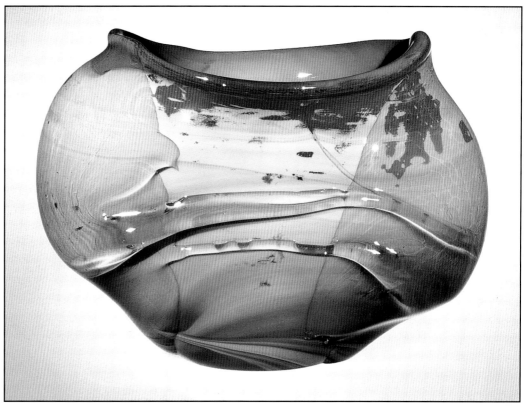

Figure 21. Vessel. Blown #475 fiberglass marbles, silver, oxide decoration. Harvey Littleton (b. 1922), United States. W. 11.4 cm; D. 11.5 cm. app. 1965. 66.4.47 *Courtesy of The Corning Museum of Glass, purchased with the aid of funds from the National Endowment for the Arts.*

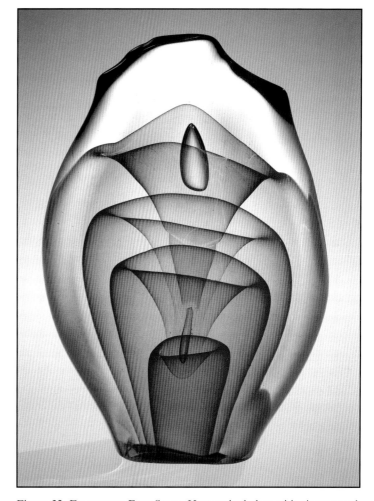

Figure 22. Emergence Four-Stage. Hot-worked glass with air trap and internal gold veiling. Dominick Labino (1910-1987), United States, Grand Rapids, Ohio. H. 22.4 cm. ca. 1975. 764.21 *Courtesy of The Corning Museum of Glass, purchased with the aid of funds from the National Endowment for the Arts.*

It is well recognized today that one of the most important acts to come out of the early Studio Glass Movement was the awarding of a Fulbright Scholarship to Dale Chihuly. Chihuly holds the distinction of being the first American glassblower to work at the famed Venini glass factory in Italy. The wealth of knowledge he absorbed and brought back to the United States proved to be an invaluable addition to propelling the Studio Glass Movement forward. Secondly, Richard Marquis, awarded a Fulbright-Hayes fellowship, became the first American to work in Murano glass at Venini. The contribution these two individuals made to the Studio Glass Movement cannot be emphasized enough. Through their training, experimenting, teaching, and crafting, these two men along with their contemporaries, men like Marvin Lipofsky and Fritz Driesbach among others, established themselves as the preeminent students of the early Studio Glass Movement. Their work and prominence continue to encourage others to embark on a path of exploration of the unique medium of glass. [Figure 23, 24]

Figure 23. Fern Green Tower. Blown, steel structure. Dale Chihuly (b. 1941), United States, Seattle, Washington. H. 335.3 cm. ca. 2000. 2000.4.6. *Courtesy of The Corning Museum of Glass, gift of the artist.*

Figure 24. Marquiscarpa #26. Blown, fused, kiln-formed, wheel-carved, assembled. Richard Marquis. United States. H. 16.2 cm. ca. 1991. 93.4.90. *Courtesy of The Corning Museum of Glass, part gift of Susan Steinhauser and Daniel Greenberg, Ruth T. Summers and the artist.*

As the 1970s gave way to the final decades of the twentieth century, studio glass exhibitions became more plentiful and artists and craftsmen became better known. Now, even galleries and museums would begin to truly accept and appreciate the glassworks done by talented individuals to be marketed as a recognized American craft.

Additionally, the Studio Glass Movement spawned a new industry for glass and glassmaking products. The important tools and materials necessary for crafting clear and colored glass rods in soft and borosilicate glass, furnaces, and annealing ovens became commercially available to the glass artist. This was extremely important for those who chose not to or were unable to build and create their own tools. Most importantly, change would soon occur in glass composition. From the earliest use of Johns Manville #475 glass marbles in the early 1960s, along with soda, beer, liquor, and other bottles in the 1960s and 1970s, to the important glass cullet offered by glass companies of the Ohio River Valley, and finally later to batch glass. This glass was specifically made for the studio glass artist and had a tremendous impact on the ability and quality of the studio glass crafted during each of these historical time periods. [Figure 25]

Figure 25. Johns Manville #475 Fiberglass marbles. Johns Manville, a Berkshire Hathaway Company. 7/8 in., ca. app. 1955-1969. *Courtesy of the author.*

Also, as time went on the debate between "art versus craft" began to take hold and pushed aside many of the other issues associated with working individually. This debate continues even today, though with less vociferous and ardent supporters on either side of the issue. What with new interest in the 1980s and 1990s in the flame- or torchwork method of crafting, the art of *pate de vere*, kiln work, cold work, and slump worked glass; little time was left for debate on any issue.

As the increasingly prominent role of women working in glass [Schiffer Publishing, 2003, book of the same name] attests, the most active interest of the artist is less in debating the affects of their craft and, more importantly, focused on the art they create. This is seen most importantly in the additions museums have made in including studio glass in their contemporary art collections, not simply in decorative craft exhibitions.

Also, the serious studio glass artist of the twenty-first century is looked upon much differently than the loner, for example, working in a tent in the woods as Josh Simpson did early in his career. Many of today's artists have established studios based not just on creativity, but a high level of professionalism as well. [Figure 26-28]

Figure 26. Josh Simpson. ca. app. early-1970s. *Courtesy of Josh Simpson.*

Figure 27. Josh Simpson Contemporary Glass. Aerial view; studio, property. ca. late-twentieth century. *Photo: Tommy Olof Elder. Courtesy of Josh Simpson.*

This means the artist must also concentrate on the business of operating a working studio, and the teamwork necessary to encourage and enable assistants, apprentices, and students the ability to develop strategies to stand out from others not just in the work they produce but the way in which they market their work.

The past ten years has brought an increased interest by the collector in building a truly personal and worthy collection, expanding the fellowship of the collecting community, and encouraging artists to maintain a healthy competition leading to a stable market intended to enhance the overall value of the works.

With schools and programs devoted to graduating students with degrees in many disciplines of the glass movement it is expected that a continuation of prolific glass artists will come forward, allowing the public to view and purchase some of the most innovative and exciting creations ever crafted in the art of glassmaking.

Figure 28. Megaplanet. Single gather. Josh Simpson. Josh Simpson Contemporary Glass. 8 in., ca. 2004. *Photo: Tommy Olof Elder. Courtesy of Josh Simpson.*

Chapter Two
Contemporary Marbles and the Studio Glass Movement

With the rapid development of the studio glass movement through the 1960s and 1970s it is not surprising that glass marble crafting emerged. What is surprising is that it did not occur until August 1974. This is the seminal date in the history of the Contemporary Marble Movement. Prior to this date little is available that indicates glass marbles were being crafted by hand on anything but a rare basis. The occurrence that brought contemporary marbles to the public occurred in Marin County, California, in the summer of 1974. A mere thirty years ago, Richard Marquis and Ro Purser, who later went on to create exciting contemporary murrini spheres, built a two glory hole furnace for use at a Renaissance festival where they dressed in period clothing and hand crafted hundreds of small 7/8" glass swirl marbles over a six week period. [Figure 29, 30]

Figure 29. Marin County Renaissance Faire, Marin County, California. ca. 1975. *Courtesy of Ro Purser.*

Figure 30. Ribbon Swirls. Rod- and cane-cut. Crafted during the Marin County Renaissance Faire, Marin County, California. Richard Marquis, Ro Purser. 7/8 in., ca. 1975. *Courtesy of the author.*

Figure 31. Murrini Sphere. Rod- and cane-cut. Pulled murrini canes, signature 1982 Noble Effort murrini cane. Richard Marquis, Ro Purser. 1-5/8 in., ca. 1982. *Courtesy of the Marble Collectors Society of America.*

Figure 32. Murrini Sphere. Rod- and cane-cut. Pulled murrini canes, signature Ro 99 murrini cane. Ro Purser. 2-1/2 in., ca. 2000. *Courtesy of the author.*

Figure 33. Jody Fine *(second from left)*, Richard Marquis *(second from right)*, Jack Wax *(far right)*. ca. mid-1970s. *Courtesy of Jody Fine.*

The uniqueness of watching these two men work with glass rods, fire, and heat captivated the crowds that attended the festival. And while these first pieces sold for just a few dollars each, that was considered to be a tidy sum for a few minutes work at something they enjoyed doing. Any of these Renaissance Faire marbles are difficult to come across in collecting today, but should you happen upon a glass swirl marble that looks like those illustrated, you may have just found one of the earliest handmade contemporary marbles.

Both Richard Marquis and Ro Purser went on to successful careers in the studio glass field. For a time these two teamed up in a business venture, "Noble Effort," in the early to mid-1980s. This partnership utilized Dick Marquis' artistic and visionary talents in the use of murrini that he studied and continued to develop upon his return from Italy, and Ro Purser brought both creative and exceptional technical skills to the partnership. Collectors prize Noble Effort murrini spheres when they come available for sale. It is easy to identify them by their Noble Effort signature cane, most often with the date. [Figure 31]

Later, after Marquis and Purser went their separate ways, Ro Purser continued to craft murrini and spheres and has produced spheres of exceptional beauty and intrigue. Simply pick one up and you find yourself continuously moving the sphere around in the palm of your hand to gaze at all of the beautiful canes designed and crafted. Many of these spheres incorporate some of the original cane work from the earlier Marquis/Purser pieces. A double treat if you are lucky enough to find one. [Figure 32]

While the birth of the Contemporary Marble Movement is rightly placed at the feet of Marquis and Purser, their own modesty indicates that they believe they were merely in the right place, doing the right thing at the right time. Both men feel it was only a matter of time before someone else would have come along, possibly within months, and done much the same as they did in California during that summer of 1974. In fact, soon thereafter, another young glass artist, Jody Fine, began an apprenticeship with Marquis and Purser. Early studio glass pioneer, Jack Wax later joined them. Together this group formed H.O.T.M.I.R.E. (Hippies Out To Make It Rich Enterprises). They continued to explore the use of glass as an artistic medium while producing swirl marbles. Spend a considerable amount of time talking with these men and you will come away with the feeling that they not only enjoyed those days of early glass making, but also found the experience of doing what few had done previously extremely liberating in the creative sense. [Figure 33]

Having had the privilege of a number of conversations with studio glass founder Harvey Littleton; during the course of extensive interviews he answered one of the most important questions regarding contemporary marbles posed, "Why did he or his students not make marbles earlier when the movement began? Why was there such a lag, twelve or more years before the first commercially successful contemporary marbles hit the marketplace? His answer was both simple and straightforward, much like the man himself. Littleton replied, "There was no money in marbles. They were children's toys. You could go to Woolworth's or the corner store and buy a bag for a dollar or less. Why would we make marbles? It didn't make sense."

He went on to add "Glass was in short supply in those early years to us. We didn't have access to Italian glass. It was expensive and not easy to come by. So we did the best we could with soda and beer bottles. Really, any glass we could find we put in the furnace and melted. That's why if you look at so many of those early pieces you'll see that the oranges are muddy, the reds look brown, the colors are all wrong. But what could we do? We were young and experimenting. It was more important for us to be able to work the glass. Make a form by blowing. Time would take care of the rest."

Well, time certainly did when it came to contemporary marbles. After a relatively slow start with few working in the spherical form, the early to mid-1980s brought forward a number of artists and craftsmen, both school trained and self taught to the movement. The works of Marquis, Purser, Fine, Maslach, and Josh Simpson were becoming more well known and with that brought others who have earned a rightful place in the early history of the Contemporary Marble Movement. These individuals included Joe St. Clair, Brian Lonsway, Steven Lundberg, David Salazar, Rolf and Genie Wald, and others. As works began to circulate among a small group of collectors, the Marble Collectors Society of America (MCSA) formed in 1975, becoming the first organization dedicated to the education and hobby of marbles and marble collecting, and to prominently highlight contemporary marbles in their publications. This was first done in the mid-1980s with the Society's color plates. Still available today, these plates illustrate some of the earlier works and provide a unique showcase for comparing pieces crafted today versus those crafted decades ago.

The Expanding World of Contemporary Marbles

The 1980s was a time of experimentation, both in crafting and selling. Purist marble collectors nearly universally scorned contemporary marbles. In fact, marble collectors did not truly view them as marbles at all. And conversely, the craft world gave short shrift to these diminutive spheres, looked upon as simply prettier "child's playthings." Neither giving justice to the intensity required by the artist or craftsman to design, develop, employ the technique, and utilize the glass medium for producing what have since become historically important pieces.

As the 1980s gave way to the last decade of the twentieth century, the first major expansion of the Contemporary Marble Movement began. More and more artists and craftsmen worked to craft marbles and larger spheres and orbs of intricate ribbon and latticinio canes, thereby creating truly unique designs that did not mimic in any way marbles that had been handmade in Germany a century earlier or spit out by machine's decades before. This would continue as these men and women began to exhibit at collector's shows all across the country in greater numbers. Here they could come together, exchange ideas, provide tips to each other, and simply enjoy each other's fellowship. Designs would come out of these shows that would hit the marketplace and a growing number of marble collectors began to embrace contemporary marbles as a true collectible in their own right. At the very least, many collectors would have a few examples in their collection to show the difference in styles and techniques from their earlier cousins.

Figure 34. Flora. Single gather. Paper-weight-Style. Harry and Kathleen Boyer. 1-1/2 in., ca. 1986. *Courtesy of the author.*

The twenty-first century has brought with it incredible growth in the Contemporary Marble Movement. With artists and craftsmen having readily available access to equipment and glass, the movement has experienced its greatest growth in the last few years alone. Much of this growth can be attributed to the quality and diversity of designs being crafted. [Figure 34-36]

Additionally, with more and more recognized institutions adding works to their permanent contemporary art collections, contemporary marbles, spheres, and orbs have to a large extent bridged the gap of the previous two decades from craft to art. In fact, now recognized by many as a truly American art form, contemporary marbles, spheres, and orbs are finding their rightful place in the collections of studio glass art collectors. Some might even contend that fewer and fewer pieces are being collected by "marble collectors" and more and more by those who simply like the form and design, and still others who have established art collections and are seeking another sculptural form.

While the demand for both traditional and more contemporary rod- and cane-cut designs continues at a regular pace, the high growth area of the movement is found most abundantly in the flame- or torchwork method of crafting. Using both soft or moretti glass and borosilicate or Pyrex® glass, it has become easy for any hobbyist to purchase a gas/oxygen torch, glass rods, graphite molds and simply begin mixing them together over the flame. While it is relatively easy to spot the works of the hobbyist, there is a growing legion of outstanding artists crafting some of the most innovative and exciting designs using the torchwork method. Names such as James Daschbach, Jerry Kelly, and Raj Kommineni; Shell Neisler, Christopher Rice, Josh Sable, Jesse Taj, and Gateson Recko, along with many others are rapidly broadening this area of the movement. It is nearly impossible to keep up with those who come in and out of the crafting process and establish themselves with collectors. [Figure 37-39]

Figure 35. Eight-Lobed Onionskin. Torchwork. Orange, white, air trap. Kris Parke. 1-1/2 in., ca. 2004. *Courtesy of the author.*

Figure 37. Murrini. Torchwork. Hummingbird, flora murrini, ribbon, rake pull. Jesse Taj. 1-1/2 in., ca. 2003. *Courtesy of the author.*

Figure 36. Rake Pull. Torchwork. Short Tailed Swallowtail; butterfly series. Drew Fritts. 1-3/4 in., ca. 2002. *Courtesy of the author.*

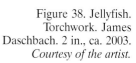

Figure 38. Jellyfish. Torchwork. James Daschbach. 2 in., ca. 2003. *Courtesy of the artist.*

Figure 39. Universe. Torchwork. Gateson Recko. 3-1/4 in., ca. 2004. *Courtesy of the author.*

In addition to the traditional means of reaching the marketplace through galleries, gift shops, and dealers, vehicles are now readily available directly to the artist/craftsman for sales such as Internet venues, including eBay®, Tias®, and Yahoo®. The avenues for works to reach the market have expanded exponentially over the past half-decade.

This author estimated during the research process in 1999-2000 for contemporary marbles and related glass art there were less than 150 artists/craftsmen and studios that had worked or were currently working in the contemporary marble, sphere, and orb field. In 2004, that number has grown to over 300 and shows no signs of slowing. Few areas in the studio arts have shown such rapid growth and it can only benefit the hobbyist with more and varied works to choose from by so many talented individuals and studios. What will be most important for the advancement of the hobby of collecting contemporary marbles, spheres, and orbs is the inclusion of more collectors with the knowledge, experience, and interest to focus their collecting on the works of those who truly inspire through their creations.

Chapter 3
More About Marbles

Figure 40. Divided Core Swirl. Multi-color divided core, alternating yellow, white outer bands. Antique handmade; Germany. 1-3/4 in., ca. app. 1850-1920. *Courtesy of the author.*

Figure 41. End-of-Day. Paneled Onionskin. Four-panels, two each, yellow/red, blue/white. Antique handmade; Germany. 1-5/8 in., ca. app. 1850-1920. *Courtesy of the author.*

Figure 42. Micas. Clear green, brown, blue, mica inclusions. Antique handmade; Germany. 11/16 - 3/4 in., ca. app. 1850-1920. *Courtesy of Stanley Block.*

Figure 43. Marble Rod Stock. Misshaped latticinio core marble rod stock pieces, dug. Antique handmade; Germany. 1-3/8 - 1-5/8 in., ca. app. 1850-1920. *Courtesy of the author.*

Ancient and Antique Handmade Marbles

The American Heritage Dictionary College Dictionary, Third Edition, defines marbles in the following way, "a. A small hard ball, usually of glass, used in children's games. b. marbles (used with a sing. verb) Any of various games played with marbles."

As round spherical objects marbles have most probably been used in children's games going back in time over 3,000 years. Found both in ancient Egyptian tombs and North American Indian burial grounds, marbles likely hold the distinction for oldest continuously played toy. With annual marble tournaments held in Wildwood, New Jersey, each spring where the American champions are crowned, and in Tinsley Green, England, on Good Friday each year, these tournaments have brought crowds and competitors together for nearly 400 years combined.

While the first marbles were undoubtedly made prior to the glass age, it is assumed that stones, nuts or fired clay pieces were used and various games played, many since lost to the ages. Marbles of pottery and stone were produced by hand in Germany as far back as the early 1800s, and some pottery marbles are also believed to have been made in England at this early date. The first modern era glass marbles are widely acknowledged to have been produced in Germany in the mid-1800s. The importance of this is striking. With America at war with itself, ships laden by the ton with glass marbles serving a dual purpose as toy and ballast were sailing from Europe to the United States where marbles were wholesaled and then sold for pennies. With popular styles like Latticinio core swirls, Joseph's Coat, Onionskin, Lutz, and End-of-Day marbles in various sizes from peewee to 2" coming from the Laucha region of Germany, it was not uncommon for children to shoot marbles before and after school, at recess, when chores were completed, or after church on Sunday. Stories have been passed from generation to generation recounting the holes in children's pockets created by the weight of marbles pulling at the seams. These handmade antique German marbles were manufactured by the tens of thousands, primarily as a cottage industry from approximately 1850-1920. [Figure 40-44]

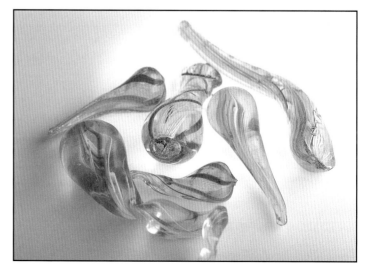

Figure 44. Marble Rod Stock. Misshaped latticinio, divided core, ribbon core marble rod stock pieces; dug. Antique handmade; Germany. 1-3/8 - 3 in., ca. app. 1850-1920. *Courtesy of the author.*

While hand cut agate and stone marbles were produced around the same time. The term "aggie" refers to the prized stone agate marbles costing considerably more than glass marbles. Many of the early agate marbles were hand ground in mills by German workers from material mined in the famed Idar-Oberstein region of Germany. As the mines became tapped out, imported material was brought in from India, Mexico, Brazil, and other countries; some of it was dyed, giving the marbles a blue, green, or even yellow color. [Figure 45]

Figure 45. Agates. Banded agates, various colors, light brown, black, blue, some with quartz crystalline. Antique handmade; Germany. 5/8 - 1-3/8 in., ca. app. 1850-1920. *Courtesy of the author.*

American Machine-Made and Foreign Manufactured Marbles

With the Industrial Revolution in full swing in the United States, glass marbles became a commodity produced in great quantities by the mid- to late-1920s. While these marbles did not have the handsome look of those imported from Germany, the cost, even in pennies, was enormously important in effectively putting the Germans out of the marble business between the World Wars.

Popularly referred to as "The Golden Age of Machine-mades," American marble manufacturers sprouted up along the Ohio River Valley and began a furious competition with each other as each sought to produce unique designs and styles; colors and novelties. Companies with names like Akro Agate, Christensen Agate, Master Marble, Peltier Glass, and Vitro Agate all competed for the attention, if not hearts, of young boys and some young girls. [Figure 46, 47]

Figure 46. Corkscrew. Akro Agate Company. Machine-made; United States. 5/8 in., ca. 1927-1935. *Courtesy of the author.*

Figure 47. Swirl. Christensen Agate Company. Machine-made; United States. 5/8 in., ca. 1927-1929. *Courtesy of Robert Block.*

With the Depression beginning in 1929, manufacturers were forced to scale back on production costs and in doing so many of the most vivid colors and designs were set aside, never to be replicated.

Following World War II, American marble manufacturers began to fail one by one. This can be attributed as a direct result to the rebuilding of Japan by the allies. Newly manufactured and imported cat's-eye marbles made it virtually impossible for American companies to compete on price. By the 1960s, nearly all marbles manufactured and sold in the United States were imported from Japan. All the while interest in marble playing, which peaked in the 1930s and 1940s, continued a steady decline. The interests of children were more apt to revolve around television and later electronic games and other mechanical and electronic toys. Today, nearly all machine-made marbles you find in stores are manufactured in China or Mexico. [Figure 48, 49]

Figure 48. Cat's-eye. Machine-made. Multi-color bands, clear glass. Japan. 1-1/2 - 5/8 in., ca. app. 1990-2000. *Courtesy of Robert Block.*

Figure 49. Confetti. Vacor de Mexico. Machine-made; Mexico. 1 in., ca. app. 1980-2000. *Courtesy of Robert Block.*

As a wave of nostalgia washed over the United States at the end of the twentieth century in the 1990s and leading into the new century, marble playing experienced somewhat of a resurgence in popularity along with other earlier childhood toys like yo-yo's, hula hoops, jacks, and other toys of the first half of the twentieth century. It is not likely this resurgence will ever come close to the popularity marbles played in children's lives in those earlier days, but much as the ancient peoples of 3,000 years ago found games could be played with round pebbles and other objects, children today find the simplicity of marble playing a healthy antidote to the video games and multitude of after school activities that provide them with little down time. Scouts continue to earn a merit belt badge and pin by learning the game of "Ringer" even today.

Chapter 4
Collecting Contemporary Marbles, Spheres, and Orbs

Building Your Collection

With so many collectibles available to the public today it is often asked, "Why collect contemporary marbles"? While the question may seem simple, the answer is certainly more complex. Marbles, spheres, and orbs are beautiful in their own right, and quite often more intricate and aesthetically pleasing than other forms of glass art.

When it comes to building a collection, whether small and inexpensive or world class, the most important thing to remember when considering a purchase is always let your heart guide you, not investment considerations. While the history of the field shows clearly that the value of contemporary marbles, spheres, and orbs has grown considerably, this can vary from artist to artist and piece to piece. The most exciting part of collecting is when your eyes light up over a piece you are considering purchasing, or one you have had in your collection for years. It is impossible to put a dollar amount on the enjoyment you will receive from your collection over time. The satisfaction you have from knowing your collection is "worth it" to you should be infinitely more "valuable" than the profit you'll reap if you decide to sell any or all of your pieces at some time.

So, while investment potential and the reputation of the artist/craftsman or studio is certainly important, it should be a secondary consideration to your personal investment in enjoying the piece itself. You can be attracted to a particular piece for the quality of its craftsmanship, design, colors or size even if you have never heard of the craftsman. And, can you purchase pieces that are known historically to increase in value? Absolutely. It is documented that the exciting and unique works by Paul Stankard, crafted as recently as two years ago, have increased in value quite rapidly over this relatively short period of time. Other artist examples are James Alloway, Christopher and Lissa Juedemann, and Christopher Rice, just to name a few whose pieces continue to increase in value. But it is certainly not limited to the few names mentioned here; there are tens of artists/craftsmen whose works should be considered for inclusion in a comprehensive contemporary collection.

There is a difference of opinion amongst experts in the antiques and collectibles field over whether it is better to own more of lesser quality than fewer of higher quality. This is not an easy question to answer. The arguments on both sides of the issue are potent and responsible. It simply comes down to your personal preference when collecting. Some choose to have a small curio cabinet of only the finest works displayed; others spread a large collection throughout various rooms and different display arrangements in their home. Do what works best for you—and what you enjoy most.

It is often said that a little knowledge is dangerous. This is the opposite of what is suggested in the collectible fields. It is impossible to have too much information. Whether through books and articles, talking with other collectors and the artists themselves, attending shows, specialized television programs, following collectible trends on the Internet, all of these things can only make you more knowledgeable and more aware of what is out there in the marketplace. You'll also find you have a heightened appreciation for the work that goes into each piece when you have a better understanding of the glass art and Contemporary Marble Movement.

As you begin to add works to your collection you will find that it is important to keep accurate records of your purchases. By recording the piece, artist, date of purchase, purchase price, and other important information, you'll establish a provenance for each piece that will enable you to quickly access information that could prove invaluable when you decide to part with a piece, either through private sale or auction, or when adding additional pieces by the same artist or studio. Additionally, this written record should be used for insurance purposes and can keep you up-to-date on comparisons of like pieces sold long after you have purchased your own.

One of the most often asked questions when it comes to a collectible like contemporary marbles, spheres, and orbs is "How should I display my collection"? There are those who believe that the only way to adequately protect their "investment in glass" is to do so by locking the pieces away in cases lined with foam or other materials to protect each piece from any damage. Others choose to display their collection in curio cabinets, museum display cases, and custom made cabinets or other ways which allow the viewing, but not touching of the works. This is a perfectly accepted manner in which to both protect the pieces and at the same time enjoy them. Still others display their collections by making them a part of their décor. There is a growing movement in the antiques and collectibles field to use antiques and collectible items as an integral part of a home or office décor. By grouping pieces of like styles or artist on display stands, whether on a bookshelf, coffee table or even in a bathroom, you get the best of everything. Not only can you see your collection up close, but you can also continually move and rearrange pieces. A beautiful display of Steven Maslach swirl marbles of different sizes in an antique American Brilliant Cut Period bowl or dish makes a glittering and dazzling attention grabber on any table. A blown glass jar filled with different style and size Josh Simpson Planets will bring more attention and get visitors talking about the most unlikely of subjects—from the otherworldly to the here and now.

A Gateson Recko Universe Marble on a brass stand sitting on the corner of a desk or end table invites the viewer to pick it up and rotate in hand. The unbelievable depth and form of the piece makes you, the collector, the purveyor and even curator of your own personal, in-home collection. There can be no better compliment to a collection than the wonderment expressed by others for the beauty and technical ability the artist/craftsman puts into their work. The passion and personality of the maker is so often a focal point of the work itself that it becomes easier for the collector to separate the works of individual artists/craftsmen into collecting versus accumulating. [Figure 50-53]

Figure 50. Vortex. Torchwork. Orange, dichroic glass vortex window, outer casing blue, orange flume. Dustin Morell. 2-1/4 in., ca. 2004. *Courtesy of the author.*

Figure 51. Swirls; Paperweight-style. Torchwork. Various ribbon, banded swirls; paperweight-style, assorted murrini cane, blue ground. Rudy Calin. 1-1/4 - 1-1/2 in., ca. 2003. *Courtesy of the author.*

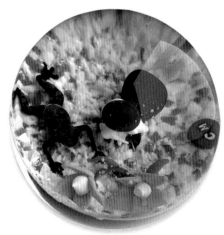

Figure 52. Gnome. Torchwork. Paperweight-style, Gnome, frog, flowers, multi-color glass ground. Lewis and Jennifer Wilson. 2-1/4 in., ca. 2002. *Courtesy of the artists.*

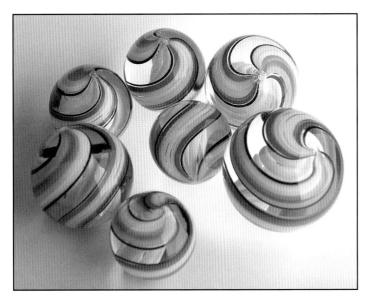

Figure 53. Latticinio Swirls. Rod- and cane-cut. White latticinio core, multi-color two-panel outer bands. *Limited edition set.* Jody Fine. Marble stock crafted at Wheaton Village Marble Weekend 2003. Jody Fine, Douglas Sweet. 7/8 - 1-5/8 in., ca. 2003. *Courtesy of the author.*

So, go ahead, be inventive! Consider tossing out all the preconceived notions you have about how and where to display your collection. You might just come up with a new and exciting way to enjoy your wonderful contemporary marbles, spheres, and orbs.

Caring For Your Collection

The most important thing to remember about glass is it is fragile. This may seem like common sense, but you would be amazed at how often you'll hear about great-grandmother's fine antique crystal being shattered after being loaded and run in the dishwasher. The same is true for contemporary handmade glass marbles, spheres, and orbs. The delicate nature of glass can be both forgiving to the artist when crafting, and extremely unforgiving to the owner after its purchase.

Therefore, the best way to protect your pieces is to use plain old common sense. Just as you would not use glass cleaner on your finest Baccarat or Steuben crystal, so to you should only use a soft cloth and tepid water with a mild or extremely well diluted dishwashing detergent to clean your pieces. Let them either air dry or wipe them carefully and lightly with a soft dry cloth. Or as others suggest, simply breath some warm air onto them and wipe carefully, you'll be surprised at how quickly their luster is restored. With hand-painted china and mineral marbles, you should use these same methods. Even though the material is harder, it is easier to remember and prevents you from doing any damage to them as well.

Since glass serves as a refractor, be sure you never place your pieces where direct sunlight will smile brightly on them. While they may look their most brilliant in this light, you risk losing your collection and home by starting a fire from the concentrated rays of light passing through the glass. Keep in mind as the seasons change and the earth moves in its orbit around the sun, you may want to move your pieces as well to keep them out of harm's way.

Chapter Five

Edition Types

Nearly all artists can place a limit on the edition of the work they are crafting. However, because both price and the market suggest otherwise, for Beetem to stop producing his signature Stardust Clambroth style pieces, Salazar to cease crafting Angelfish, or Wald to never make another Beachball would be detrimental to their overall business and a loss to the expanding collecting community. [Figure 54-56]

Figure 54. Clambroth. Rod- and cane-cut. Stardust Clambroth. Multi-color, dichroic glass. Geoffrey Beetem. 1-3/8 in., ca. 2001. *Courtesy of the author.*

Figure 55. Aquarium scene. Single gather. Paperweight-style, multi-layer, kelp, barnacles, coral, ange-lfish murrini canes. *Limited edition 43/50.* David Salazar. 1-3/4 in., ca. 1998. *Courtesy of the author.*

Figure 56. Banded Swirl. Rod- and cane-cut. Beachball. Six-panels, multi-color, beachball design. Rolf and Genie Wald. 1-1/2 in., ca. 2000. *Courtesy of the author.*

What can greatly affect market price is an artist who crafts a signature style piece, ceases after a run of pieces and gives every indication the style or design will not be revived. An artist should not designate works to be limited edition pieces solely on the basis of saying they are crafted infrequently. It is important to remember the work should always bear the appropriate artist's mark indicating it is a true limited edition, or at the very least associated paperwork should be provided indicating the same. A problem occurs when the artist comes back after some time has passed to craft more of the same pieces. This can greatly alter the market value for the earlier works, most often because the newer pieces are sold for a considerably higher price than the previous works would likely bring. Also, the quality can be quite different. It is strongly recommended that you research the artist, their work history and availability, and their proclivity to produce very carefully. This should help to ensure the works you are purchasing while being ones you personally like, are from regular stock or open edition production stock, or just as important, limited editions.

What Contemporary Works to Collect

As you decide what works to collect or add pieces to make your collection even grander, the variety of what is available can be both astounding and confusing. In order to more easily define the works of artists and craftsmen available, four major categories have been established that cover most if not all of the work being crafted today. These categories are applicable to all contemporary handmade marbles, spheres, and orbs, whether rod- and cane cut, flame- or torchwork, china or others. These groups are regular stock or open edition production stock, prototypes, limited editions, and experimental pieces. Because artist proof pieces are by far the smallest subgroup they are not included as a fifth category, but rather a specialty within the well-established previous four categories. As your collection grows, decisions on which group a particular marble should be placed can be based on a common understanding of the definition of each of these categories.

Glass, by its very nature, is both a beautiful and limited material in which artists can express their creativity. The yearly output of studio glass artists is most often restricted by their own physical capability to craft. While each artist spends a disparate amount of time crafting, whether it be only marbles, spheres, and orbs, or other glass works, such as ornaments, goblets, paperweights, perfumes, sculptural objects, etc., the number of marbles made can be as few as a handful or well into the hundreds. This partly depends on whether the artist is a sole practitioner of their work or oversees studio workers who then produce the artist's designs.

Regular Stock or Open Edition Production Stock

Most marbles can be referred to as regular stock or open edition production stock. While it is easy for an artist to place a limit on their work, you will not often see this being done. The reason being the experience the artist has when creating each piece is both unique and personal. The artists express their creativity so that as many collectors as possible can enjoy their most affordable works, all the while attempting to make a living for themselves and their families. So while the design and colors may be similar, each piece is unique unto itself. There will always be subtle differences from piece to piece, whether cut from a rod or crafted over the torch. Even hand painted china marbles of the same design will have variations in color density and slight differences in the drawing, as each is hand crafted.

Regular stock or open edition production stock marbles are those styles and designs an artist or studio is recognized as producing on an ongoing basis, oftentimes from year to year. It is relatively easy for the more advanced collector to identify these works since they are the most common types, most often crafted. Just as the production process limits the quantity an artist produces during the calendar year; artists may add and delete styles from their regular stock selection. These works are easiest to find available directly from the artist or studio, dealers, in gallery shops, and gift and museum shops, as well as via the Internet.

An artist may retire from production a regular stock or open edition production stock marble; however, the designation should not change since the marble was not produced under any other auspices during its run. Just as automobiles go through an evolution in design and engineering during their life cycle, so too do many handmade contemporary marbles.

The value of an artist's regular stock or open edition production stock work will generally rise and fall in value dependent on current market conditions, especially while the style is still being produced and made available by the artist. Once the artist ceases to craft the style, it is likely the marble's value will begin to raise within a short time, though this is not always the case. Artist's prices can often fluctuate during the time works are in production. This can vary greatly from dealer to dealer, gallery-to-gallery, dependent on geographic location and the power and global reach of the Internet.

Figure 57. Banded Swirl. Rod- and cane-cut. Aventurine glass. Rolf and Genie Wald. 1-1/8 in., ca. 2004. *Courtesy of the author.*

Figure 58. Joseph's Coat. Rod- and cane-cut. Three-color, reverse twist. Fritz Lauenstein. 1-5/8 in., ca. 2003. *Courtesy of the author.*

Figure 59. Coreless Banded Swirl. Rod- and cane-cut. Multi-color bands, clear core. Jody Fine. 1-5/8 in., ca. 2003. *Courtesy of the author.*

Regular or production stock marbles should but may not always bear the artist's mark and date. [Figure 57-59]

Prototypes

During the concept phase of designing, testing, and refining a work in glass, through this process an artist will oftentimes design and craft a small number of prototype pieces. Because these marbles are so-called "works in progress," they are rarely made available to the contemporary collector through regular market routes. Artists often keep or destroy their prototype marbles from the stock pulled to produce the final pieces. Prototypes often exhibit a rougher, less refined look than the final pieces, and so hold less appeal for most collectors.

Sometimes an artist releases a prototype design to gauge the collecting public's reaction to the style or design. If a prototype is indeed sold, the artist usually signs the piece with a "P," though seldom are more than three prototypes produced much less released. Prototype marbles should always bear the artist's mark, date, and a designation in some manner as a prototype. This will most often assure the piece's value will increase higher with time than other marbles. [Figure 60, 61]

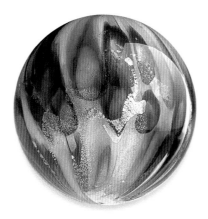

Figure 60. End-of-Day. Onionskin Cloud. Rod- and cane-cut. Multi-color dichroic glass, white base. *Prototype.* Geoffrey Beetem. 2 in., ca. 2004. *Courtesy of the author.*

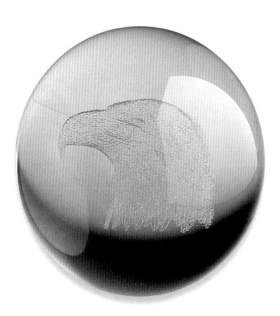

Figure 61. Laser Crystal. Single gather. Eagle bust, laser imploded dots in crystal. *Prototype.* Image 3 Crystal, license from Laser Design International. 2-7/8 in., ca. 2002. *Courtesy of the author.*

Limited Editions

Many, many collectibles are produced in limited editions. Think of United States Mint Commemorative coins, U.S. Postal Service Commemorative stamps, artist's serigraph prints, limited edition decorative plates, and many of the collectibles found in your local Hallmark store. Much like paperweights, an artist intentionally crafts limited edition marbles, spheres, and orbs in a short or limited run. Most truly recognized limited editions do not exceed twenty-five or fifty pieces in the contemporary marble field. On rare occasions an edition of one hundred will be set. Limited editions may be crafted as such due to a unique, difficult or complex design. Set apart from others produced from regular stock or open edition production stock, limited edition pieces generally take more time on the artist's part, and the process and complexity of the design does set the work apart from others by the artist or studio. A marble dealer may request a limited edition, which is another way to release to the collecting community a premium marble by a well-established or up-and-coming artist. Oftentimes, the studio artist who produces various forms of contemporary handmade glass art will seek input from those in the field who are most knowledgeable about what would make a good collectible limited edition.

These marbles can begin to rise in value immediately after production and release. And while the value of a limited edition marble will be set by varying forces, namely the artist, dealer, and other collectors, if there is little demand for the pieces, their value will be artificially defined or decline quickly. Most often though, limited edition marbles are highly sought after by collectors. Much of the collectible nature depends on the size of the edition produced. Are there 25, 50 or 100 marbles in the edition? Is the edition comprised of more than one marble, thus creating a limited edition set?

Limited edition marbles will often be available to the collector at a premium price, which can be as low as twice the artist's regular price to as high as four times the price for the same artist's regular stock or open edition production stock pieces. These marbles must always bear the artist's mark, date, and some form of appropriate numbering by the artist.

The limited edition marble can be numbered in various ways. It can be done straight from one through the total edition size. The artist can also remove the prototype marbles, subtract them from the total, and begin the numbering at three or four of the total edition size.

If you decide to acquire a limited edition marble and it is from a set or series of more than one, secure the entire series to be sure you have the comprehensive limited edition crafted.

Given the choice between a limited edition and a regular stock or open edition production stock marble, and liking them both equally, you would be wise to purchase the limited edition marble. However, be sure the work is truly a limited edition and not simply one that is indicated as limited in number at the time of crafting. It is also advised that if your concern is future value of the limited edition, get to know the artist's full body of work, museum and gallery collections. If the artist producing limited editions, or what are described as "limited in nature," is well known in the field it is likely there will be an artificially higher demand for this artist's work. [Figure 62, 63]

Figure 62. Jim Davis Master Marble Maker Family Collection. Rod- and cane-cut. Various styles. *Limited edition 27/200.* Steve, Rick, Mike, John, Mark, and Joe Davis. Marbles: 1-1/2 in., Box: 6-3/4 x 6-3/4 x 2-1/4 in., ca. 2004. *Courtesy of the author.*

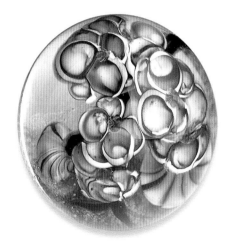

Figure 63. Onionskin. Rod- and cane-cut. Yellow, blue murrini stars, orange, blue base. *Sea Tac Limited edition 29/33.* David Salazar. 1-11/16 in., ca. 1999. *Courtesy of the author.*

Experimental Works

As difficult as it is to acquire prototype marbles from a particular artist, experimental marbles are even more difficult to acquire directly from an artist or on the secondary market. These can include artist error pieces as well. This is so for one primary reason: artists generally tend to release only what they view to be their finest quality works. Few artists who like to craft in glass do so from a continuous point of expertise; therefore, a considerable amount of glass or other material will be used in crafting experimental designs. It is difficult to place a value on these marbles. Most often it is arbitrary and fluctuates greatly from artist to artist and piece to piece. Most experimental pieces will bear the artist's mark even though they are experiments in the crafting process. These marbles serve primarily to enhance the body of the artist's work. [Figure 64, 65]

Figure 65. Animal Skin. Ocelot. Rod- and cane-cut. Graal technique, graded gray/brown, white base. Artists error. Incorrect image of spots on backside, spine on underbelly. One of three known. Mark Matthews. 1-1/2 in., ca. 2001. *Courtesy of the author.*

Figure 64. Flora. Single gather. Multi-layer, paperweight-style, torchwork ruffled pansies, stems, leaves, aventurine glass banded ground. *Experimental 1-X.* David Salazar. 2-1/8 in., ca. 2003. *Courtesy of the author.*

Chapter Six
The Artist's Mark

One of the most hotly debated subjects within the Contemporary Marble Movement over the years continues to be the concern for the artist's mark. Both artists and collectors differ on the subject of signed work. That is, the craftsman's mark intentionally placed on the sphere to ensure permanent identification. What was not even considered an issue in the days of antique handmade, machine-made or even early contemporary marbles has taken on an increasingly higher level of importance proportionate to the heightened interest in collectible contemporary marbles, spheres, and orbs.

Many of the earliest handmade contemporary marble artisans rarely if ever signed their works. Some artist's/craftsmen consider their body of work able to speak for itself. The thought of disturbing the completely clean spherical nature of the work is antithetical to what the artist strives to achieve—the perfect glass sphere. Just as those artists, many from the earlier generation of students of the Contemporary Marble Movement, were concerned with the aesthetic nature and value of their pieces, today's craftsmen are equally as interested in the preservation and provenance of the works they produce. Artists like Jody Fine, Steven Maslach, and many of the studio glass houses do not, as a practice, signature mark their works. While they may do so upon request by the collector, as a general rule they adhere to the art-for-art's-sake philosophy that drew them to first create handmade marbles. Or, they may not craft the works themselves in their entirety, but rather design them for others in their studio to actually produce.

While an unsigned marble may be identified as belonging to the work of a particular artist or studio, the artist's mark, in whatever form it takes, is a direct link between the work and the craftsman. Just as you would immediately search for the Galle, Daum Nancy, Steuben, Tiffany, or other mark on a piece of antique or contemporary decorative glass, so too does the collector of the contemporary sphere. Such artist's marks can be distinctive additions to a craftsman's work and may be formed by scribing, hot metal imprinting, diamond-bit setting or by the increasingly popular use of a signature cane. This is especially true for the artists who are extremely proficient in the crafting of murrini cane. They will use exquisite cane pieces in their works and will take care to incorporate them as part of their marking. Such signed marbles cannot however be undeniably linked to the artist who produced them. If an artist changes his mark over time, varies from piece to piece, does not mark the work at the time of crafting or until it is sold, or varies the pronouncements on their own marks, confusion can be raised. Many of today's contemporary marble artists are dating their marbles in order to leave a lasting presence upon the art world.

For practical purposes, the form of signing a craftsman chooses is personal. However, as a collector, you would be well advised to seek those marbles that are crafted and signed with equal care by the artist. Viewing an artist's signature will no doubt teach you much about their personality as well. Is the artist's mark done in a quality manner with effort and care? Is the marking form unique? Are initials, last name or full name scratched onto the pole? Does the marking do anything to take away from the piece by being either too large or too small? These are all questions you must answer for yourself. Examples you will see as you collect will serve you best to give you a true visual image of the various forms of the artist's mark.

Trademark and Copyright Use

Today, there has been an ever increasing interest on the artists part regarding the applicability of trademarks and copyrights on works they design and produce. It is a difficult issue in the creative arts field and one that will surely be viewed more closely as the field grows and artists' works become more prolific. The United States Patent and Trademark Office offers these definitions and criteria, though for more detailed information it is advised to follow-up with the agency directly.

1. "What Is a Trademark?

A trademark is a word, name, symbol or device which is used in trade with goods to indicate the source of the goods and to distinguish them from the goods of others.

Trademark rights may be used to prevent others from using a confusingly similar mark, but not to prevent others from making the same goods or from selling the same goods or services under a clearly different mark. Trademarks which are used in interstate or foreign commerce may be registered with the Patent and Trademark Office."

2. "What Is a Copyright?

Copyright is a form of protection provided to the authors of "original works of authorship" including literary, dramatic, musical, artistic, and certain other intellectual works, both published and unpublished. The 1976 Copyright Act generally gives the owner of copyright the exclusive right to reproduce the copyrighted work, to prepare derivative works, to distribute copies or phonorecords of the copyrighted work, to perform the copyrighted work publicly, or to display the copyrighted work publicly.

The copyright protects the form of expression rather than the subject matter of the writing. For example, a description of a machine could be copyrighted, but this would only prevent others from copying the description; it would not prevent others from writing a description of their own or from making and using the machine."

Chapter Seven
Crafting Contemporary Marbles, Spheres, and Orbs

Studio Glass Works

As has been discussed, the studio glass piece is one that is produced by artists or their representatives working in collaboration in a small studio dedicated to producing a limited number of glass art objects in a given time period. These studio glass houses may have as few as one or two craftsmen and apprentices or as many as ten to twenty people working together, each with individual assignments to ensure the quality production of contemporary glass.

Many of the most popular and collectible handmade contemporary marble, sphere, and orb craftsmen work alone, especially those crafting in the torchwork method and hand-painted china pieces. Whether for reasons of cost containment or enjoyment of the solitude of working with hot glass and glazes while listening to operatic and popular music, art is inherently a very personal experience and challenge. These artists produce high-quality work readily identifiable by the experienced collector, while other master glass artists have seen their studios grow in size to necessitate the supervised employment of other glass craftsmen.

Figure 66. Ribbon Swirl. Rod- and cane-cut. Multi-color, dichroic glass. Michael Hansen, Nina Paladino Caron. 1-7/8 in., ca. 2003. *Courtesy of the author.*

Oftentimes the studio glass artist working a furnace or crucible will produce marbles in very limited numbers and only two or three times during the calendar year. Those working in the torchwork and other methods have greater flexibility. Constantly aware of the life span of their furnace, torch, and tools, other forms of contemporary glass produced, and the market availability of their marbles, spheres, and orbs, these artists can set their production schedule to suit their own needs.

Other glass studios, employing many to handle the glass—from pulling the rods to signing the works—maintain an ongoing schedule, ensuring continual placement and ready availability of their work in the public domain throughout the year.

Whether the artist is a sole practitioner of the craft or works as the master craftsman overseeing a staff, the contemporary pieces produced are all individually crafted and released to the public only after the artist has approved the final pieces for release. [Figure 66-68]

Figure 67. Vortex. Torchwork. Dichroic, rake pull. Dustin Morell. 1-3/4 in., ca. 2004. *Courtesy of the author.*

Decorative Glass House Works

Once the studio glass artists of the West Coast of the United States became proficient at crafting contemporary spheres that gained public acceptance as true forms of contemporary glass art, the decorative glass houses of the Mid-Atlantic and Mid-Western United States saw the advantage of a natural addition to their already large line of decorative glass art. Studios such as Gibson Glass, Hamon Handcrafted Glass, House of Glass, and Prestige Glass, are but a few of the hundreds of decorative studio glass houses operating in the United States since the early 1900s to the present day.

These glass houses have a unique and interesting history in the glass movement of the United States. Primarily segmented in the heavily rich natural resource states of West Virginia, Ohio, and Indiana, these glass houses relied on their abundance of sand and natural gas to produce functional items like dishes, glasses, lamps, and also decorative items that were then sold through major retailers throughout the United States and Europe. As the United States entered World War II, the need for resources to

Figure 68. Ribbon Swirl. Rod- and cane-cut. Dichroic core, ribbons. Geoffrey Beetem. 2 in., ca. 2003. *Courtesy of the author.*

Figure 69. End-of-Day. Lobed Core Onionskin. Rod- and cane-cut. Gibson Glass. Charles Gibson. 1-3/4 in., ca. 2002. *Courtesy of the author.*

Figure 70. End-of-Day. Cloud Onionskin. Rod- and cane-cut. Light brown base, dark brown overlay glass. St. Clair Glass Work. Attributed to Joe St. Clair. 1-5/8 in., ca. 1985. *Courtesy of the Marble Collectors Society of America.*

support the war effort forced the closing of many of the functional and decorative glass houses. With the war's end and without a new generation to follow in the footsteps of their fathers or grandfathers, the functional and decorative glass house movement fell on hard times.

A small number of glass houses continue to keep the tradition alive. The market is supplied with both inexpensive and expensive glassware bought through catalog, department store, and gift shop sales, while the marbles, spheres, and orbs produced by glass houses such as Gibson Glass, House of Glass, and Prestige Glass are the true production-style handmade contemporary glass marble. Many of the styles are reminiscent of earlier antique styles with a contemporary flair, such as Onionskin, Swirl, and End-of-Day varieties; however, these marbles are easily identifiable as glass-house marbles primarily due to the lower level of lead in the glass needed to produce them. The color combinations will most always follow those already being utilized for other glass house items, and the more advanced contemporary marble art collector, while finding them collectible, desires these marbles less than others.

Many beginning collectors will feel their way into the collectible contemporary marble hobby by acquiring works from these glass houses. These pieces are seldom signed by the studio and are rarely made by the namesake artist of the glass house. However, many of the early Charles Gibson and Joe St. Clair marbles are quite collectible, even if they can be difficult to positively identify by date or direct linkage to the owners crafting the pieces themselves.

Also of note are the glass craftsmen who have left the glass house to work on their own conception and production of contemporary marbles, spheres, and orbs. Again, many of these marbles will generally exhibit a lower quality than the studio glass artist works, primarily due to the nature of the training or experience the glass craftsman has acquired through those years in producing production-style glass items. The glass of these artists will often exhibit lesser quality techniques and crystal clarity than the studio artist's work. This is not true in all cases as is noted by the works of Eddie Seese, formerly of Fenton Glass, and Steve Davis and his brothers, who grew up with their father having been a glass factory worker. However, these works will most likely be signed, and while produced at a more rapid pace than those of the studio glass artist, they will be easily traceable to the glass craftsman. [Figure 69-71]

Figure 71. Flora. Single gather. Paperweight-style, red flora, center air trap, pink ground. House of Glass. Joe Rice. 1-3/4 in., ca. 1999. *Courtesy of the Marble Collectors Society of America.*

Artist's/Craftsman's Work

While the origins of handmade marbles have been discussed in detail in earlier chapters, the mass production of machine-made marbles in the early to mid-twentieth century effectively eliminated the need and desire to craft handmade marbles for play. Therefore, as demand for marbles as toys increased early in the century and waned during the later decades of the 1900s, marbles as glass collectibles have taken on a variety of forms. The detailed craftsmanship exhibited by the finest artists in the contemporary marble field is in many ways as much an attribute of the early handmade marbles as it is of studio glasswork. Whether the craftsman is sitting at a bench behind a gas/oxygen torch holding a myriad number of pre-made glass rods and creating small one inch marbles or nearly 2-1/2 inch spheres; or grasping a glass stock cane the thickness of a tree limb to pull a large cane; or hand-rolling and grinding, polishing and glazing, painting and firing the exquisite hand-painted china marbles reminiscent of antique German china marbles—each craftsman is artistic in their own right.

As the hobby of collecting these already varied spheres continues to grow, the designs, sizes, and types of handmade contemporary marbles, spheres, and orbs will likely flourish to meet the demands of the collecting community. Highly sought-after contemporary glass marbles, spheres, and orbs are primarily produced in two manners, and the processes have been refined quite considerably over the last thirty years. As you compare the antique handmade and machine-made marbles to those handcrafted by trained and talented artists throughout the pages of this book, take the time to become more familiar yourself with these processes, both of which allow the artist to control the final sphere they seek to produce. By doing so you will gain an even greater appreciation for the imagination and ability brought to bear in crafting "true contemporaries."

The Crafting Process

In the process known as cane-cut or rod-cut, the glass cane or rod is developed through heating to the desired size by layering smaller rods of glass, whether clear or colored to create the various styles of marbles desired. These can be swirls, clambroths, end-of-days, Indians, micas, or opaque marbles. Once the glass rod, or stock has been produced, the end is heated in a furnace or over a torch and rounded using a hand-held marble device. Once the marble has been properly heated, it is twisted or pulled to create the swirl or the helix and cut with a glass scissor or shear. Keeping in mind that the glass is nearly molten hot throughout these stages the artist must be sure that the development of the rod is exact in order to achieve the desired marble. Wearing special safety eye ware, the artist crafts each piece individually and must ensure that once the final work has been cut from the rod or cane, it is cooled properly in an annealing oven to prevent shattering from great degrees of temperature change.   After the marble has been properly annealed, the artist must then use the lapidary process on the pontils in order to achieve the absolute smoothness on both the top and bottom poles to complete the sphere making process. [Figure 72-86]

Figure 73. After the glass is picked up it is necessary to heat it in the glory hole so it becomes malleable and more easily worked. *Photo: John Heisch and Jodene Goldenring Fine. Courtesy of the artist.*

Figure 74. In the crafting process it is important to shape the color on the marver when it has reached a temperature allowing it to be worked. *Photo: John Heisch and Jodene Goldenring Fine. Courtesy of the artist.*

Figure 72. Marble Set-Up. Rod- and cane-cut. The artist works with a variety of colored glass to achieve the desired design. Here, colored glass is picked up out of the soaking oven. Jody Fine. ca. 2004. *Photo: John Heisch and Jodene Goldenring Fine. Courtesy of the artist.*

Figure 75. The colored glass is now pulled into a long cane; often times 6-8 feet in length, sometimes even longer. *Photo: John Heisch and Jodene Goldenring Fine. Courtesy of the artist.*

Figure 76. Having chosen the color stock to be used to craft the completed marbles, the artist lays them out in a predetermined pattern. This prevents a random design from occurring. *Photo: John Heisch and Jodene Goldenring Fine. Courtesy of the artist.*

Figure 77. With the colors chosen and pattern determined; the glass canes are now put into the "cage." This holds them in place as the process proceeds. *Photo: John Heisch and Jodene Goldenring Fine. Courtesy of the artist.*

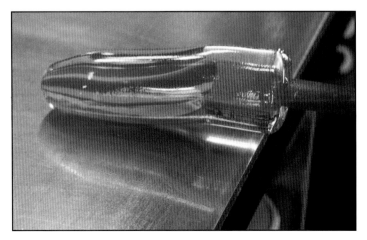

Figure 78. A small piece of previously made stock is now heated. This piece will become the marbles core. *Photo: John Heisch and Jodene Goldenring Fine. Courtesy of the artist.*

Figure 79. The artist encases the core in clear glass as the complex process continues in what appears to be a series of seamless operatic movements. *Photo: John Heisch and Jodene Goldenring Fine. Courtesy of the artist.*

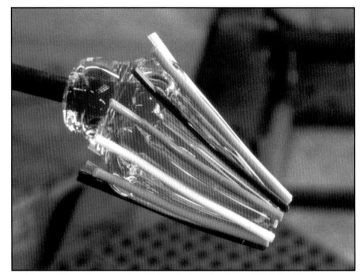

Figure 80. The "cage," having served to hold the glass rods in place in a predetermined pattern allows them to now be "picked up" and melted to the core. *Photo: John Heisch and Jodene Goldenring Fine. Courtesy of the artist.*

Figure 81. The punty with glass is now placed in the glory hole where more clear glass is picked up to cover the rods and core. *Photo: John Heisch and Jodene Goldenring Fine. Courtesy of the artist.*

Figure 82. The entire glass mass is now pulled into a bar of marble stock. *Photo: John Heisch and Jodene Goldenring Fine. Courtesy of the artist.*

Figure 83. After the stock has been made and cut, smaller stock pieces can be picked up from the soaking oven. *Photo: John Heisch and Jodene Goldenring Fine. Courtesy of the artist.*

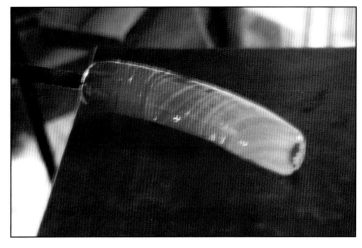

Figure 84. Marble stock is now heated again and twisted to the desired tightness of the completed marble. *Photo: John Heisch and Jodene Goldenring Fine. Courtesy of the artist.*

Figure 85. Using a graphite mold, the artist shapes the marble attached to the rod and completes the necessary rounding to achieve a nearly completed sphere. *Photo: John Heisch and Jodene Goldenring Fine. Courtesy of the artist.*

Figure 86. A finished marble is now ready to separate from the stock and be placed in an annealing oven to cool. This is necessary and allows the piece to set and prevents it from cracking or shattering. *Photo: John Heisch and Jodene Goldenring Fine. Courtesy of the artist.*

The second common process for crafting handmade contemporary glass marbles, spheres, and orbs is referred to as the single-gather technique. This involves gathering a glob of glass from a glory hole or done over a gas/oxygen torch, whether one or more colors. The glass can be molded and incised with objects, or through a process of building or decorating successive layers onto the end of a punty the artist/craftsman reaches the desired size of the finished piece. This process is achieved through the heating process similar to the cane- or rod-cut style, and the glob of glass is rounded in special wooden or graphite blocks producing the marble, which is cut or tapped off the end of the punty. Cooling in an annealing oven is necessary in this process as well to avoid cracking or shattering the glass. [Figure 87-98, Figure 99]

Figure 89. Design elements are then worked and marvered to the tubes surface. *Courtesy of the artist.*

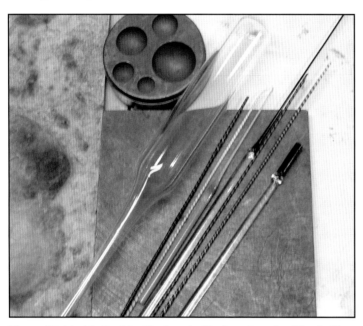

Figure 87. Marble Set-Up. Torchwork. Single gather. Sea Floral. Glass rods, tube; graphite mold required to craft sea floral marble. Jerry Kelly. ca. 2004. *Courtesy of the artist.*

Figure 90. Heat is then applied to melt the completed design to the surface glass. *Courtesy of the artist.*

Figure 91. Additional marvering is required to achieve a final smooth finish. *Courtesy of the artist.*

Figure 88. The artist preheats the host tube surface in preparation for design. *Courtesy of the artist.*

Figure 92. The artist must continue to heat the design evenly so that no portion cools too quickly. This is extremely important to allow for continued crafting. *Courtesy of the artist.*

Figure 93. The design must now be melted smooth with the surface of the host glass. *Courtesy of the artist.*

Figure 94. Using a graphite mold, the bottom of the piece is rounded in the appropriate size indented half circle in the mold. *Courtesy of the artist.*

Figure 95. A punty is now attached to the bottom of the completed design and heat is applied. *Courtesy of the artist.*

Figure 96. The piece is continuously heated as it is removed and the tube is removed from the top of the marble. *Courtesy of the artist.*

Figure 97. Having had the tube removed from the marbles top pole, it is heated and rounded much like the bottom pole was earlier. *Courtesy of the artist.*

Figure 98. While still hot the piece is placed in the graphite mold and final shaping is done to ensure the work is round. It is now ready to be removed from the punty and placed in an annealing oven to slowly cool. This process allows the piece to set and prevents it from cracking or shattering. *Courtesy of the artist.*

Figure 99. Marble Set-up. Torchwork. Single gather. Swirl. Six-stage set-up. Clear glass, eight light blue glass stringers applied, initial shaping, multi-colored glass and gold aventurine glass stringers applied, glass is twisted to desired tightness, rake pull to enable stringers to swirl, completed swirl. Bruce Breslow. 2-1/4 - 1-1/4 in., ca. 2002. *Courtesy of the artist.*

Chapter Eight
Grading

All of the marbles illustrated in this book have been assigned a value that can be reviewed in the Associated Value Index at the back of this book. In order to establish accurate values and evaluate a marble in your collection, it is important to define what retail price and mint condition really mean. Additional categories of grading and classification will be provided in this section. Due to the fact that contemporary marbles, spheres, and orbs are decorative and ornamental objects and therefore not subject to the stresses of their "plaything" predecessors, nearly all handmade contemporary works are classified as mint. The designations and numerical terms established by the Marble Collectors Society of America (MCSA) are today's most widely used and accepted condition forms in the hobby, and thus are appropriate for use in the case of contemporary marbles, spheres, and orbs as well. However, because of the artistic nature of the contemporary field, definitions have been expanded for the specific use in determining throughout this book how to define the category a particular work can fall within.

When seeking additions to your collection, you will need to evaluate each marble based on a number of factors: the artist/craftsman; the clarity of the glass; the design and colors incorporated in the piece; and whether the marble, sphere or orb is a limited edition, prototype, experimental or regular stock or open edition stock piece. As was discussed earlier, artist's proof pieces can be categorized in a number of ways and should therefore be treated on a piece-by-piece basis.

Mint. 9.6-10.0. This refers to a work that is new or unmarred in its original condition. The term wet-mint is applied when the piece has not left the artist's studio and has most likely been handled only by the artists themselves. This marble, sphere or orb will be in the best possible condition. All aspects of the work are near perfect as can be reasonably achieved by the artist or craftsman. The color, clarity, and execution of design leave no doubt that the piece was crafted with the finest care. All intentional markings by the artist are flawless. The artist's mark, date, number, and any other identifying marks are easily readable and well placed in an appropriate place on the piece. Any accompanying certificate, art card, box or paper issued with this piece are intact and in original clean condition. Value of works in this category will likely be higher than the regular retail price for a similar work in mint condition.

Marbles, spheres, and orbs in this category may have changed hands as little as once, oftentimes going only from the artist through an intermediary before reaching its owner. Nearly all contemporary handmade marbles, spheres, and orbs in your collection will likely be in mint condition as a result of the relatively young nature of the hobby. Though it is possible to acquire rare, early contemporary marbles in mint condition because the processes and techniques were much less refined than those used by artists during the last decade or two, it is best to consult with a reputable dealer or other hobbyist to authenticate the quality of the piece. Works in this category will generally be available for the full retail price, though some may be higher for rare or unusual styles in mint condition.

Near Mint. 9.1-9.50 The work's surface is nearly free from wear or pitting, though the piece may show some minor scratches that may occur during packing, unpacking or multiple changing of hands. The colors should be vibrant, crisp, and clean, and if the piece is crafted of glass, the glass should be very nearly crystal clear. Any unintentional internal air bubbles should be minimal at best. Any associated paperwork should be included with the work. A piece in near mint condition will generally be valued at 15%-25% less than the full retail mint price. These marbles, spheres, and orbs are oftentimes referred to as Excellent or Very Good.

Good. 8.5-8.90 Works in this category will show well but may have a few small dings, surface scratches, minor wear, and somewhat hazy glass. The core or design of the piece must be easily seen and should be without large chips or fractures. These pieces will be either signed or unsigned and valued at 50% less than the retail price of a like item in the mint or near mint category. Marbles, spheres, and orbs in this category can be difficult to identify and provenance to a specific artist. No accompanying paperwork will be associated with this work, and it may show some of the wear and handling as that of a better piece in excellent condition. Valuing these items becomes more difficult, therefore they command much less than an artist-marked piece in mint or near mint condition.

Collectible. >8.40 These will be the least desirable pieces for many of the opposite reasons already identified. A marble, sphere or orb in fair condition may have surface chips, dings, and surface cloudiness. There may also be fractures under the surface, though the piece must be complete. Many will be unsigned though should be easily identified to a specific artist. Most of these pieces will have no associated paperwork or provenance. With the exception of an extremely unusual design or if the work was crafted by an artist no longer working in the field, such a signed piece would be recommended as an addition to a collection for style or artist name only. Works in collectible or fair condition will generally be valued at less than 75% of the mint condition value.

Valuating

It is important to keep in mind that the retail price is different from the associated or market value of a particular piece. While many artists continually produce many of the same style marble or a slight variation of a time-tested and collected piece over the course of years, the associated value of the works you collect may be higher than the actual regular retail price for a like item. Subtle differences in the design, color, and glass will affect the associated value much more than they will the retail price. The retail price is that price usually paid an artist, dealer or collector for a particular work.

Retail prices are affected by a number of factors: their source, type, and total number crafted; and whether they are signed, dated, numbered, limited edition, prototype, experimental, or least often an artist's proof. Also factored in are the artist or craftsman, desirability, condition, and material used in producing the work, and more often than not today, the effects of availability via the Internet.

The fluctuation in the price of raw materials such as gas or glass can affect the retail price as well. Also, an artist or craftsman may design and produce such a limited quantity that the mere lack of available pieces by a particular artist at a given time will cause prices to jump abruptly, though possibly artificially for a short span of time.

Prices paid for an artist's work will fluctuate beyond or below the retail price when a piece comes up at auction. Remember, two interested collectors can greatly run the price of either a rather common available marble, or even a rare piece much higher at auction than that same piece could expect to be sold for at a meet, art show, gallery, or through the Internet. The same is true for a collector who greatly pursues the works of a particular artist or a particular style of work. These collectors are usually given the first opportunity to view an artist's newest works and therefore will likely pay a premium for that opportunity. It is not unheard of for a collector to pay three to four times the regular retail price for a new or vintage contemporary in order to add it to their collection. A word of caution when comparing marble prices you are considering purchasing: as glass art and handmade collectible crafts, marbles, spheres, and orbs are a commodity and will therefore sell for prices as high as a collector is willing to pay for a particular piece. Be sure your financial and preferred collector status arrangements with the artist, dealer or collector are firmly agreed on when you become involved in this level of collecting. As is true in any collectible hobby, the rule of thumb is practical, "Buyer, Beware!" Become as knowledgeable as possible about the hobby. Then you will find that your offer-price or trade-for a specific piece will be respected, and you will receive equitable treatment in return.

Chapter 9
More About Marbles, Spheres, and Orbs

The primary focus of this book, as discussed earlier, is to compare and contrast marbles from earlier time periods with marbles, spheres, and orbs crafted by studio glass artists and others since the founding of the Contemporary Marble Movement. By doing so, the reader and collector should find that many of the works have either a definitive direct or indirect relationship to previously made antique handmade or machine-made marbles. Therefore, wherever possible, works are categorized closest with those that came before them. In all cases this was only done to most accurately reflect the general style or design of the work and is based in nearly all instances on the author's research and observation.

In the last five years or so there is a body of work emerging that I have termed and refer to as "novel and inventive contemporary" or "true contemporary" marbles, spheres, and orbs. These are works that have no direct distinguishable relationship with any previous marble handcrafted or machine-made. With that being said, there may be one or more varieties of antique handmade or machine-made marbles that are not discussed in this book. The reason for this being these marbles have no discernable contemporary handmade or machine produced marble to relate the work too. The bibliography will provide a detailed reference listing of other books and resources more appropriate for those seeking additional and extended information on the hobby of marble collecting itself.

Through the following pages you will be dazzled by a variety of marbles, spheres, and orbs. As you will see, many of these works cannot be considered marbles at all regardless of the category they may be listed in. One simple fact sets them apart—they are true works of studio art. They should be classified as fine art. After all, the works are the embodiment of extremely high levels of artistic and technical achievement. While there will be numerous illustrations accompanying most of the styles, in some instances there were few if any available examples. In one or two cases no contemporary examples either exist or were available of particular styles previously produced. In each of the following paragraphs a concerted effort has been made to describe the various styles of marbles as succinctly as possible. Additionally, wherever possible the subjects have been treated in generally recognized marble collecting chronological order within accepted categories; i.e., non-glass handmade marbles, handmade glass marbles, machine-made marbles, etc. Therefore, the earliest handmade marbles are discussed and illustrated first, though the same might not hold true for antique handmade marbles. In this category these marbles are discussed in industry-accepted order by category, and alphabetized within each category. Ultimately, the details that are most important for you the reader to be informed of are the variety of marbles in each category and the approximate dating of their styles. Dates of ancient, antique German handmade marbles, and machine-made marbles have been rounded to the closest decade. There is no intent to mislead the reader by doing so. On the contrary, these dates are simply generalized for historically important perspective and analysis. All of these marbles are currently available either directly from their manufacturers, as in the case of machine-made marbles from Mexico and other countries, or on the secondary market through collectors, dealers, the Internet, and other venues. It can never be stressed enough in any book or publication on a collectible that the best collector is the one who spends the necessary time to become knowledgeable. The key to a successful and happy collecting career is not just the attainment of a particular piece or artist's work, but the accurate information that goes into feeling most comfortable with your purchase.

Ancient, Mineral, and Handmade Non-Glass Marbles, Spheres, and Orbs

Clay Marbles (Originally produced: Ancient to 1920): One of the easiest marble forms to recognize. With millions of these still in existence, clay marbles have little eye appeal. Used from ancient times to colonial times and later, clay marbles may have been used as ballast in ships keels sailing across the Atlantic from Europe. Clay marbles can be found in their natural form, as well as having been dyed in various colors and foil coated. [Antique: Figure 100], [Contemporary: Figure 101-106]

Figure 102. Clay. Rod- and cane-cut. Multi-color guinea-style, art clay/glass hybrid. Steve Parent. 1-3/16 in., ca. 2001. *Courtesy of the author.*

Figure 100. Clay. Antique handmade; Germany. 5/8 in., ca. app. 1850-1920. *Courtesy of Stanley Block.*

Figure 101. Clay. Rod- and cane-cut. Blue, white swirl, art clay/glass hybrid. Steve Parent. 3/4 in., ca. 2001. *Courtesy of the author.*

Figure 103. Clay. Rod- and cane-cut. Multi-color checkerboard, murrini-style; crockery-style swirl; guinea-style, art clay/glass hybrid. Steve Parent. 3/4 - 1-3/16 in., ca. 2001. *Courtesy of the author.*

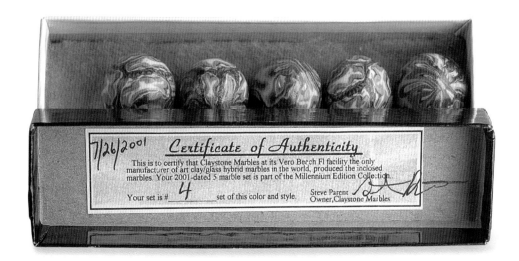

Figure 104. Clay. Rod- and cane-cut. Multi-color, yellow, orange murrini starfish, art clay/glass hybrid. *Claystone Marbles 2001 Millenium Edition; Set No. 4.* Steve Parent. 3/4 in., ca. 2001. *Courtesy of the author.*

Figure 105. Clay. Single gather. Multi-color assorted swirls, slags, patches; Sculpti® Clay. Emily Block, Kevin Block. 1/2 - 3/4 in., ca. 2003. *Courtesy of Emily Block, Kevin Block.*

Figure 106. Clay. Rod- and cane-cut. Fruit, flora, holiday symbols, hand-painted. Attributed to James Kirkland. 3/4 in., ca. app. 2000-2003. *Courtesy of the author.*

Figure 107. Crockery. Antique handmade; Germany. 3/4 in., ca. app. 1850-1920. *Courtesy of Stanley Block.*

Crockery Marbles (Originally produced: 1850-1930): Made from more than one color of clay, these marbles are most often white. Because they are fired at temperatures higher than clay marbles, crockery marbles are denser. Some marbles will exhibit blue, green or a swirling of colors. [Antique: Figure 107-109], [Contemporary: Figure 110]

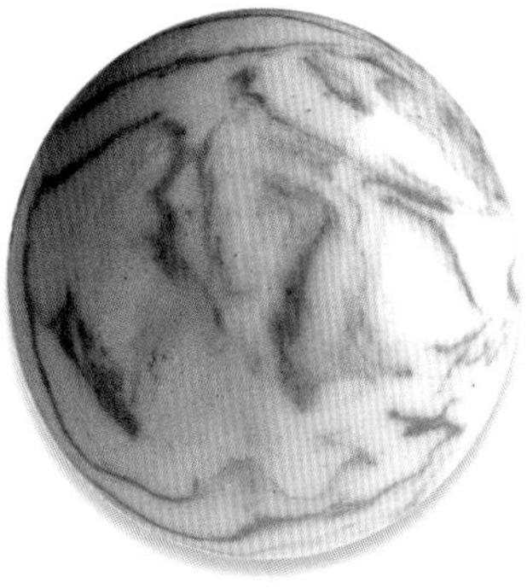

Figure 109. Stoneware. Antique handmade; Germany. 1 in., ca. app. 1850-1920. *Courtesy of Stanley Block.*

Figure 108. Crockery. Antique handmade; Germany. 3/4 - 1 in., ca. app. 1850-1920. *Courtesy of Stanley Block.*

Figure 110. Stoneware. Torchwork. Swirled color bands, white base, glazed. Dinah Hulet. 1-1/2 in., ca. 1997. *Courtesy of the author.*

Bennington Marbles (Originally produced: 1850-1930): While Bennington marbles closely resemble the pottery manufactured in Bennington, Vermont, there is no concrete evidence that marbles were ever crafted there. In fact, it is accepted by collectors that these marbles were imported from Germany. The salt glaze used in the firing process causes the look of Bennington marbles. Many of these marbles have "eyes," or spots on the surface. The marbles touching each other while in the firing stage causes this to occur. Because of the relative worth of these marbles, it is unlikely that contemporary examples exist, as they would have little if any appeal to the collecting market. [Antique: Figure 111-113]

Figure 111. Bennington. Fancy. Blue with "eyes," glazed. Antique hand-made; Germany. 11/16 in., ca. app. 1850-1920. *Courtesy of Stanley Block.*

Figure 112. Bennington. Pink, black; glazed. Antique handmade; Germany. 19/32 in., ca. app. 1850-1920. *Courtesy of Stanley Block.*

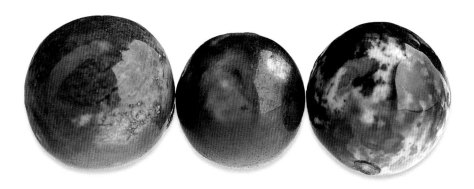

Figure 113. Bennington. Multi-color, glazed. Antique handmade; Germany. 1/2 - 3/4 in., ca. app. 1850-1920. *Courtesy of Stanley Block.*

China Marbles (Originally produced: 1850-1930): Clay marbles are fired at an extremely high temperature. China marbles are denser than either the clay or crockery marbles discussed earlier. The beauty of China marbles is that most are painted and many glazed. Decoration on these marbles can be quite elaborate or as simple as circular lines, some intersecting. Other designs include crows feet, bull's eyes, floral, and least common of all—scenic painted designs. [Antique: Figure 114-117], [Contemporary: 118-183]

Figure 117. China. Lined, painted, glazed. Antique handmade; Germany. 1-3/4 in., ca. app. 1850-1920. *Courtesy of the author.*

Figure 114. China. Red helix, crow's feet, leaves, lined, painted, glazed. Antique handmade; Germany. 3/4 in., ca. app. 1850-1920. *Courtesy of Stanley Block.*

Figure 115. China. Checkerboard, painted, glazed. Antique handmade; Germany. 3/4 in., ca. app. 1850-1920. *Courtesy of Stanley Block.*

Figure 118. China. Single gather. Lined, painted, glazed. Gregg Pessman. 1-1/4 in., ca. app. 2002. *Courtesy of the author.*

Figure 116. China. Lined, painted, glazed. Antique handmade; Germany. 3/4 - 7/8 in., ca. app. 1850-1920. *Courtesy of Stanley Block.*

Figure 119. China. Single gather. Lined, painted, glazed, unglazed. *Experimental.* Nadine Macdonald. 1 - 1-3/8 in., ca. 2001-2003. *Courtesy of the author.*

Figure 120. China. Single gather. Lined, pinwheel, leaves, berries, painted, glazed. Nadine Macdonald. 1-9/16 in., ca. 1999. *Courtesy of the author.*

Figure 121. China. Single gather. Lined, painted, glazed. Robert Brown. 1-1/4 in., ca. 1991. *Courtesy of the author.*

Figure 122. China. Single gather. Star, lined, crackled, painted, glazed. Tom Thornburgh. 1-1/8 - 1-1/4 in., ca. 2002. *Courtesy of the author.*

Figure 123. China. Single gather. Lined, multi-color helix, painted, glazed. Nadine Macdonald. 1 in., ca. 2003. *Courtesy of the author.*

Figure 124. China. Single gather. Lined, etched, painted, glazed. Nadine Macdonald. 1-1/8 in., ca. 2000. *Courtesy of the author.*

Figure 125. China. Single gather. Lined, flora, painted, glazed. Tom Thornburgh. 1-5/16 in., ca. 2002. *Courtesy of the author.*

Figure 126. China. Single gather. Lined, flora, painted, glazed. Nadine Macdonald. 7/8 in., ca. 2002. *Courtesy of the author.*

Figure 127. China. Single gather. Cape Cod Wild Garden. Flora, red base, painted, glazed. Nadine Macdonald. 1 in., ca. 2002. *Courtesy of the author.*

Figure 128. China. Single gather. Cape Cod Fern and Flora. Flora, fauna, painted, glazed. Nadine Macdonald. 2 in., ca. 1999. *Courtesy of the author.*

Figure 129. China. Single gather. Cape Cod Fern and Flora. Flora, fauna, black base, painted, unglazed. Nadine Macdonald. 2 in., ca. 1999. *Courtesy of the author.*

Figure 130. China. Single gather. Japanese Rose Hip. Flora, pinwheel, painted, glazed. Nadine Macdonald. 1-1/16 in., ca. 1999. *Courtesy of the author.*

Figure 131. China. Single gather. Japanese Rose Hip. Tiffany-style flora, rose flora, pinwheel; flora, pinwheel, black base, painted, glazed. Nadine Macdonald. 1-1/8 - 1-1/4 in., ca. 2001. *Courtesy of the author.*

Figure 132. China. Single gather.
Flora, pinwheel, painted, glazed.
Gregg Pessman. 1-3/8 in., ca. 2004.
Courtesy of the author.

Figure 133. China. Pennsylvania Dutch.
Single gather. Hex sign design, painted,
glazed. Nadine Macdonald. 1-3/8 in., ca.
2004. *Courtesy of the author.*

Figure 134-135. China. Single gather. Nailsea.
Spider web design, painted, glazed. Nadine
Macdonald. 7/8 in., ca. 2003. *Courtesy of the
author.*

Figure 138. China. Pinwheel. Single gather. Brown base, painted, crackled, glazed. Tom Thornburgh. 1-3/16 in., ca. 2002. *Courtesy of the author.*

Figure 136. China. Stars and Bars. Single gather. Multi-color bars, stars at poles, painted, glazed. Gregg Pessman. 1-1/2 in., ca. 2002. *Courtesy of the author.*

Figure 137. China. Stars. Single gather. Multi-color helix, stars, painted, glazed. Gregg Pessman. 1-1/2 in., ca. 2002. *Courtesy of the author.*

Figure 139. China. Millefiori. Single gather. Multi-color millefiori, yellow base, painted, glazed. Nadine Macdonald. 1-1/2 in., ca. 2000. *Courtesy of the author.*

Figure 140. China. Fruit and Flora. Single gather. Tiffany-style, stained glass design, painted, unglazed. Nadine Macdonald. 1 - 1-9/16 in., ca. 2001. *Courtesy of the author.*

Figure 143. China. Dragonfly and Flora. Single gather. Tiffany-style, stained glass design, painted, unglazed. Nadine Macdonald. 1-3/8 in., ca. 2003. *Courtesy of the author.*

Figure 141. China. Flora. Single gather. Tiffany-style, stained glass design, painted, glazed. Nadine Macdonald. 2 1/4 in., ca. 2003. *Courtesy of the author.*

Figure 144. China. Geometric. Single gather. Multi-color checkerboard design, painted, glazed. Gregg Pessman. 2-1/8 in., ca. 2003. *Courtesy of the author.*

Figure 142. China. Flora. Single gather. Tiffany-style, stained glass design, painted, glazed. Nadine Macdonald. 1-3/8 in., ca. 2003. *Courtesy of the author.*

Figure 145. China. Geometric. Single gather. Multi-color checkerboard design, painted, glazed. Gregg Pessman. 1-1/4 in., ca. 2003. *Courtesy of the author.*

Figure 148. China. Pinwheel. Single gather. Flora, multi-color pinwheel, painted, glazed. Gregg Pessman. 1-1/2 in., ca. 2003. *Courtesy of the author.*

Figure 146. China. Geometric. Single gather. Multi-color checkerboard design, painted, glazed. Gregg Pessman. 1 in., ca. 2003. *Courtesy of the author.*

Figure 149. China. Flora. Single gather. Painted, glazed. Gregg Pessman. 1-3/8 in., ca. 2002. *Courtesy of the author.*

Figure 147. China. Banded Swirl. Single gather. Multi-color, painted, glazed. Nadine Macdonald. 15/16 - 1-1/16 in., ca. 2003. *Courtesy of the author.*

Figure 150. China. Flora. Single gather. Flora, pigs, light green base, painted, glazed. Gregg Pessman. 1-1/2 in., ca. 2002. *Courtesy of the author.*

Figure 151. China. Bennington. Single gather. Mottled red, green, yellow, painted, glazed. Robert Brown. 1-3/4 in., ca. 1989. *Courtesy of the author.*

Figure 152. China. Single gather. Slag; rose; wildflower; slag; swirl, painted, glazed. Robert Brown. 1/2 - 1-3/8 in., ca. 1990-1991. *Courtesy of the author.*

Figure 153. China. Flora. Single gather. Flora, white base, painted, glazed. Robert Brown. 1-1/4 in., ca. 1990. *Courtesy of the author.*

Figure 154. China. Single gather. Intersecting line; pinwheel; flora; rose, painted, unglazed, glazed. Robert Brown. 7/8 - 1 in., ca. 1989-1991. *Courtesy of the author.*

Figure 155. China. Scenic. Single gather. Cornfield scene, pinwheel back, painted, glazed. Gregg Pessman. 1-1/4 in., ca. 2002. *Courtesy of the author.*

Figure 158. China. Scenic. Single gather. Can-Can dance scene, multi-color pinwheel, painted, glazed. Gregg Pessman. 1-3/8 in., ca. 2002. *Courtesy of the author.*

Figure 156. China. Scenic. Single gather. Schoolhouse scene, apple at top pole, painted, glazed. Gregg Pessman. 1-3/8 in., ca. 2002. *Courtesy of the author.*

Figure 159. China. Scenic. Single gather. Ballerina dancers scene, pinwheel, painted, glazed. Gregg Pessman. *Commission.* 1-1/2 in., ca. 2001. *Courtesy of Emily Block.*

Figure 157. China. Scenic. Single gather. Schoolhouse, marble playing scene, painted, glazed. Gregg Pessman. 1-3/8 in., ca. 2003. *Courtesy of the author.*

Figure 160. China. Scenic. Single gather. Amusement park scene, painted, glazed. Gregg Pessman. 1-1/2 in., ca. 2002. *Courtesy of the author.*

Figure 161. China. Scenic. Single gather. Flying pigs scene, crescent sun, blue base, painted, glazed. Gregg Pessman. 1-3/8 in., ca. 2003. *Courtesy of the author.*

Figure 162. China. Scenic. Single gather. Happy Birthday, sixteen candles, multi-color, painted, glazed. Nadine Macdonald. 1-1/8 in., ca. 2000. *Courtesy of the author.*

Figure 163. China. Single gather. Intertwined hearts, Cape Cod fern, gold embellishment, painted; glazed. *Commission.* Nadine Macdonald. 1-1/2 in., ca. 2001. *Courtesy of Ann Block.*

Figure 164-165. China. Single gather. Assorted pink hearts, Cape Cod fern, gold embellishment, painted, glazed. *Commission.* Nadine Macdonald. 1-1/2 in., ca. 2001. *Courtesy of Emily Block.*

Figure 166. China. Scenic. Single gather. Halloween witch, ghost, bats, cat, tombstone, moon, candy corn on reverse, orange base, painted, glazed. Nadine Macdonald. 1-1/8 in., ca. 1989. *Courtesy of Robert Block.*

Figure 167. China. Scenic. Single gather. Halloween witch, jack-o-lantern, orange base, painted, glazed. Nadine Macdonald. 1 in., ca. 1989. *Courtesy of the author.*

Figure 168-169. China. Scenic. Single gather. Christmas poinsettia, holly, berries on reverse, painted, glazed. Robert Brown. 1-3/4 in., ca. 1997. *Courtesy of the author.*

Figure 170-171. China. Scenic. Single gather. Christmas flora, holly, berries on reverse, painted, glazed. Tom Thornburgh. 1-3/8 in., ca. 2001. *Courtesy of the author.*

Figure 172. China. Single gather. Twin wreath, leaves, berries, gold base; Cape Cod Fern Garden, red base; flora, gold base, painted, unglazed. Nadine Macdonald. 7/8 - 1-1/4 in., ca. 1999-2000. *Courtesy of the author.*

Figure 173. China. Apple. Single gather. White base, painted, glazed. Robert Brown. 1-1/4 in., ca. 1991. *Courtesy of the author.*

Figure 174. China. Clown. Single gather. White base, painted, glazed. Tom Thornburgh. 1-3/8 in., ca. 2000. *Courtesy of the author.*

Figure 175. China. Clown. Single gather. White base, painted, glazed. Tom Thornburgh. 1-1/2 in., ca. 2000. *Courtesy of the author.*

Figure 176-177. China. Scenic. Single gather. Marble Collectors Society of America (MCSA) logo, assorted multi-color marbles on reverse, painted, glazed. *Commission.* Gregg Pessman. 1-3/8 in., ca. 2002. *Courtesy of the author.*

Figure 178. China. Scenic. Single gather.
Dutch village scene, blue delft, painted, glazed.
Gregg Pessman. 1-3/8 in., ca. 2003. *Courtesy of
the author.*

Figure 182. China. Scenic. Single
gather. Angel, night sky, floral, blue
base, painted, glazed. Coralee Smith.
1-3/8 in., ca. 2001. *Courtesy of the
author.*

Figure 179. China. Scenic. Single gather.
Schoolhouse scene, painted, glazed. Gregg
Pessman. 1-1/2 in., ca. 2003. *Courtesy of the
author.*

Figure 183. China. Scenic. Single gather.
Desert scene, cactus, mountains,
painted, glazed. Coralee Smith. 2-3/8 in.,
ca. 2003. *Courtesy of the author.*

Figure 180-181. China. Scenic. Single gather. Post office, farm
scene, gold pinwheel, painted, unglazed. Nadine Macdonald.
1-3/8 in., ca. 1999. *Courtesy of the author.*

Carpet Balls (Originally produced: 1850-1930): Used in games, among them one similar to Bocce. Carpet Balls are glazed, crockery pieces believed to have been manufactured in the United Kingdom. Ranging in size from 3" to 3-1/2", and occasionally even larger, they are most often glazed after having been covered with painted designs including intersecting lines, and flora, and mocha ware. [Antique: Figure 184, 185], [Contemporary: Figure 186, 187]

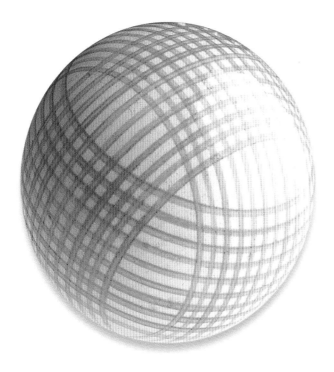

Figure 184. Carpet Ball. Intersecting yellow lines, white base, glazed. Antique handmade; Germany. 3-1/4 in., ca. app. 1850-1930. *Courtesy of Robert Block.*

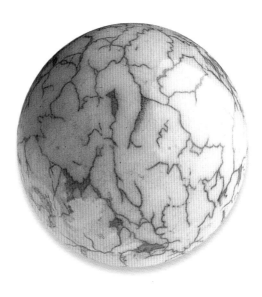

Figure 185. Carpet Ball. Blue spider web swirling, white base, glazed. Antique handmade; Germany. 2-1/2 in., ca. app. 1850-1930. *Courtesy of Robert Block.*

Figure 186. Carpet Ball. Green flora, leaves, white base, glazed. China. 3-1/4 in., ca. 2004. *Courtesy of Claire Block.*

Figure 187. Carpet Ball. Blue flora, green flora, white base, glazed. China. 3-1/4 in., ca. 2004. *Courtesy of Claire Block.*

Agate Marbles (Originally produced: 1850 - present): These marbles are discussed separately from other stone and mineral marbles and spheres because of their unique position in the production and playing they attained at the height of their popularity with children. Though they are still prized as collectibles by many marble collectors. [Antique and Contemporary: Figure 188, 189]

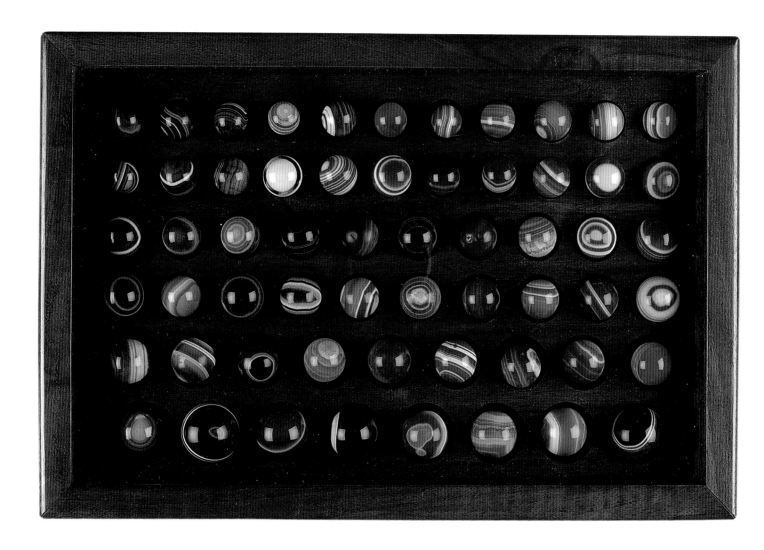

Figure 188. Agate. Antique hand cut, contemporary banded, bull's-eye, various colors, natural, dyed. Marbles: 3/4 - 1-1/4 in. Box: L. 14 x W. 9 in., ca. app. 1800-2003. *Courtesy of the author.*

Figure 189. Agate. Antique hand cut, banded, bull's-eye, various colors, natural, dyed. 3/4 in., ca. app. 1800-1930. *Courtesy of the author.*

Agate is so named because of its banded crystalline quartz composition. Agate is most often found as nodules in former volcanic rock cavities having displaced gases. Agate often filled cracks and fissures in volcanic rock. Other times this gemstone has been found free of any other mineral having been washed from volcanic areas, found in streams, dry lake beds, and other igneous sites. Once agate is cut it often reveals the type and amount of quartz within the mineral. These bandings may be multicolored or various shades of the same color. The most common agate type is chalcedony, an extremely fine and tight-grained variety of quartz found in various colors. Chalcedony is found associated with common quartz, smoky quartz, amethyst, jasper, and carnelian.

The agate used in playing marbles during peak production is commonly believed to be from the 1800s - early-1900s. First found in rich brown tones in the Idar-Oberstein region of Germany, this beautiful gemstone was hand cut and ground with noticeable faceting by skilled workers in factory settings. Later pieces were cut into cubes and placed in large tumblers to remove the facets and make them as smooth as possible. Children prized agate marbles because of their relative rarity and expense compared to glass marbles. While agate was heat-treated, acid soaked, and boiled in solutions to enhance color, the most sought after agates from the region are untreated. Mineralogists must view altered gemstones carefully to ascertain if the color is natural to the stone or aided by man.

As the mines of the Idar-Obersterin region became depleted, agate was shipped in from numerous countries, including, India, Brazil, and Mexico. Nearly all of this material was treated in some manner to enhance the natural grayish color exhibited. Though not commonly found, dyed agates of black, blue, green, and yellow in mint condition are prized by collectors.

Much like other minerals and gemstones, agates have become commercially popular in large sizes as decorative objects. [Figure 190]

Figure 190. Agate. Antique hand cut, contemporary banded, bull's-eye, various colors, natural, dyed. 5/8 - 1 in., ca. app. 1800-1930. *Courtesy of the author.*

Mineral Marbles (Originally produced: Ancient to present): First believed to be ocean rounded and polished pebbles used by ancient peoples for various games, the mineral marbles most often associated with the hobby of marble collecting were shaped on large mechanical grinding machines, a vast multitude of spheres and smaller marbles are beautiful pieces in their own right. Today, a diverse and extensive collection of mineral marbles, spheres, and orbs can be assembled and displayed quite nicely. The primary market for these pieces are not marble collectors, but rather mineral collectors, decorators, and designers. You name the mineral or gemstone and it is quite likely you will be able to readily attain a spherical piece. There are literally hundreds of varieties of mineral marbles. It is important to keep in mind that much like contemporary handmade marbles, spheres, and orbs, mineral pieces are not spherical in order to play with, but rather as collectibles. There is an abundance of literature, mostly anecdotal, on the subject of minerals for metaphysical or medicinal properties. [Figure 191-196]

Figure 191. Mineral. Dry Head Agate; Utah, United States. 1-1/2 in., ca. late-1990s. *Courtesy of the author.*

Figure 195. Mineral. Sodalite; Brazil. 1-1/2 in., ca. late-1990s. *Courtesy of the author.*

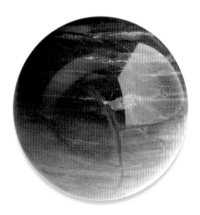

Figure 192. Mineral. Petrified Wood, Arizona, United States. 1-7/8 in., ca. late-1990s. *Courtesy of the author.*

Figure 196. Mineral. Golden Rutilated Quartz; Mexico. 1-1/4 in., ca. late-1990s. *Courtesy of the author.*

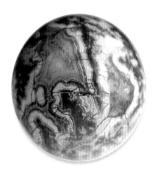

Figure 193. Mineral. Crazy Lace Agate; Mexico. 1-1/2 in., ca. late-1990s. *Courtesy of the author.*

Figure 194. Mineral. Fluorite in Limestone; Canada, Tigereye; Brazil. 1-1/2 in.; 1-1/4 in., ca. late-1990s. *Courtesy of the author.*

Below is a listing of known mineral marbles in one-inch size. Many of these and more are available in larger sphere and orb sizes in excess of 5-1/2" diameter. This listing was made available courtesy of www.SpheresToYou.com.

Agate, Assorted	Goldstone	Pectolite, Blue (Larimar)
Agate, Black Banded	Hematite	Petrified Palm Wood
Agate, Brown Banded	Holmquisite	Petrified Wood
Agate, Golden	Howlite	Picasso Marble
Agate, Golden Banded	Jade, Blue	Quartz, Hematoid
Agate, Orange Banded	Jade, Dark	Quartz, Red
Agate, Peach	Jade, Light	Quartz, Rose
Agate, Silver Banded	Jasper, Black	Quartz, Rose Star
Amber	Jasper, Green Tree	Quartz, Rose Star Pale Transulcent
Amethyst	Jasper, Indian Fancy	Quartz, Smokey
Ametrine	Jasper, Leopard Skin	Rhodochrosite
Amazonzite	Jasper, Picture	Rhodonite
Aquamarine	Jasper, Polychrome	Richtorite
Aquamarine with Actinolite	Jasper, Rainforest	Ruby
Aventurine	Jasper, Red	Ruby, Fuschite
Azurite	Jasper, Red Breciated	Ruby Zoisite
Bloodstone, Spotted	Jasper, Red Snakeskin	Rutilated Quartz
Bloodstone	Jasper, Green Zebra	Rutilated Quartz, Gold
Blue Opal	Jet	Rutilated Quartz, Gold Tinged
Bustamite	Labradorite	Rutilated Quartz, Pink-Tinged
Bustamite, Richtorite	Lapis	Rutilated Quartz, Silver Rutile
Calcite, Golden	Lapis, Snowflake	Rutilated Quartz, White Rutile
Canyon Wonderstone	Lodolite	Sapphire
Carnelian	Malachite	Sapphire, Black Star
Charoite	Mariposite	Seraphenite
Chiastalite	Magnesite	Sodalite
Chrysocolla, from Stalagite	Meteorite	Spanish Olivine
Chrysocolla in Quartz	Mookaite	Sugilite
Chrysocolla in Black	Morganite	Sunstone/Moonstone
Chrysocolla in Matrix	Obsidian, Mohagany	Thulite
Coral, Red	Obsidian, Snowflake	Tiger Eye
Coral, Indonesian	Obsidian, Rainbow	Tiger Eye, Blue
Crystal Quartz	Onyx	Tiger Eye, Green
Dalmation Stone	Onyx, Black	Tiger Eye, Red
Dinosaur Bone	Onyx, Pampas	Tiger Iron
Dinosaur Coprolite	Opal, Andean	Tourmaline, Shocking Pink
Dumortierite	Opal Andean Pink	Tourmaline, Black (Schorl)
Fluorite, Blue	Opal, Imperial Cat's Eye	Turquoise
Fluorite, Purple/Green	Opal, Louisana	Unikite
Fluorite, Purple	Opal, Mexican Fire (Orange)	Variscite, Australian
Fuschite, Green	Opal, Mexican Fire (Multi-Color)	Volcanic Glass, Green
Galena	Opal,Oregon	Walrus Ivory Tusk
Garnet, Star	Opalite, Lavendar	

Handmade Glass Marbles, Spheres, and Orbs

Swirls

Banded and Coreless Swirl Marbles (Originally produced: 1850-1920): With an outer surface or subsurface layer of various colored repeating bands these marbles have no design core. Banded marbles can be transparent, translucent or opaque. Coreless appear as though they should have had a crafted center design core. [Antique: Figure 197-201], [Contemporary: Figure 202-229]

Figure 197. Banded Swirl. Multi-color, clear glass. Antique handmade; Germany. 3/4 in., ca. app. 1850-1920. *Courtesy of Stanley Block.*

Figure 198. Banded Swirl. Blue bands, gold aventurine glass. Antique handmade; Germany. 3/4 in., ca. app. 1850-1920. *Courtesy of Stanley Block.*

Figure 199. Banded Swirl. Clear olive/green base, subsurface white bands. Antique handmade; Germany. 11/16 in., ca. app. 1850-1920. *Courtesy of Stanley Block.*

Figure 200. Banded Swirl. Red, clear glass. Antique handmade; Germany. 11/16 in., ca. app. 1850-1920. *Courtesy of Stanley Block.*

Figure 201. Banded Swirl. Golden yellow, gold aventurine glass. Antique handmade; Germany. 3/4 in., ca. app. 1850-1920. *Courtesy of Stanley Block.*

Figure 202. Banded Swirl. Torchwork. Clear brown base, green band. Bruce Troeh. 7/8 in., ca. 2000. *Courtesy of the artist.*

Figure 203. Banded Swirl. Rod- and cane-cut. Light-green, gold aventurine glass bands, clear green base. Dudley Giberson. 1-1/4 in., ca. 1990s. *Courtesy of the author.*

Figure 204. Banded Swirl. Torchwork. Gold aventurine glass bands, white bands, blue base. Bruce Troeh. 3/4 in., ca. 2002. *Courtesy of the author.*

Figure 205. Banded Swirl. Rod- and cane-cut. Red, white bands, alternating blue band, mica, clear glass. William Murray. 1-1/8 in., ca. 2001. *Courtesy of the author.*

Figure 206. Banded Swirl. Rod- and cane-cut. Orange, white, yellow, white bands, dark blue base, blizzard mica. Steve Davis. 2 in., ca. 2003. *Courtesy of the author.*

Figure 209. Banded Swirl. Rod- and cane-cut. Yellow, orange bands, alternating orange/red, blue/green dichroic glass base. Eddie Seese. 1-1/2 in., ca. 2003. *Courtesy of the artist.*

Figure 207. Banded Swirl. Rod- and cane-cut. Red, yellow, blue bands, opaque white base. Unsigned. Unidentified. 1-1/2 in., ca. 1990s. *Courtesy of the author.*

Figure 210. Banded Swirl. Rod- and cane-cut. Red, orange bands, purple, orange bands, orange dichroic glass over dark green base. Eddie Seese. 1-3/8 in., ca. 2003. *Courtesy of the author.*

Figure 208. Banded Swirl. Rod- and cane-cut. Multi-color bands, green aventurine glass base. Steve Davis. 1-1/2 in., ca. 2003. *Courtesy of the author.*

Figure 211. Banded Swirl. Rod- and cane-cut. Multi-color bands, green aventurine glass, dark blue base. Steve Davis. 1-1/2 in., ca. 2003. *Courtesy of the author.*

Figure 214. Banded Swirl. Torchwork. Multi-color lightning bolt bands, purple base. Unsigned. Unidentified. 1-1/4 in., ca. app. 2001-2003. *Courtesy of the author.*

Figure 212. Banded Swirl. Torchwork. Green, turquoise blue bands, dichroic bands, reverse rake pull. Shell Neisler. 1-1/2 in., ca. 2004. *Courtesy of the author.*

Figure 215. Banded Swirl. Torchwork. Red, white, gold aventurine glass bands, transparent blue base. Drew Fritts. 1-7/8 in., ca. 2003. *Courtesy of the author.*

Figure 213. Banded Swirl. Rod- and cane-cut. Assorted multi-color banded opaque base, clear base, some with gold aventurine glass. Dale Danowski, Matthew Potter. 5/8 - 7/8 in., app. ca. 2000-2003. *Courtesy of the author.*

Figure 216. Banded Swirl. Torchwork. Red, orange, yellow, blue aventurine glass bands, transparent blue base. Drew Fritts. 1-7/8 in., ca. 2003. *Courtesy of the author.*

Figure 217. Banded Swirl. Rod- and cane-cut. Multi-color bands, red aventurine glass, folded. Rolf and Genie Wald. 7/8 in., ca. 2002. *Courtesy of the artist.*

Figure 218. Banded Swirl. Rod- and cane-cut. Multi-color bands, folded. Jody Fine. 7/8 in., ca. 2003. *Courtesy of the author.*

Figure 219. Banded Swirl. Rod- and cane-cut. Multi-color lobed bands, orange/green, silver dichroic glass, dark blue base. Eddie Seese. 1-3/4 in., ca. 2003. *Courtesy of the artist.*

Figure 220. Banded Swirl. Rod- and cane-cut. Blue, purple bands, black, green dichroic glass base. Eddie Seese. 1-3/8 in., ca. 2003. *Courtesy of the artist.*

Figure 221. Banded Swirl. Rod- and cane-cut. Yellow, orange bands, blue bands. Robert Lichtman. 1-3/8 in., ca. 1987. *Courtesy of the author.*

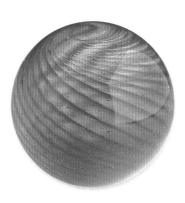

Figure 222. Banded Swirl. Rod- and cane-cut. Turquoise, blue bands, clear base. Bermuda Glass Blowing Studio, Bermuda. 1-3/4 in., ca. app. 1990-1995. *Courtesy of the Marble Collectors Society of America.*

Figure 223. Banded Swirl. Torchwork. Alternating multi-color bands, black, clear base. Unsigned. Unidentified. 1-1/4 in., ca. app. 2001-2003. *Courtesy of the author.*

Figure 224. Banded Swirl. Rod- and cane-cut. Multi-color thin bands, clear base. Harry Besett. 1-1/2 in., ca. 2003. *Courtesy of the author.*

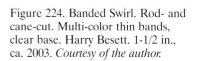

Figure 225. Banded Swirl. Rod-
and cane-cut. Red, green bands,
yellow bands. Phillip Nolley. 1-1/2
in., ca. 1990s. *Courtesy of the artist.*

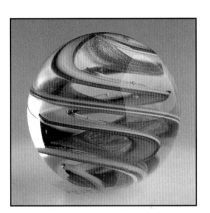

Figure 226. Banded Swirl. Single
gather. Pink, yellow, white, gold
aventurine glass, clear base. David
Salazar. 1-3/8 in., ca. 2002.
Courtesy of the author.

Figure 228. Banded Swirl. Rod- and cane-cut.
Four-panel, red, white, blue with mica,
signature cane. *Limited edition 4/25.* Rolf and
Genie Wald. 1-1/2 in., ca. 2002. *Courtesy of
the author.*

Figure 227. Banded Swirl. Rod- and cane-cut.
Alternating multi-color bands, black, clear
base. Robert Dane. 2 in., ca. 1986. *Courtesy of
the Marble Collectors Society of America.*

Figure 229. Banded Swirl. Single gather. Torchwork. Multi-
color; various bands; clear base. David Salazar *(front three)*;
Christopher Robinson *(back)*. 7/8 - 1 in., ca. 2003; ca. app.
2000. *Courtesy of the author.*

Clambroth Swirl Marbles (Originally produced: 1850-1920): Typically composed of an opaque milky-white base with either single or multiple colored evenly spaced bands, clambroth swirl band colors are most often blue, green or light red/pink. Rare examples of this type of marble are composed of a black, blue or other colored base glass. Additionally, some of these marbles will have various alternating colored surface bands in a repetitive pattern. [Antique: Figure 230-232], [Contemporary: Figure 233-237]

Figure 230. Clambroth. Wide, Pink, green, blue bands, opaque white base. Antique handmade; Germany. 11/16 in., ca. app. 1850-1920. *Courtesy of Stanley Block.*

Figure 231. Clambroth. Pink bands, opaque white base. Antique hand-made; Germany. 3/4 in., ca. app. 1850-1920. *Courtesy of Stanley Block.*

Figure 232. Clambroth. Narrow, pink, green, blue bands, opaque white base. Antique handmade; Germany. 3/4 in., ca. app. 1850-1920. *Courtesy of Stanley Block.*

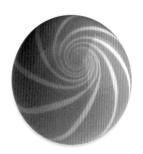

Figure 233. Clambroth. Torchwork. White bands, light-blue base. Drew Fritts. 1-1/4 in., ca. 1999. *Courtesy of the author.*

Figure 234. Clambroth. Torchwork. Yellow, pink bands, white base. *Prototype.* Drew Fritts. 1-1/4 in., ca. 1999. *Courtesy of the author.*

Figure 235. Clambroth. Rod- and cane-cut. Stardust Clambroth. Multi-color bands, dichroic glass base. Geoffrey Beetem. 1-3/8 in., ca. 2001. *Courtesy of the author.*

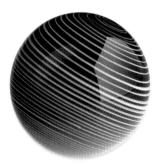

Figure 236. Clambroth. Torchwork. Black, white, shadow effect. Mike Edmundson. 1-1/2 in., ca. 2004. *Courtesy of the author.*

Figure 237. Clambroth. Rod- and cane-cut. Brown, white, gold aventurine glass bands, pink base; blue, gold aventurine bands, light-blue base; red, blue latticinio bands, pink base. Dale Danowski. 5/8 - 7/8 in., ca. app. 1995-1999. *Courtesy of the author.*

Divided Core Swirl Marbles (Originally produced: 1850-1920): Constructed of three or more white or colored glass bands, when the divided core marble is twisted by the craftsmen from its host cane, a core is formed containing open space between the bands. Bands of three, four, five, and even six add beauty to these distinctive marbles. [Antique: Figure 238-240], [Contemporary: Figure 241-248]

Figure 240. Divided Core Swirl. Multicolor bands, white base, alternating white, yellow outer bands, clear glass. Antique handmade; Germany. 1-3/4 in., ca. app. 1850-1920. *Courtesy of the author.*

Figure 238. Divided Core Swirl. Multi-color bands, white base, yellow, white outer bands, clear glass. Antique handmade; Germany. 1-5/8 in., ca. app. 1850-1920. *Courtesy of the author.*

Figure 239. Divided Core Swirl. Multi-color bands, white base, yellow outer bands, clear glass. Antique handmade; Germany. 1-9/16 in., ca. app. 1850-1920. *Courtesy of the author.*

Figure 241. Divided Core Swirl. Torchwork. Yellow, blue bands, black outer bands, clear glass. Unsigned. Unidentified. 7/8 in., ca. app. 2001-2003. *Courtesy of the author.*

Figure 242. Divided Core Swirl. Rod-and cane-cut. Yellow, red, white bands, blue, yellow outer bands, clear glass. Phillip Nolley. 1-1/2 in., ca. 2002. *Courtesy of the artist.*

Figure 243. Divided Core Swirl. Torchwork. Pink, white bands, surrounded by white bands, multi-color outer bands, clear glass. Cuneo Furnace, Steven Maslach. 1-1/4 in., ca. app. 1990-1995. *Courtesy of the Marble Collectors Society of America.*

Figure 246. Divided Core Swirl. Rod- and cane-cut. Red, white bands, transparent blue outer bands, clear glass. Unsigned. Unidentified. 1-3/4 in., ca. app. 2001-2003. *Courtesy of the author.*

Figure 245. Divided Core Swirl. Rod- and cane-cut. Black, white, yellow, red bands, clear glass. Phillip Nolley. 1-3/4 in., ca. 2002. *Courtesy of the artist.*

Figure 247. Divided Core Swirl. Torchwork. Black, white core, multi-color frit; gold aventurine glass, clear glass. Bruce Troeh. 1-3/8 in., ca. 2002. *Courtesy of the artist.*

Figure 244. Divided Core Swirl. Torchwork. Dark blue bands, gold aventurine glass, clear glass. Bruce Troeh. 1-3/8 in., ca. 2002. *Courtesy of the artist.*

Figure 248. Divided Core Swirl. Rod- and cane-cut. Multi-color core, black, reverse twist, clear glass. Fritz Lauenstein. 2 in., ca. 2004. *Courtesy of the artist.*

Indian Swirl Marbles: (Originally produced: 1850-1920): With an opaque black glass base, Indian swirl marbles have surface bands of white and/or various colored glass. Some of these marbles show unbroken bands from top to bottom, others appear with bits of color that have been stretched or pulled in the crafting process. [Antique: Figure 249-251], [Contemporary: Figure 252-254]

Figure 249. Indian Swirl. Yellow, black base. Antique handmade; Germany. 7/8 in., ca. app. 1850-1920. *Courtesy of Stanley Block.*

Figure 252. Indian Swirl. Torchwork. Orange, blue, gold aventurine glass, black base. Christopher Robinson. 7/8 in., ca. app. 1995-1999. *Courtesy of the author.*

Figure 250. Indian Swirl. Multi-color, black base. Antique handmade; Germany. 11/16 in., ca. app. 1850-1920. *Courtesy of Stanley Block.*

Figure 253. Indian Swirl. Torchwork. Red, green, yellow, blue, black base. Christopher Robinson. 7/8 in., ca. app. 1995-1999. *Courtesy of the author.*

Figure 251. Indian Swirl. White, black base. Antique handmade; Germany. 1 in., ca. app. 1850-1920. *Courtesy of Stanley Block.*

Figure 254. Indian Swirl. Torchwork. Yellow, green, blue, black base. Christopher Robinson. 1/2 in., ca. app. 1995-1999. *Courtesy of the author.*

Latticinio Core Swirl Marbles (Originally produced: 1850-1920): Consisting of a central lattice-like core of interweaving fine bands of white or colored glass. In most instances these marbles will have outer bands of one or more colored glass in repeating patterns. [Antique: Figure 255-257], [Contemporary: Figure 258-272]

Figure 255. Latticinio Core Swirl. Yellow core, red, green bands. Antique handmade; Germany. 1-3/4 in., ca. app. 1850-1920. *Courtesy of the author.*

Figure 258. Latticinio Core Swirl. Rod- and cane-cut. Multi-color core, multi-color bands, clear glass. *Limited Edition 2/25.* Jody Fine. 1-5/8 in., ca. 2002. *Courtesy of the author.*

Figure 256. Latticinio Core Swirl. White core, red, yellow, green bands. Antique handmade; Germany. 7/8 in., ca. app. 1850-1920. *Courtesy of the author.*

Figure 257. Latticinio Core Swirl. White core, red, yellow, blue, white; red, white, green, yellow bands. Antique handmade; Germany. 1-1/2 in., ca. app. 1850-1920. *Courtesy of the author.*

Figure 259. Latticinio Core Swirl. Rod- and cane-cut. Multi-color core, multi-color bands, aventurine, clear glass. Jody Fine. 7/8 in., ca. 2003. *Courtesy of the author.*

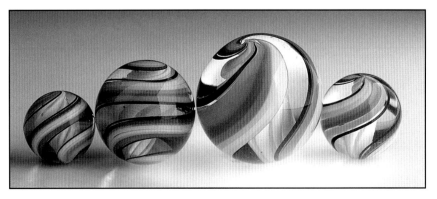

Figure 260. Latticinio Swirls. Rod- and cane-cut. White latticinio core, multi-color, two-panel outer bands. *Limited edition set.* Jody Fine. Marble stock crafted at Wheaton Village Marble Weekend 2003. Jody Fine, Douglas Sweet. 7/8 - 1-5/8 in., ca. 2003. *Courtesy of the author.*

Figure 261. Latticinio Core Swirl. Rod- and cane-cut. Yellow core, yellow, white, black, clear glass. Dudley Giberson. 1-1/4 in., ca. app. 1990-1995. *Courtesy of the author.*

Figure 262. Latticinio Core Swirl. Rod- and cane-cut. White core, red, yellow, blue, aventurine, clear glass. Gibson Glass, attributed to Charles Gibson. 1-5/8 in., ca. app. 1990-1997. *Courtesy of the author.*

Figure 263. Latticinio Core Swirl. Rod- and cane-cut. Blue, white core, blue, clear glass. Unsigned. Unidentified. 1-3/8 in., ca. app. 2001-2003. *Courtesy of the author.*

Figure 265. Latticinio Core Swirl. Rod- and cane-cut. Orange, green core, orange, green, blue, yellow, black, clear glass. Ken Rosenfeld. 1-3/8 in., ca. 2002. *Courtesy of the author.*

Figure 266. Latticinio Core Swirl. Rod- and cane-cut. Fused, half and half, tan, black lavender, white latticinio half; blue, yellow, green banded half, clear glass. Robert Dane. 1-1/4 in., ca. app. 1983-1987. *Courtesy of the Marble Collectors Society of America.*

Figure 264. Latticinio Core Swirl. Rod- and cane-cut. White, lavender core, white, red, green, aventurine, clear glass. Ken Rosenfeld. 1-3/8 in., ca. 2002. *Courtesy of the author.*

Figure 267. Latticinio Core Swirl. Rod-and cane-cut. Black core, white, grey, green, clear glass. Teign Valley Glass, England. 1-3/8 in., ca. app. 1990-1997. *Courtesy of the Marble Collectors Society of America.*

Figure 270. Latticinio Core Swirl. Rod- and cane-cut. White core, black, white, reverse twist *(left)*; red, black, yellow, black, reverse twist *(right)*, clear glass. Rolf Greiner-Adams, Germany. 1 in., ca. 2001. *Courtesy of the author.*

Figure 268. Latticinio Core Swirl. Rod- and cane-cut. White core, transparent red, blue, clear glass. Robert Lichtman. 1-3/4 in., ca. 1987. *Courtesy of the author.*

Figure 271. Latticinio Swirl. Rod- and cane-cut. White core, clear red, white, pink bands. Cuneo Furnace. Steven Maslach. 2-1/4 in., ca. 2000. *Courtesy of the author.*

Figure 269. Latticinio Core Swirl. Rod-and cane-cut. White core, transparent green, purple dichroic bands, green, lavender, clear glass. Eddie Seese. 1-3/8 in., ca. 2003. *Courtesy of the artist.*

Figure 272. Latticinio Swirl. Ribbon Swirl. Rod- and cane-cut. Multi-color ribbon core, outer latticinio bands, dichroic glass. James Alloway. 3 in., ca. 2004. *Courtesy of the author.*

Figure 273. Peppermint Swirl. Red, blue, white base. Antique handmade; Germany. 1/2 – 3/4 in., ca. app. 1850-1920. *Courtesy of Stanley Block.*

Figure 274. Peppermint Swirl. Rod- and cane-cut. Red, blue, white base. Gibson Glass, attributed to Charles Gibson. 1-3/8 in., ca. 1998. *Courtesy of the author.*

Peppermint Swirl Marbles (Originally produced: 1850-1920): An opaque white base and surface bands of alternating blue and red colored glass, some thick, others thin, characterize the construction of peppermint swirls. It is generally accepted these marbles first appeared at the U.S. Centennial Exposition in Philadelphia, Pennsylvania, as a tribute to America's 100th birthday. [Antique: Figure 273], [Contemporary: Figure 274-276]

Figure 275. Peppermint Swirl. Rod- and cane-cut. Red, blue, mica, white base. Mark Matthews. 1-3/4 in., ca. 1990. *Courtesy of the author.*

Figure 276. Peppermint Swirl. Torchwork. Red, blue, white base. Kris Parke. 1-7/8 in., ca. 2004. *Courtesy of the author.*

Ribbon Core Swirl Marbles (Originally produced: 1850-1920): Marbles with a flat central core band of color usually found to be rather wide are referred to as ribbon core swirl marbles. From no twist at all to four twists, some tight others more elongated, the thickness of the ribbon can vary greatly from marble to marble. These marbles can be either single or double ribbon core pieces, depending if one or two ribbons of white or colored glass are present. Most often you will see these marbles exhibit a core made up of a solid color with other colored bands overlaid or placed next to the center ribbon. [Antique: Figure 277-279], [Contemporary: Figure 280-331]

Figure 277. Ribbon Swirl. Red, white, blue, outer blue bands, transparent glass. Antique handmade; Germany. 1-1/8 in., ca. app. 1850-1920. *Courtesy of the author.*

Figure 278. Ribbon Swirl. Red, yellow, green, outer white bands, clear glass. Antique handmade; Germany. 1-1/4 in., ca. app. 1850-1920. *Courtesy of the author.*

Figure 279. Ribbon Swirl. Red, yellow, white bands, clear glass. Antique handmade; Germany. 1-1/8 in., ca. app. 1850-1920. *Courtesy of Stanley Block.*

Figure 280. Ribbon Swirl. Rod- and cane-cut. Single ribbon, red, grey, white, black, clear glass. Robert Dane. 2-1/4 in., ca. 1980s. *Courtesy of the author.*

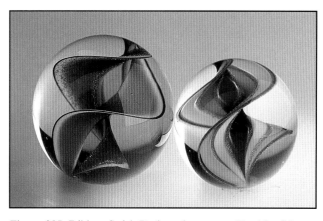

Figure 285. Ribbon Swirl. Rod- and cane-cut. Double ribbon, pink, white, red, blue, white, gold aventurine glass; single ribbon, red, white, blue, green, gold aventurine glass, blue aventurine glass, clear glass. Dudley Giberson. 1-1/4 - 1-1/2 in., ca. app. 1990-1997. *Courtesy of the author.*

Figure 281. Ribbon Swirl. Flag. Rod- and cane-cut. Single ribbon, red, white, yellow, blue, gold aventurine glass, clear glass. *Limited edition 1/100.* Rolf and Genie Wald. 1-1/2 in., ca. 1995. *Courtesy of the author.*

Figure 286. Ribbon Swirl. Torchwork. Single ribbon, red, green, blue, clear glass. Rudy Calin. 1-1/4 in., ca. 2003. *Courtesy of the artist.*

Figure 283. Ribbon Swirl. Torchwork. Single ribbon, light blue, pink *(left)*; red, white *(right)*, clear glass. Bruce Troeh. 5/8 - 3/4 in., ca. 2003. *Courtesy of the author.*

Figure 282. Ribbon Swirl. Rod- and cane-cut. Single ribbon, yellow, brown, gold aventurine glass, clear glass. Dudley Giberson. 1-5/8 in., ca. app. 1990-1995. *Courtesy of the author.*

Figure 287. Ribbon Swirl. Torchwork. Single ribbon, amber brown, white, clear glass. William Murray. 1-1/4 in., ca. 2002. *Courtesy of the author.*

Figure 284. Ribbon Swirl. Rod- and cane-cut. Single ribbon, pink, blue, white, black, white, clear glass. Jody Fine. 1-1/4 in., ca. 1980. *Courtesy of the author.*

Figure 288. Ribbon Swirl. Rod- and cane-cut. Single ribbon, multi-color, green aventurine glass, clear glass. Harry and Kathleen Boyer. 1-1/2 in., ca. app. 1990-1995. *Courtesy of the author.*

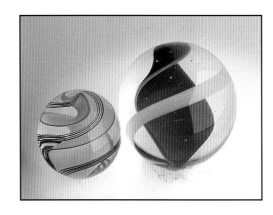

Figure 291. Ribbon Swirl. Rod- and cane-cut. Single ribbon, light blue, red, black outer bands *(left)*; red, blue, white outer band *(right)*. Cuneo Furnace. Steven Maslach. 7/8 - 1-1/4 in., ca. 1980s. *Courtesy of the author.*

Figure 289. Ribbon Swirl. Torchwork. Single ribbon, yellow, red, green, blue, clear glass. Unsigned. Unidentified. 1-3/8 in., ca. app. 2001-2003. *Courtesy of the author.*

Figure 292. Ribbon Swirl. Rod- and cane-cut. Single ribbon, yellow, pink, black bands, lavender, pink, black band, clear glass. Fred Widner. 1-1/8 in., ca. 1993. *Courtesy of the author.*

Figure 293. Ribbon Swirl. Torchwork. Single ribbon, blue, black, white, green aventurine glass, clear glass. Jody Fine. 1-1/4 in., ca. app. 1990-1995. *Courtesy of the Marble Collectors Society of America.*

Figure 290. Ribbon Swirl. Torchwork. Single ribbon, pink, lavender, blue; gold aventurine band, clear glass. Chuck Pound. 1-3/8 in., ca. 2002. *Courtesy of the author.*

Figure 294. Ribbon Swirl. Torchwork. Single ribbon, tan, green, red, black *(left)*; blue, tan, red, black *(middle)*; green, tan, red, black *(right)*, clear glass. Jerry Kelly. 1-1/8 - 1-1/4 in., ca. 2003. *Courtesy of the author.*

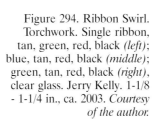

Figure 295. Ribbon Swirl. Torchwork. Single ribbon, green, tan, red, black, clear glass. Jerry Kelly. 1-7/8 in., ca. 2002. *Courtesy of the author.*

Figure 299. Ribbon Swirl. Rod- and cane-cut. Purple, blue, white, gold aventurine glass, brown band *(left)*; green aventurine glass, blue, red, gold aventurine glass *(middle)*; blue, white, pink, purple *(right)*, clear glass. Dudley Giberson, Jody Fine. 1-3/8 in., ca. app. 1993-1998, ca. app. 1980-1985 *Courtesy of the author.*

Figure 296. Ribbon Swirl. Rod- and cane-cut. Double ribbon, multi-color, gold aventurine glass; single ribbon, multi-color, red, blue aventurine glass; single ribbon, multi-color, gold aventurine glass, clear glass. Rolf and Genie Wald. 7/8 in., ca. 2002. *Courtesy of the author.*

Figure 300. Ribbon Swirl. Rod- and cane-cut. Purple, multi-color, lavender, yellow, white outer bands, clear glass. Cuneo Furnace. Steven Maslach. 1-1/8 - 1-3/8 in., ca. 2002. *Courtesy of the author.*

Figure 297. Ribbon Swirl. Rod- and cane-cut. Double ribbon; single ribbon, gold aventurine, red aventurine glass, green ribbons, multi-color outer ribbons, clear glass. Rolf and Genie Wald. 1-1/8 in., ca. 2004. *Courtesy of the author.*

Figure 298. Ribbon Swirl. Rod- and cane-cut. Assorted single ribbon, various ribbon colors, multi-color outer ribbons, clear glass. Cuneo Furnace. Steven Maslach. 7/8 - 1-1/8 in., ca. app. 1995-1999. *Courtesy of the author.*

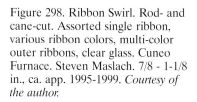

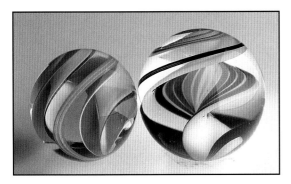

Figure 301. Double Ribbon, Single Ribbon Swirl. Rod- and cane-cut. Double ribbon, lavender, white, red, lavender, green outer bands; single ribbon, white, multi-color, black outer bands, clear glass. Cuneo Furnace. Steven Maslach. 1-1/8 - 1-1/4 in., ca. 2002. *Courtesy of the author.*

Figure 304. Ribbon Swirl. Torchwork. Chartreuse, murrini canes, blue base. Beth Tomasello. 1-1/4 in., ca. app. 2003. *Courtesy of the author.*

Figure 302. Ribbon Swirl. Rod- and cane-cut. White, multi-color, ghost latticinio, yellow outer bands, reverse twist, *third generation #3*; blue, light blue, chartreuse, pink, red outer bands, reverse twist, clear glass. Fritz Lauenstein., 1-9/16 in., ca. 2003-2004. *Courtesy of the author.*

Figure 303. Ribbon Swirl. Torchwork. Black, white, clear glass. Dan Grumbling. 1-1/8 in., ca. 2002. *Courtesy of the artist.*

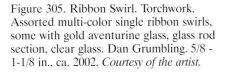

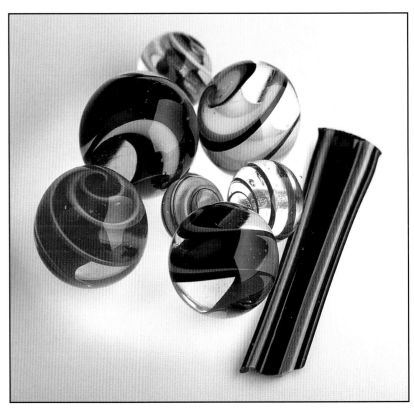

Figure 305. Ribbon Swirl. Torchwork. Assorted multi-color single ribbon swirls, some with gold aventurine glass, glass rod section, clear glass. Dan Grumbling. 5/8 - 1-1/8 in., ca. 2002. *Courtesy of the artist.*

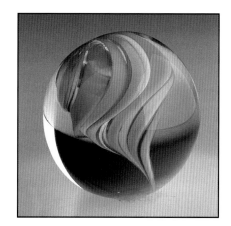

Figure 306. Ribbon Swirl. Rod- and cane-cut. Multi-color, end of cane, clear glass. David Grant Maul. 1-5/8 in., ca. 1993. *Courtesy of the Marble Collectors Society of America.*

Figure 307. Ribbon Swirl. Rod- and cane-cut. Chartreuse, green, blue, white, clear glass. Unsigned. Unidentified. 1-1/2 in., ca. app. 2001-2003. *Courtesy of the author.*

Figure 310. Ribbon Swirl. Torchwork. Double ribbon, lavender, green, clear glass. Jody Fine. 1-1/4 in., ca. app. 1990-1995. *Courtesy of the Marble Collectors Society of America.*

Figure 308. Ribbon Swirl. Rod- and cane-cut. Double ribbon, blue, white, orange, clear glass. Richard Marquis. 7/8 in., ca. 1976. *Courtesy of the author.*

Figure 309. Ribbon Swirl. Rod- and cane-cut. Four-vane, purple, yellow/gold, clear glass. *Limited edition 48/50. 1ˢᵗ Annual Canadian Marble Meet.* Francis Coupal. 1-1/2 in., ca. 2002. *Courtesy of the author.*

Figure 311. Ribbon Swirl. Torchwork. White bands, red, blue outer bands, clear glass. VWT. Unidentified. 1-5/8 in., ca. 2002. *Courtesy of the artist.*

Figure 312. Ribbon Swirl. Torchwork. Multi-color ribbon, multi-color filigrana, yellow base, clear glass. Greg Hoglin., 1-3/16 in., ca. 2002. *Courtesy of the author.*

Figure 313. Ribbon Swirl. Torchwork. Multi-color ribbon, red/brown base. Elizabeth Root. 1-1/4 in., ca. 2003. *Courtesy of the author.*

Figure 314. Ribbon Swirl. Rod- and cane-cut. Alternating latticinio ribbons, lavender, yellow, blue, multi-color dichroic, red base. Eddie Seese. 1-3/4 in., ca. 2003. *Courtesy of the author.*

Figure 315. Ribbon Swirl. Rod- and cane-cut. Fused, half and half multi-color ribbons. Robert Dane. 1-1/4 in., ca. app. 1983-1987. *Courtesy of the Marble Collectors Society of America.*

Figure 316. Ribbon Swirl. Rod- and cane-cut. Black ribbon, outer white latticinio ribbon. William Burchfield. 1-3/4 in., ca. app. 1990-1995. *Courtesy of the author.*

Figure 317. Ribbon Swirl. Rod- and cane-cut. Black, white ribbon, air trap, clear glass. Michael Hansen, Nina Paladino Caron. 1-3/4 in., ca. 2001. *Courtesy of the author.*

Figure 318. Ribbon Swirl. Rod- and cane-cut. Red, pink, white ribbon, clear glass. Michael Hansen, Nina Paladino Caron. 1-3/4 in., ca. 2001. *Courtesy of the author.*

Figure 319. Ribbon Swirl. Rod- and cane-cut. Blue, turquoise blue, green, white ribbon, air trap, clear glass. Michael Hansen, Nina Paladino Caron. 1-3/4 in., ca. 2001. *Courtesy of the author.*

Figure 320. Ribbon Swirl. Rod- and cane-cut. Multi-color, clear glass. David Salazar. 1-1/4 - 1-3/8 in., ca. 2003. *Courtesy of the author.*

Figure 321. Ribbon Swirl. Rod- and cane-cut. Assorted multi-color swirls, clear glass. Robert LaGrand. ca. 2003. *Courtesy of the author.*

Figure 323. Ribbon Swirl. Rod- and cane-cut. White ribbon, red, gold aventurine glass, blue, gold aventurine glass. William Burchfield. 1-1/2 in., ca. app. 1990-1995. *Courtesy of the author.*

Figure 322. Ribbon Swirl. Rod- and cane-cut. White ribbon, red. William Burchfield. 1-1/2 in., ca. app. 1990-1995. *Courtesy of the author.*

Figure 324. Ribbon Swirl. Rod- and cane-cut. Red, white ribbon, multi-color canes, gold aventurine glass. *(top view)* William Burchfield. 1-3/4 in., ca. app. 1990-1995. *Courtesy of the author.*

Figure 325. Ribbon Swirl. Rod- and cane-cut. Red, white ribbon, multi-color canes, gold aventurine glass. *(side view)* William Burchfield. 1-3/4 in., ca. app. 1990-1995. *Courtesy of the author.*

Figure 326. Ribbon Swirl. Rod- and cane-cut. Multi-color, clear glass. William Burchfield. 1-1/2 in., ca. app. 1993-2000. *Courtesy of the author.*

Figure 327. Ribbon Swirl. Rod- and cane-cut. Yellow, white, light blue, blue, gold aventurine glass. Dudley Giberson. 1-1/4 in., ca. app. 1993-1998. *Courtesy of the Marble Collectors Society of America.*

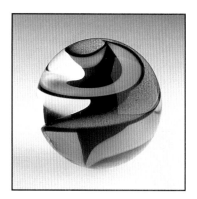

Figure 330. Ribbon Swirl. Rod- and cane-cut. Red, light blue, green aventurine glass. Dudley Giberson. 1-1/4 in., ca. app. 1993-1998. *Courtesy of the author.*

Figure 328. Ribbon Swirl. Rod- and cane-cut. Red, orange, lavender, clear glass. Michael Hansen, Nina Paladino Caron. 2-1/4 in., ca. 1992. *Courtesy of the author.*

Figure 329. Ribbon Swirl. Rod- and cane-cut. Purple, white, blue, green aventurine glass. Dudley Giberson. 1-1/8 in., ca. app. 1993-1998. *Courtesy of the author.*

Figure 331. Ribbon Swirl. Rod- and cane-cut. White ribbon, multi-color. Fritz Lauenstein. 2 in., ca. app. 1990-1995. *Courtesy of the author.*

Solid Core Swirl Marbles (Originally produced: 1850-1920): With a central core of white or colored glass packed closely so that no open space is noticeable between them, solid core swirl marbles may have a core of one or more colors, some overlaid with other colored bands. [Antique: Figure 332-334], [Contemporary: Figure 335-354]

Figure 335. Solid Core Swirl. Rod- and cane-cut. Red, white, blue, clear glass. Robert Lichtman. 1-1/4 in., ca. app. 1986-1989. *Courtesy of the Marble Collectors Society of America.*

Figure 332. Solid Core Swirl. White, outer yellow, green bands. Antique handmade; Germany. 1-1/2 in., ca. app. 1850-1920. *Courtesy of the author.*

Figure 333. Solid Core Swirl. Yellow, red, green, white outer caged bands. Antique handmade; Germany. 1-1/4 in., ca. app. 1850-1920. *Courtesy of the author.*

Figure 336. Solid Core Swirl. Rod- and cane-cut. Blue, white, green aventurine glass, clear glass. William Burchfield. 1-1/4 in., ca. app. 1995-2000. *Courtesy of the author.*

Figure 334. Solid Core Swirl. White, red, blue, green, yellow outer caged bands. Antique handmade; Germany. 1-9/16 in., ca. app. 1850-1920. *Courtesy of Robert Block.*

Figure 337. Solid Core Swirl. Rod- and cane-cut. Green, yellow, orange. Frank Oddu. 1-1/4 in., ca. 2001. *Courtesy of the author.*

Figure 338. Solid Core Swirl. Rod- and cane-cut. Red, white, green, mica, red, green aventurine glass, clear glass. Steve Davis. 1-1/2 in., ca. 2003. *Courtesy of the author.*

Figure 339. Solid Core Swirl. Rod- and cane-cut. White, mica, multi-color transparent surface bands, clear glass. Steve Davis. 1-1/2 in., ca. 2003. *Courtesy of the author.*

Figure 340. Solid Core Swirl. Torchwork. Multi-color, red, transparent outer bands *(left)*; multi-color *(right)*, clear glass. Christopher Robinson. 3/4 - 7/8 in., ca. app. 1995-2000. *Courtesy of the author.*

Figure 341. Solid Core Swirl. Rod- and cane-cut. Multi-color, green aventurine glass, green, blue, lavender outer bands, clear glass. David Salazar. 1-3/8 in., ca. 2002. *Courtesy of the author.*

Figure 342. Solid Core Swirl. Rod- and cane-cut. Transparent red, white core, white bands, white, dichroic blue glass outer bands, clear glass. Eddie Seese. 2 in., ca. 2003. *Courtesy of the author.*

Figure 343. Solid Core Swirl. Rod- and cane-cut. Multi-color, reverse twist, clear glass. Rolf Greiner-Adams, Germany. 1 in., ca. 2001. *Courtesy of the author.*

Figure 344. Solid Core Swirl. Rod- and cane-cut. Red dichroic glass, yellow, lime, red, chartreuse, pink outer bands, clear glass. Eddie Seese. 1-1/4 in., ca. 2003. *Courtesy of the author.*

Figure 345. Solid Core Swirl. Torchwork. Blue, green, red, gold aventurine glass, black outer bands, clear glass. Jerry Park. 1-3/8 in., ca. 2003. *Courtesy of the author.*

Figure 346. Solid Core Swirl. Rod-
and cane-cut. Multi-color, purple,
blue outer bands, clear glass. Cuneo
Furnace. Steven Maslach. 1-1/4 in.,
ca. 1995-2000. *Courtesy of the
author.*

Figure 349. Solid Core Swirl. Rod-
and cane-cut. Black, pink, orange,
green outer bands, clear glass.
Douglas Sweet. 1-1/2 in., ca. 2001.
Courtesy of the author.

Figure 350. Solid Core Swirl. Rod- and cane-
cut. Barber Pole. Red, white, blue, gold,
blizzard mica, clear glass. *Limited Edition
"MB."* Rolf and Genie Wald. 2 in., ca. 2001.
Courtesy of the author.

Figure 347. Solid Core Swirl. Rod- and
cane-cut. Multi-color, transparent
purple outer bands, clear glass. Eddie
Seese. 1-3/4 in., ca. 2003. *Courtesy of
the author.*

Figure 348. Solid Core Swirl. Rod- and
cane-cut. Orange, gray, white outer
bands. Phillip Nolley. 1-3/4 in., ca. 2002.
Courtesy of the artist.

Figure 351. Solid Core Swirl. Rod- and cane-cut. Barber Pole Set. Red, white,
blue, gold, blizzard mica, clear glass. Marbles, Square, Egg, Top, Cane. *Limited
Edition "MB."* Rolf and Genie Wald. Marbles: 1/2 - 1-1/2 in., Square: 3/4 in., Egg:
1-1/2 in., Top: 1-5/8 in., Cane: 2-1/8 in., ca. 2001. *Courtesy of the author.*

Figure 353. Solid Core Swirl. Rod-and cane-cut. Multi-color, green aventurine glass. Jody Fine. 7/8 in., ca. 2003. *Courtesy of the author.*

Figure 352. Solid Core Swirl. Rod- and cane-cut. White, light blue, red, mica, reverse twist. James Holmes. 2-3/8 in., ca. app. 1980-1985. *Courtesy of the Marble Collectors Society of America.*

Figure 354. Solid Core Swirl. Rod- and cane-cut. Black core, lutz, white, blue, green, orange, red bands. Rolf Wald. 2-1/4 in., ca. 1990. *Courtesy of the Marble Collectors Society of America.*

Joseph's Coat Swirl Marbles (Originally produced: 1850-1920): Named for the biblical figure Joseph and his coat of many colors, these marbles exhibit a beautiful assortment of outer layer colored glass bands. These bands were most often packed extremely close together on the base glass rod and do not typically allow any clear glass to show between them. [Antique: Figure 355-357], [Contemporary: Figure 358-372]

Figure 355. Joseph's Coat. Multi-color, clear core. Antique hand-made; Germany. 1-9/16 in., ca. app. 1850-1920. *Courtesy of Robert Block.*

Figure 357. Joseph's Coat. Multi-color, solid core. Antique hand-made; Germany. 13/16 in., ca. app. 1850-1920. *Courtesy of Stanley Block.*

Figure 359. Joseph's Coat. Rod- and cane-cut. Multi-color, reverse twist. Fritz Lauenstein. 1-9/16 in., ca. 2001. *Courtesy of the author.*

Figure 356. Joseph's Coat. Multi-color, clear core. Antique handmade; Germany. 5/8 in., ca. app. 1850-1920. *Courtesy of Stanley Block.*

Figure 358. Joseph's Coat. Rod- and cane-cut. White, red, green, reverse twist. Fritz Lauenstein. 1-9/16 in., ca. 2004. *Courtesy of the author.*

Figure 360. Joseph's Coat. Rod- and cane-cut. Multi-color, clear glass, reverse twist. Fritz Lauenstein. 1-9/16 in., ca. 2003. *Courtesy of the author.*

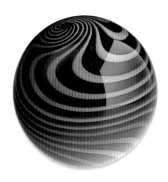

Figure 361. Joseph's Coat. Rod-and cane-cut. Pink, green aventurine glass, reverse twist. Fritz Lauenstein. 1-9/16 in., ca. 2001. *Courtesy of the author.*

Figure 364. Joseph's Coat. Rod- and cane-cut. Red, black, yellow, lavender, gold aventurine glass. Rolf and Genie Wald. 1-1/8 in., ca. 1999. *Courtesy of the author.*

Figure 367. Joseph's Coat. Rod- and cane-cut. Multi-color, gold aventurine glass, reverse twist. *Limited edition. MB #3.* Crafted from marble stock made at First Annual Marble Weekend, Wheaton Village, Millville, New Jersey. Rolf and Genie Wald. 2 in., ca. 2002. *Courtesy of the author.*

Figure 362. Joseph's Coat. Rod-and cane-cut. Green, blue, white. John K. Talmage. 1-5/8 in., ca. 2003. *Courtesy of the author.*

Figure 368. Joseph's Coat. Rod- and cane-cut. Multi-color, reverse twist, gold aventurine glass. Rolf and Genie Wald. 7/8 in., ca. 2002. *Courtesy of the author.*

Figure 365. Joseph's Coat. Rod- and cane-cut. Black, orange, yellow. Steve Davis. 1-1/2 in., ca. 2003. *Courtesy of the author.*

Figure 369. Joseph's Coat. Torchwork. Multi-color, double reverse twist. Drew Fritts. 1-7/8 in., ca. 2003. *Courtesy of the author.*

Figure 363. Joseph's Coat. Rod-and cane-cut. Blue, orange, white. Douglas Sweet. 1-1/2 in., ca. 2001. *Courtesy of the author.*

Figure 366. Joseph's Coat. Rod- and cane-cut. Green, red, yellow, blue, orange, gold aventurine glass. Rolf and Genie Wald. 1-1/2 in., ca. 2004. *Courtesy of the author.*

Figure 370. Joseph's Coat. Torchwork. Black, yellow, gold, red, orange, gold aventurine glass, double reverse twist. Drew Fritts. 1-7/8 in., ca. 2003. *Courtesy of the author.*

Figure 371. Joseph's Coat. Torchwork. Blue, red, orange, yellow, green, gold aventurine glass. Drew Fritts. 1-7/8 in., ca. 2003. *Courtesy of the author.*

Figure 372. Joseph's Coat. Rod- and cane-cut. Multi-color, end of cane, clear glass. Eddie Seese. 1-5/8 in., ca. 2003. *Courtesy of the author.*

Mica Marbles (Originally produced: 1850-1920): Quite simply, this marble is a transparent clear or colored glass marble with embedded flakes of the natural mineral mica. Extremely heavy use of mica gives rise to the term "blizzard mica." [Antique: Figure 373, 374], [Contemporary: Figure 375-377]

Figure 373. Mica. Brown glass, mica *(left)*; green glass, mica *(right)*. Antique handmade; Germany. 1-1/16 - 1-1/8 in., ca. app. 1850-1920. *Courtesy of the author.*

Figure 374. Mica. Blue glass, mica *(left)*; brown glass, mica *(center)*; green glass, mica *(right)*. Antique handmade; Germany. 3/4 - 1-1/8 in., ca. app. 1850-1920. *Courtesy of Stanley Block.*

Figure 375. Mica. Rod- and cane-cut. Red, blizzard mica. Bart and Kerry Zimmerman. 2 in., ca. app. 1983-1988. *Courtesy of the Marble Collectors Society of America.*

Figure 376. Mica. Rod- and cane-cut. Green, blizzard mica. William Murray. 1-1/4 in., ca. 2001. *Courtesy of the author.*

Figure 377. Mica. Rod- and cane-cut. Blue, blizzard mica. Bart and Kerry Zimmerman. 1-7/8 in., ca. app. 1983-1988. *Courtesy of the Marble Collectors Society of America.*

Paperweight/Millefiori Marble (Originally produced: 1850-1920): Reminiscent of earlier Italian and later French paperweights; these marbles are crafted in a similar manner. Using various colored and sized handcrafted millefiori canes, deliberate patterns and designs are most often set up with a clear glass dome encasing the interior. On occasion the marble's base will be the remnants of glass from another type of marble. [Antique: Figure 378], [Contemporary: Figure 379-382]

Figure 378. Paperweight. Red, green, white, blue millefiori cane, clear ground. Antique handmade; Germany. 1-1/2 in., ca. app. 1850-1920. *Courtesy of Stanley Block.*

Figure 379. Paperweight. Torchwork. Multi-color millefiori cane, gold aventurine glass, blue ground, rake pull reverse. Greg Hoglin. 1-1/8 in., ca. 2003. *Courtesy of the author.*

Figure 380. Paperweight. Single gather. Red, green, green aventurine glass, millefiori canes, center cane, four surrounding canes, clear glass. Tony Parker. 1-1/2 in., ca. 1992. *Courtesy of the Marble Collectors Society of America.*

Figure 381. Paperweight. Single gather. Center red flora millefiori cane, red, white triangular canes, green, white millefiori canes, five-point center stars, clear glass. Tony Parker. 1-3/4 in., ca. 1992. *Courtesy of the Marble Collectors Society of America.*

Figure 382. Paperweight. Torchwork. Center flora millefiori cane, yellow, orange, white canes, blue, white canes, white ground. James Hart. 1-5/8 in., ca. 2001. *Courtesy of the author.*

Figure 383. Sulphide. Single gather. Walking dog, clear glass. Antique handmade; Germany. 1-3/4 in., ca. app. 1850-1920. *Courtesy of the author.*

Sulphide Marbles (Originally produced: 1850-1920): One of the most easily identified of all marble types, sulphide marbles are typically crafted of a clear glass with a ceramic figure inserted in the marble's center. These marbles can be crafted of colored glass with a white to silvery colored figure and can also be clear or colored glass with a hand-painted figure encased. Those that are rare include human and mythical figures, while the more common subjects are animals, such as rabbits, cows, and sheep. [Antique: Figure 383-387], [Contemporary: Figure 388-411]

Figure 384. Sulphide. Single gather. Lion, clear glass. Antique handmade; Germany. 2 in., ca. app. 1850-1920. *Courtesy of the author.*

Figure 385. Sulphide. Single gather. Cow, clear glass. Antique handmade; Germany. 1-3/8 in., ca. app. 1850-1920. *Courtesy of the author.*

Figure 386. Sulphide. Single gather. Big Horn Sheep, clear glass. Antique handmade; Germany. 2 in., ca. app. 1850-1920. *Courtesy of Stanley Block.*

Figure 387. Sulphide. Single gather. Rabbit, blue glass. Antique handmade; Germany. 1-3/4 in., ca. app. 1850-1920. *Courtesy of Stanley Block.*

Figure 388. Sulphide. Single gather. Boy with bat, cap, painted, clear glass. Joe St. Clair. 2 in., ca. app. 1982-1986. *Courtesy of the author.*

Figure 389. Sulphide. Single gather. Snail, painted, clear glass. House of Glass. Joe Rice. 2-1/8 in., ca. app. 1990-1995. *Courtesy of the author.*

Figure 390. Sulphide. Single gather. Abraham Lincoln bust, red, white, blue glass frit ground, clear glass. Joe St. Clair. 2 in., ca. app. 1982-1986. *Courtesy of the author.*

Figure 391. Sulphide. Single gather. Lyndon B. Johnson bust, clear glass. Joe St. Clair. 2 in., ca. app. 1982-1986. *Courtesy of the Marble Collectors Society of America.*

Figure 392. Sulphide. Single gather. Gerald R. Ford bust, clear glass. Joe St. Clair. 2 in., ca. app. 1982-1986. *Courtesy of the Marble Collectors Society of America.*

Figure 393. Sulphide. Single gather. Baby bird, egg, painted, colored glass. House of Glass. Joe Rice. 2-1/8 in., ca. 1990-1995. *Courtesy of the author.*

Figure 394. Sulphide. Single gather. Cow, painted, clear glass. Gibson Glass. Charles Gibson. 2-1/8 in., ca. 1997. *Courtesy of the author.*

Figure 395. Sulphide. Single gather. Dog, painted, clear glass. Rick Davis. 1-7/8 in., ca. app. 2003. *Courtesy of the author.*

Figure 398. Sulphide. Single gather. Kitten, painted, clear glass. Gibson Glass. Charles Gibson. 2-1/4 in., ca. 1999. *Courtesy of the author.*

Figure 396. Sulphide. Single gather. Penguin, painted, clear glass. Boyd Miller, Tom Thornburgh. 2-7/8 in., ca. 2001. *Courtesy of the author.*

Figure 399. Sulphide. Single gather. Turtle, painted, clear glass. Sam Hogue. 2 in., ca. 1997. *Courtesy of the Marble Collectors Society of America.*

Figure 400. Sulphide. Single gather. Pig, painted, clear glass. Jim Davis. 1-1/2 in., ca. 1999. *Courtesy of the author.*

Figure 397. Sulphide. Single gather. Woman in prayer, painted, clear glass. Ray Laubs. 2-1/4 in., ca. 2001. *Courtesy of the author.*

Figure 406. Sulphide. Torchwork. Cat, gemstones, green aventurine glass. *(front)* Paul and Dee Snell. 1-1/4 in., ca. 2001. *Courtesy of the artists.*

Figure 401. Sulphide. Single gather. Sheep, resting, clear glass. Sam Hogue. 2 in., ca. 1997. *Courtesy of the author.*

Figure 407. Sulphide. Torchwork. Cat, gemstones, green aventurine glass. *(back)* Paul and Dee Snell. 1-1/4 in., ca. 2001. *Courtesy of the artists.*

Figure 404. Sulphide. Single gather. Eagle, air trap bubble back, clear glass. Ray Laubs. 2-1/8 in., ca. 2003. *Courtesy of the artist.*

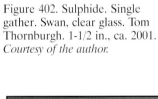

Figure 402. Sulphide. Single gather. Swan, clear glass. Tom Thornburgh. 1-1/2 in., ca. 2001. *Courtesy of the author.*

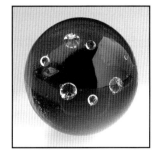

Figure 408. Sulphide. Torchwork. Angel, gemstones, red glass. *(front)* Paul and Dee Snell. 1-1/4 in., ca. 2001. *Courtesy of the artists.*

Figure 405. Sulphide. Single gather. Baby's block, painted, clear glass. Tom Thornburgh. 1-1/2 in., ca. 2001. *Courtesy of the author.*

Figure 403. Sulphide. Single gather. Elf, clear glass. Tom Thornburgh. 1-1/2 in., ca. 2001. *Courtesy of the author.*

Figure 409. Sulphide. Torchwork. Angel, gemstones, red glass. *(back)* Paul and Dee Snell. 1-1/4 in., ca. 2001. *Courtesy of the artists.*

Figure 410. Sulphide. Single gather. Duck, hat, painted, clear glass. Jim Davis. 2-1/4 in., ca. app. 1995-2000. *Courtesy of the author.*

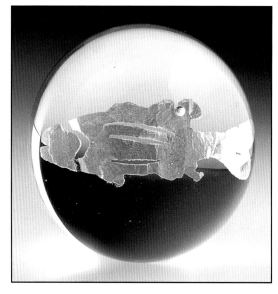

Figure 411. Sulphide. Single gather. Eisenglas (mica) fish, clear glass. Harry Besett. 2-1/2 in., ca. 2003. *Courtesy of the author.*

Figure 412. End-of-Day. Cloud. Rod- and cane cut. Red, white, blue, stretched, pulled, clear glass. Antique handmade; Germany. 3/4 in., ca. app. 1850-1920. *Courtesy of Stanley Block.*

End-of-Day

Cloud (Originally produced: 1850-1920): Typically constructed of a transparent glass base, end-of-day cloud marbles may have a glass core of colored glass or exhibit no core at all. In the crafting process bits of various colored glass are fused to the core, though these colored bits most often show no occurrence of extensive stretching. These marbles are referred to as end-of-day pieces because it is generally believed that glass factory workers first began to craft them at the day's end with leftover glass. Whether they were done so for their own family use has not been documented with any historical certainty. The same holds true for distinctly unusual mables in all those that follow in the end-of-day category. [Antique: Figure 412-414], [Contemporary: Figure 415-422]

Figure 413. End-of-Day. Cloud. Rod- and cane cut. Red, white, blue, white base; red, yellow, mica, white base, stretched, pulled. Antique handmade; Germany. 3/4 - 1 in., ca. app. 1850-1920. *Courtesy of Stanley Block.*

Figure 415. End-of-Day. Cloud. Rod- and cane-cut. Red, green, splotches, stretched colored glass, aventurine green glass, white base. Unsigned. Unidentified. 1-1/2 in., ca. app. 1995-1999. *Courtesy of the author.*

Figure 414. End-of-Day. Cloud. Rod- and cane cut. Blue, green splotches, stretched colored glass, white base. Antique handmade; Germany. 1-1/2 in., ca. app. 1850-1920. *Courtesy of Stanley Block.*

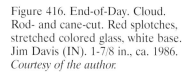

Figure 416. End-of-Day. Cloud. Rod- and cane-cut. Red splotches, stretched colored glass, white base. Jim Davis (IN). 1-7/8 in., ca. 1986. *Courtesy of the author.*

Figure 421. End-of-Day.
Cloud. Torchwork. Multi-color
splotches, stretched colored
glass, clear base. Daniel
Ambrose. 1-1/4 in., ca. 2002.
Courtesy of the author.

Figure 417. End-of-Day. Cloud. Rod-
and cane-cut. Green, pink, tan, gold
aventurine splotches, stretched colored
glass, white base. Bobbie Seese. 1-3/4 in.,
ca. 2004. *Courtesy of the author.*

Figure 422. End-of-Day. Cloud. Rod-
and cane-cut. Multi-color splotches,
stretched colored glass, green aventurine glass, white base. Unsigned.
Unidentified. 1-5/8 in., ca. 1990s.
Courtesy of the author.

Figure 418. End-of-Day. Cloud. Rod- and cane-cut.
Blue, white, stretched colored glass. Blue base. Robert
Lichtman. 2-3/8 in., ca. 1987. *Courtesy of the Marble
Collectors Society of America.*

Figure 419. End-of-Day. Cloud. Rod- and cane-cut.
Multi-color splotches, stretched colored glass, white
base. *(side view)* Robert Lichtman. 2-3/8 in., ca. 1987.
Courtesy of the Marble Collectors Society of America.

Figure 420. End-of-Day. Cloud. Rod- and cane-cut.
Multi-color splotches, stretched colored glass, white
base. *(top view)* Robert Lichtman. 2-3/8 in., ca. 1987.
Courtesy of the Marble Collectors Society of America.

Figure 423. End-of-Day. Onionskin. Rod- and cane-cut. Red, green, white base; red, green, yellow, white base; red, blue, mica, white base. Antique handmade; Germany. 3/4 - 1 in., ca. app. 1850-1920. *Courtesy of Robert Block.*

Onionskin (Originally produced: 1850-1920): With a typical construction of a transparent glass base and a core of transparent or colored glass, end-of-day onionskin marbles exhibit a core comprised of bits of various colored glass. These fused colored glasses and core were then pulled or stretched when the marble was constructed. [Antique: Figure 423, 424], [Contemporary: 425-473]

Figure 424. End-of-Day. Onionskin. Rod- and cane-cut. Blue, white, green, yellow. Antique handmade; Germany. 1 in., ca. app. 1850-1920. *Courtesy of Stanley Block.*

Figure 426. End-of-Day. Onionskin. Rod- and cane-cut. Orange, brown, yellow, white, swirled. Steve Davis. 2-1/4 in., ca. 2003. *Courtesy of the author.*

Figure 427. End-of-Day. Onionskin. Rod- and cane-cut. Multi-color, pulled, stretched, clear glass. David Salazar. 1 in., ca. 2001. *Courtesy of the author.*

Figure 425. End-of-Day. Onionskin. Rod- and cane-cut. Green, purple, white, air trap bubbles, clear glass. Eddie and Bobbie Seese. 2 in., ca. 2003. *Courtesy of the author.*

Figure 428. End-of-Day. Onionskin. Rod- and cane-cut. Orange, red, blue, green, air trap, end-of-cane, clear glass. Jim Davis (IN). 1-5/8 in., ca. 2000. *Courtesy of the author.*

Figure 429. End-of-Day. Onionskin. Torchwork. Multi-color, gold aventurine glass, twist, clear glass. Jerry Park. 1-1/2 in., ca. 2001. *Courtesy of the author.*

Figure 430. End-of-Day. Onionskin. Rod-and cane-cut. Multi-color, swirled, twist, clear glass. Robert Lichtman. 1-5/8 in., ca. 1987. *Courtesy of the Marble Collectors Society of America.*

Figure 435. End-of-Day. Torchwork. Multi-color, gold aventurine glass, pulled, stretched. Robert Livesy. Rod- and cane-cut. Pink, green, blue, orange, pulled, stretched. Phillip Nolley. Rod- and cane-cut. Red, white, blue, pulled, stretched. Jim Davis (IN). 1-1/2 in., 1-5/8 in., 1-1/4 in., ca. 1987, 2001, 2002. *Courtesy of the author.*

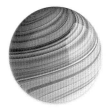

Figure 433. End-of-Day. Onionskin. Rod- and cane-cut. Multi-color, white base. Robert Hamon. 1 in., ca. app. 1986-1990. *Courtesy of the author.*

Figure 431. End-of-Day. Onionskin. Rod- and cane-cut. White, lavender, yellow, end-of-cane, clear glass. Jim Davis. 1-1/4 in., ca. app. 1995-1999. *Courtesy of the author.*

Figure 436. End-of-Day. Onionskin. Rod-and cane-cut. Brown, green, dark brown/green base. David Salazar. 1-3/4 in., ca. 2002. *Courtesy of the author.*

Figure 434. End-of-Day. Rod-and cane-cut. Multi-color, pulled, stretched. Phillip Nolley. 1-3/4 in., ca. 2002. *Courtesy of the artist.*

Figure 432. End-of-Day. Onionskin. Rod- and cane-cut. Multi-color, red aventurine glass, white base. Robert Hamon. 1 in., ca. app. 1986-1990. *Courtesy of the author.*

Figure 437. End-of-Day. Onionskin. Rod-and cane-cut. Multi-color, black base *(left)*; multi-color, white base *(right)*. Robert Lichtman. 1 - 1-1/8 in., ca. 1987-1988. *Courtesy of the author. (left) Courtesy of the Marble Collectors Society of America. (right)*

Figure 438. End-of-Day. Onionskin. Rod-and cane-cut. Multi-color, two-panels, clear glass separating. Jim Davis. 1-5/8 in., ca. app. 1998-2000. *Courtesy of the author.*

Figure 441. End-of-Day. Onionskin. Torchwork. Multi-color, gold, blue aventurine glass, pulled, stretched, white base. George Pavliscak. 1-1/8 in., ca. 2002. *Courtesy of the artist.*

Figure 439. End-of-Day. Onionskin. Rod-and cane-cut. Red, green, white, gold aventurine glass, pulled, stretched. Harry and Kathleen Boyer. 1-5/8 in., ca. app. 1985-1989. *Courtesy of the Marble Collectors Society of America.*

Figure 442. End-of-Day. Onionskin. Torchwork. Multi-color, gold, blue aventurine glass, pulled, stretched. George Pavliscak. 1-1/8 in., ca. 2002. *Courtesy of the artist.*

Figure 443. End-of-Day. Onionskin. Torchwork. Gold aventurine glass, pulled, stretched, black base *(left)*; multi-color reverse chevron, gold aventurine glass *(right)*. George Pavliscak. 1-1/4 in., ca. 2002. *Courtesy of the author.*

Figure 440. End-of-Day. Onionskin. Torchwork. Multi-color, gold aventurine glass, black base. Mark Capel. 3/4 in., ca. 1995. *Courtesy of the author.*

Figure 444. End-of-Day. Onionskin. Torchwork. Gold aventurine glass, pulled, stretched, black base. George Pavliscak. 1-1/8 - 1-1/4 in., ca. 2002. *Courtesy of the author.*

Figure 445. End-of-Day. Onionskin. Rod-and cane-cut. Gold aventurine glass, black base. Harry and Kathleen Boyer. 1-3/8 in., ca. app. 1995-1999. *Courtesy of the author.*

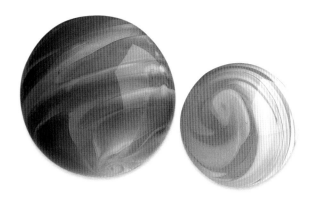

Figure 447. End-of-Day. Onionskin. Torchwork. Purple, pink, pulled, stretched, lavender glass *(left)*; pink, white, pulled, stretched, lavender glass *(right)*. Jerry Park. 1-5/8 in., 1-1/4 in., ca. 2002. *Courtesy of the author.*

Figure 446. End-of-Day. Onionskin. Rod-and cane-cut. Purple, lavender, white, pulled, stretched, clear glass. Steve Davis. 1-1/2 in., ca. 2002. *Courtesy of the author.*

Figure 448. End-of-Day. Onionskin. Torchwork. Blue, white, pulled, stretched, light blue glass. Jerry Park. 1-1/2 in., ca. 2002. *Courtesy of the author.*

Figure 450. End-of-Day. Onionskin. Torchwork. Red, blue, white, gold aventurine glass. George Pavliscak. 1-1/4 in., ca. 2003. *Courtesy of the author.*

Figure 449. End-of-Day. Onionskin. Torchwork. Purple, blue, green, turquoise blue, dichroic glass. *Experimental.* Drew Fritts. 1-3/4 in., ca. 2003. *Courtesy of the author.*

Figure 451. End-of-Day. Onionskin. Torchwork. Red, yellow, orange bands, pulled, stretched. Drew Fritts. 1-3/4 in., ca. 2003. *Courtesy of the author.*

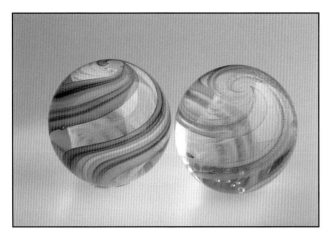

Figure 452. End-of-Day. Onionskin. Rod- and cane-cut. Multi-color bands, translucent white core, clear glass. David Salazar. 1-1/4 in., ca. 2003. *Courtesy of the author.*

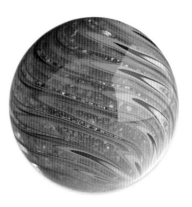

Figure 455. End-of-Day. Onionskin. Rod- and cane-cut. Multicolor bands, pulled, stretched, blizzard mica, red base. Boyd Miller. 1-3/4 in., ca. 2003. *Courtesy of the author.*

Figure 453. End-of-Day. Onionskin. Rod- and cane-cut. Multi-color bands, pulled, stretched, clear glass. Eddie Seese. 1-3/4 in., ca. 2003. *Courtesy of the author.*

Figure 454. End-of-Day. Onionskin. Rod- and cane-cut. Multi-color bands, pulled, stretched, white base. Boyd Miller. 1-3/4 in., ca. 2003. *Courtesy of the author.*

Figure 456. End-of-Day. Onionskin. Rod- and cane-cut. Multicolor frit, pulled, stretched, lavender base *(left)*. Robert Lichtman. Multi-color bands, frit, pulled, stretched, white base *(right)*. Phillip Nolley. 1-1/2 in., ca. app. 1993-1997, 2002. *Courtesy of the author. Courtesy of the artist.*

Figure 457. End-of-Day. Onionskin. Rod- and cane-cut. Multi-color frit, pulled, stretched. Robert Lichtman. 1-1/2 in., ca. app. 1993-1997. *Courtesy of the author.*

Figure 462. End-of-Day. Onionskin. Rod- and cane-cut. Multi-color bands, blizzard mica. Rolf and Genie Wald. 1-7/8 in., ca. 1991. *Courtesy of the Marble Collectors Society of America.*

Figure 461. End-of-Day. Onionskin. Rod- and cane-cut. Multi-color bands, mica. Rolf and Genie Wald. 7/8 - 1-1/8 in., ca. 2002. *Courtesy of the author.*

Figure 458. End-of-Day. Onionskin. Rod- and cane-cut. Multi-color bands, pulled, stretched, latticinio, gold aventurine glass, black base. William Burchfield. 1-1/2 in., ca. app. 1993-1997. *Courtesy of the author.*

Figure 463. End-of-Day. Onionskin. Torchwork. Multi-color bands, pulled, stretched. Teri Conklin. 1-1/2 in., ca. 2003. *Courtesy of the author.*

Figure 459. End-of-Day. Onionskin. Rod- and cane-cut. Multi-color bands, mica. Rolf and Genie Wald. 1-1/8 in., ca. 2004. *Courtesy of the author.*

Figure 460. End-of-Day. Onionskin. Rod- and cane-cut. Multi-color bands, mica. Rolf and Genie Wald. 1-1/2 in., ca. 2004. *Courtesy of the author.*

Figure 464. Rod- and cane-cut. Chartreuse, light blue, pulled, stretched, Nailsea-style. Eddie Seese. 1-3/4 in., ca. 2001. *Courtesy of the artist.*

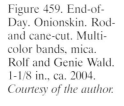

Figure 465. End-of-Day. Onionskin. Torchwork. Multi-color bands, blizzard mica, white base, reverse twist. *Experimental.* Drew Fritts. 1-7/8 in., ca. 2002. *Courtesy of the author.*

Figure 469. End-of-Day. Onionskin. Torchwork. Red, orange, yellow, lavender, green, blue, purple, black bands, reverse twist. *(view one)* Ben Walsh. 2-1/4 in., ca. 2003. *Courtesy of the artist.*

Figure 466. End-of-Day. Onionskin. Torchwork. Multi-color, gold aventurine glass, pulled, stretched, reverse chevron. George Pavliscak. 1-1/8 in., ca. 2002. *Courtesy of the artist.*

Figure 470. End-of-Day. Onionskin. Torchwork. Red, orange, yellow, lavender, green, blue, purple, black bands, reverse twist. *(view two)* Ben Walsh. 2-1/4 in., ca. 2003. *Courtesy of the artist.*

Figure 467. End-of-Day. Onionskin. Torchwork. Multi-color dichroic bands, blue, black base, reverse twist. George Pavliscak. 1-1/8 in., ca. 2002. *Courtesy of the artist.*

Figure 471. End-of-Day. Onionskin. Torchwork. Multi-color, black base, reverse twist. *Experimental.* Drew Fritts. 7/8 - 1 in., ca. 2003. *Courtesy of the author.*

Figure 468. End-of-Day. Onionskin. Torchwork. Multi-color dichroic bands, green base, red base, reverse twist. George Pavliscak. 1-1/8 in., ca. 2002. *Courtesy of the artist.*

Figure 472. End-of-Day. Onionskin. Rod- and cane-cut. Blue, white, blizzard mica, clear glass. Terry Crider. 2 in., ca. app. 1983-1990. *Courtesy of the Marble Collectors Society of America.*

Figure 473. End-of-Day. Onionskin. Rod- and cane-cut. Multicolor, mica, clear glass. Douglas Sweet. 1-5/8 in., ca. app. 1985-1990. *Courtesy of the author.*

Paneled Cloud or Onionskin (Originally produced: 1850-1920): The differences in the construction of these end-of-day marbles compared with the two types discussed previously are the noticeably distinctive grouping of different colored glasses. Most often comprised of four panels, two each of alternating colors, some may have only two panels and extremely rare examples of eight panels have been noted. [Antique: Figure 474-477], [Contemporary: 478-482]

Figure 474. End-of-Day. Paneled Onionskin. Red, blue, white. Antique handmade; Germany. 1-1/2 in., ca. app. 1850-1920. *Courtesy of the author.*

Figure 475. End-of-Day. Paneled Onionskin. Red, blue, white. Antique handmade; Germany. 3/4 in., ca. app. 1850-1920. *Courtesy of Robert Block.*

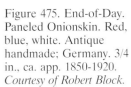

Figure 478. End-of-Day. Paneled Onionskin. Rod- and cane-cut. Six panel, orange, white, yellow, transparent blue wrap, clear glass. Russell Stankus. 2 in., ca. app. 1984-1988. *Courtesy of the Marble Collectors Society of America.*

Figure 476. End-of-Day. Paneled Onionskin. Paperweight. Red, blue, green, white, extensive diamond cuts. Antique handmade; Germany. *(top view)* 2 in., ca. app. 1850-1920. *Courtesy of the author.*

Figure 477. End-of-Day. Paneled Onionskin. Paperweight. Red, blue, green, white, extensive diamond cuts. Antique handmade; Germany. *(side view)* 2 in., ca. app. 1850-1920. *Courtesy of the author.*

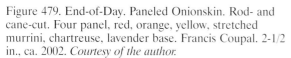

Figure 480. End-of-Day. Paneled Onionskin. Rod- and cane-cut. Four panel, orange, yellow, stretched murrini, chartreuse, blue base, blizzard mica. Francis Coupal. 1-7/8 in., ca. 2003. *Courtesy of the author.*

Figure 479. End-of-Day. Paneled Onionskin. Rod- and cane-cut. Four panel, red, orange, yellow, stretched murrini, chartreuse, lavender base. Francis Coupal. 2-1/2 in., ca. 2002. *Courtesy of the author.*

Figure 481. End-of-Day. Paneled Onionskin. Rod- and cane-cut. Six panel, yellow, chartreuse, stretched murrini, lavender, blue bands. Francis Coupal. 1-5/8 in., ca. 2003. *Courtesy of the author.*

Figure 482. End-of-Day. Paneled Onionskin. Rod- and cane-cut. Six panel, yellow, orange, stretched murrini, lavender, blue bands. Francis Coupal. 1-7/8 in., ca. 2003. *Courtesy of the author.*

Figure 483. End-of-Day. Lobed Onionskin. Blue, white, six-lobe. Antique handmade; Germany. 7/8 in., ca. app. 1850-1920. *Courtesy of the author.*

Lobed (Originally produced: 1850-1920): These end-of-day marbles are comprised of much the same basic glass compositions of other marbles in this category. The craftsman pulling the center glass in repetitive spacing from top to bottom, thus leaving a groove appearance causes the lobes that occur. These marbles have been noted to have sixteen or more lobes surrounding the core. [Antique: Figure 483, 484], [Contemporary: Figure 485-489]

Figure 484. End-of-Day. Lobed Onionskin. Red, green, white, four-lobe. Antique handmade; Germany. 3/4 in., ca. app. 1850-1920. *Courtesy of the author.*

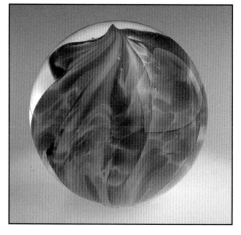

Figure 485. End-of-Day. Lobed Onionskin. Rod- and cane-cut. Six lobe, red, white, clear glass. Jim Davis (IN). 1-7/8 in., ca. 1986. *Courtesy of the Marble Collectors Society of America.*

Figure 486. End-of-Day. Lobed Onionskin. Rod- and cane-cut. Twelve-lobe, black, white. Jim Davis. 1-1/2 in., ca. 1999. *Courtesy of the author.*

Figure 487. End-of-Day. Lobed Onionskin. Rod- and cane-cut. Twelve-lobe, multi-color, clear glass. Mike Davis. 1-7/8 in., ca. 2003. *Courtesy of the artist.*

Figure 488. End-of-Day. Lobed Onionskin. Rod- and cane-cut. Six-lobe, multi-color. Steve Davis. 2-1/4 in., ca. 2003. *Courtesy of the author.*

Figure 489. End-of-Day. Paneled Onionskin. Torchwork. Four panel, multi-color, twisted, modified lobe. Kris Parke. 1-1/2 in., ca. 2004. *Courtesy of the author.*

Lutz or Aventurine Glass

There are a variety of lutz type marbles handcrafted during the time period of other antique handmade marbles, that is, approximately 1850-1920. Many of the characteristics of lutz marbles include those of banded, Indian, onionskin, ribbon, and other glass marbles discussed earlier. Therefore, the most notable difference in these marbles is the inclusion of aventurine glass, a man-made material also referred to as goldstone, a man-made artificial mineral.

Commonly referred to by both marble and other glass collectors as "lutz," this is a true misnomer in the collecting field. There is no evidence to support the contention that Nicholas Lutz, a extremely well documented nineteenth century glassblower, first in his native Germany and later as a major contributor to the works of the American and Sandwich Glass Company, Massachusetts, ever used goldstone in his work, or for that matter crafted any marbles at all.

In nature, the mineral aventurine is a form of quartz flecked with the mineral mica. For hundreds of years, and with continuous success, glassmakers have artificially produced gems by imitating nature, most recently in laboratory conditions that mimic nature's forces through a speeded up process.

Aventurine glass, made with finely ground copper, is commonly known as "goldstone," or in the case of marble collectors, "lutz." Myths are hard to debunk, especially when the vernacular becomes a regular part of the lexicon and commentary on a subject as it has with marble collecting. [Antique: Figure 490, 491], [Contemporary: Figure 492-496]

Figure 490. Lutz. Ribbon Lutz Swirl. Rod- and cane-cut. Blue, yellow, white, gold aventurine glass. Antique handmade; Germany. 3/4 in., ca. app. 1850-1920. *Courtesy of Stanley Block.*

Figure 491. Lutz. Banded Lutz Swirl. Rod- and cane-cut. Green, white, gold aventurine glass. Antique handmade; Germany. 3/4 in., ca. app. 1850-1920. *Courtesy of Stanley Block.*

Figure 492. Goldstone. Gold aventurine glass, manmade. 2 in., ca. 2000. *Courtesy of Emily Block.*

Figure 496. Lutz. Swirl. Rod- and cane-cut. Assorted. Solid core swirls, spinning top, gold aventurine glass, clear glass. Rolf and Genie Wald. 1 - 1-1/8 in., ca. app. 1995-2002. *Courtesy of the author.*

Figure 493. Lutz. Banded Lutz Swirl. Rod- and cane-cut. Purple, green, gold aventurine glass. John Hamon Miller. 1-1/4 in., ca. 2003. *Courtesy of the author.*

Figure 494. Lutz. Reverse Twist Onionskin. Rod- and cane-cut. Multi-color, gold aventurine glass, reverse twist. Rolf Greiner-Adams, Germany. 1-1/8 in., ca. 2001. *Courtesy of the author.*

Figure 495. Lutz. Banded. Rod- and cane-cut. Red, white, gold aventurine glass. Mark Matthews. 1-1/4 in., ca. 2000. *Courtesy of the author.*

American Machine-Made and Foreign Manufactured Glass Marbles and Contemporary Works

As technology advanced in the earlier decades of the twentieth century, so too did the notion that to produce and sell more toys to children the use of machinery would be a natural progression in the evolution of marble making.

While the German cottage industry workers continued to produce marbles by hand, the innovations in the United States a decade or more prior to World War I led an Ohio man, Martin F. Christensen, to develop a machine that could produce as round a sphere mechanically as possible. You could say a war was now being waged between ourselves and competitors overseas to see who would produce a marble of near perfection in rolling. The battle was won fairly rapidly by the Americans for a couple of reasons, one being, machine-made marbles had no pontils—the area at the top and bottom of the marble where it was sheared off the host rod by the craftsman, and then polished down. Second, simple economics took root. The machinery utilized by the Americans greatly outstripped the productivity of the Germans, thus, dramatically reducing the price per unit.

And so, not too many years after the end of World War I, American ingenuity and business had won the war of marble production, effectively resulting in the end of the era of handmade marbles. Some might argue that marbles as a collectible might have been started as early as 1920 or so, rather than the added near fifty-years that followed.

From the middle of the 1920s through the 1940s the "Golden Age of Machine-made Marbles" followed, primarily through United States production. Companies began to sprout along the Ohio River Valley—those most well known with dates of operation included names like, M.F. Christensen & Son Company (Akron, Ohio, 1905-1918), Christensen Agate Company (Cambridge, Ohio, 1927-1929), Akro Agate Company (Akron, Ohio, 1914-1916, Clarksburg, West Virginia, 1916-1951), and, Peltier Glass Company (Ottawa, Illinois, 1881-present).

Names given to particular marble styles for marketing purposes included, Akro Agate Corkscrew, Akro Agate Popeye, and Peltier National Line Rainbo, among others. Certainly history documents by the late 1920s-early 1930s and the advent of the Great Depression two companies, Akro Agate Company and Peltier Glass Company were acknowledged as the largest producers of machine-made marbles. It is important to remember throughout the writings of the previous discussion on handmade German antique marbles, and now this chapter on American and foreign machine-made marbles that these items were produced by the thousands, hundreds of thousands, and then millions over the years. While it may be argued that craftsmen on off time, as fancies for themselves, children, friends or families, made a very, very few pieces, marble crafting and producing was a true production industry—the purpose to bring a "child's plaything" to market.

As the Depression dragged into the Second World War, marble makers had to concern themselves with cost and the need for glass for the war effort. During this period the more vividly colored marbles became available less and less and more and more desirable by schoolchildren.

Following a first wave of manufactures in the mid- to late 1920s until the onset of World War II, marble manufacturers production increased immensely. These diminutive round toys, for which near countless games could be played, among these the popular Ring Taw were met by additional companies and thus added competition. The two largest to enter the market around the war years were the Master Marble Company and Vitro Agate Company. Sadly, the uniqueness of the Akro Agate Company was not enough to prevent it from discontinuing business in the very early 1950s. And further change came quickly!

With the end of the war and the United States policy of rebuilding Japan in the far East, technology and machinery were introduced and thus allowed the Japanese to produce and export an even newer marble design—one you could say hit the American market by storm—the Cat's-eye. As the era of prosperity in America from the 1950s edged into the early 1960s, American marble companies began to fade quickly, replaced by the marbles manufactured overseas.

As social turbulence in America rose and raged from the 1960s through much of the 1970s, marble production and children playing with them steadily declined. In part caused by the advent of computer technology and all the resulting advantages of color television, as well as more organized after school activities, a general decline in "nostalgia" toys became quite evident. During this time marble production shifted dramatically due to even cheaper labor and resources to America's neighbor to the south, Mexico. Today, having bridged the twentieth to twenty-first century, Vacor de Mexico and Jabo-Vitro in the United States are recognized as the largest of all marble manufacturers.

While smaller companies profit across the globe, Vacor de Mexico and Jabo-Vitro marbles are those most likely to be found in toy and specialty shops today. With the resurgence in nostalgia in the late 1980s through the present, marbles are being packaged and sold with game book instructions. Marbles are being used in the medical field in occupational therapy, as well as in activity games for children of various ages. These games with their near Rube Goldberg like chutes and colorful plastic and wood construction pieces allow for the creation of imaginative and intriguing projects. And yes, all these years later, if you happen upon a school yard you just might catch a group of kids "knuckling down" involved in a serious game of marble playing.

For the purposes of this book, it is not the authors intention to delve into details on the history of machine-made marble companies, nor the types and styles each company produced. Rather, the more important goal to be achieved for the reader is to visualize the contemporary handmade marble artist or craftsmen's works and how they relate to those made by machine today or during an earlier time. Therefore, a brief description of the most common machine-made style marbles handcrafted and corresponding explanations of construction are provided in this chapter.

Transitional Marbles (Originally produced: 1890-1915): Recognized as being amongst the first true American-made marbles, these slag style marbles have one pontil and were likely manufactured/crafted using a number of different processes, both by hand and machine; hence the term "transitional." Through the pot gathering of a glob of molten glass on the end of the punty rod and either the process of rounding a single marble off that end or permitting glass to slowly drop from the punty's end into a machine by one worker, a second worker could cut the streaming glass, thereby creating individual globs of glass allowed to then become rounded.

As time progressed in the transition from handmade to machine-made marbles, many believe later marbles in this category were fully manufactured by machine. With the glass streaming from a furnace and running through a marble shearing mechanism each glass glob would then be sent through a series of rollers that would continually round the glass into a marble. However, because these glass globs were not rotated on all axes a cut off mark still remains from the earlier shearing. [Figure 497, 498]

Figure 497. Transitional. Handmade. United States. 11/16 in., ca. app. 1880-1910. *Courtesy of Stanley Block.*

Figure 498. Transitional. Handmade. United States. 7/8 - 11/16 in., ca. app. 1880-1910. *Courtesy of Robert Block.*

Cat's-eye Marbles (Originally produced: 1950-present): First manufactured in Japan beginning in the early 1950s, the migration of production has found its way to Mexico and lesser producing countries.

Cat's-eye marbles are likely to be the most common of all machine-made marbles being produced continuously today. These marbles are mainly manufactured using primary and variations on primary colors. The unique appeal of these marbles to a growing number of collectors stem from the subtle differences in color and construction, and more importantly, from their almost whimsical cat's-eye appearance. [Figure 499, 500]

Figure 499. Cat's-eye. Multi-color bands, clear glass. Machine-made. Japan. 5/8 in., ca. app. 1960-1980. *Courtesy of Robert Block.*

Figure 500. Cat's-eye. Multi-color bands, clear glass. Machine-made. Japan. 1/2 - 5/8 in., ca. app. 1990-2000. *Courtesy of Robert Block.*

Corkscrew Marbles (Originally produced: 1920-present): Quite likely the most common and easy to identify by collectors, the corkscrew's design is much as its name implies. Through the use of two or more colored glasses being run through the marble making machine at one time and entering the shearing mechanism simultaneously, colors of different densities were stratified. As the glass from the machinery stream entered the machine's cup and passed through a hole in its bottom, the cup's spinning ability created a twirled corkscrew pattern. Of course, the number of colors in the marble was determined by the number of different colored glasses being forced through the various nozzles of the machine. If the cup was not spinning, then a patch was created. The number of nozzles that had glass flowing through them when the glass stream was created determined the number of different colored spirals in the corkscrew, or the number of different color patches. A corkscrew marble is identified as such by virtue of its having no less than two spirals of color that rotate around the marble from pole to pole without intersecting. [Machine-made: Figure 501-503], [Contemporary: Figure 504, 505]

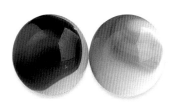

Figure 504. Corkscrew. Torchwork. Red, yellow, blue, clear glass. Scott Patrick. 7/8 in., ca. app. 1995-1999. *Courtesy of the author.*

Figure 501. Corkscrew. Akro Agate Company. Machine-made. Black, yellow, white. United States. 11/16 in., ca. app. 1927-1935. *Courtesy of Robert Block.*

Figure 502. Corkscrew. Akro Agate Company. Machine-made. Blue, yellow. United States. 11/16 in., ca. app. 1927-1935. *Courtesy of Robert Block.*

Figure 503. Corkscrew. Akro Agate Company. Machine-made. Red, white, yellow, white. United States. 11/16 in., ca. app. 1925-1935. *Courtesy of Robert Block.*

Figure 505. Corkscrew. Torchwork. Red, yellow twist, clear glass, purple, green dichroic glass. Kristen Shields. 1 in., ca. 2003. *Courtesy of the author.*

Figure 506. Guinea. Christensen Agate Company. Machine-made. Guinea *(left)*; Guinea Cobra *(right)*. United States. 5/8 - 11/16 in., ca. app. 1925-1935. *Courtesy of Robert Block.*

Guinea Marbles (Originally produced: 1920-1940): So named it is believed due to the marble's colors appearing similar to those of guinea cocks on the ground of the marble factory guinea marbles are manufactured with a transparent glass base. The marble will then be littered with colored bits of glass that have been melted, stretched, and pulled by machine. Most of these marbles are clear based, though a rare number can be found to have amber yellow, cobalt blue, and even reportedly a ruby red base.

Because of the highly collectible nature of these marbles, the most difficult to find in this style is referred to as a guinea-cobra. Quite simply, this marble is one of a transparent clear glass base with colored bits of glass only found within or under the marbles surface; all on one side, and none on the outside surface. [Machine-made: Figure 506], [Contemporary: 507-511]

Figure 507. Guinea. Rod- and cane-cut. Multi-color, gold aventurine, black base. Robert Livesy. 1-1/2 in., ca. 2001. *Courtesy of the author.*

Figure 508. Guinea. Rod- and cane-cut. Multi-color, clear glass. Sam Hogue. 1-3/4 in., ca. 2002. *Courtesy of the author.*

Figure 509. Guinea. Torchwork. Multi-color, blue base. *Limited edition. Amana Marble Meet 25th Anniversary.* Mike Edmundson. 1 in., ca. 2002. *Courtesy of the author.*

Figure 510. Guinea. Torchwork. White, blue, green transparent glass. Chuck Pound. 5/8 in., ca. 2003. *Courtesy of the author.*

Figure 511. Guinea. Rod- and cane-cut. Red, green aventurine glass. Phillip Nolley. 1-3/4 in., ca. 2002. *Courtesy of the artist.*

Patch (Originally produced: 1920-present): The characteristics of patch marbles are similar to those of corkscrew, the glass streamed through the machine to this point, then a patch marble resulted. [Machine-made: Figure 512-515], [Contemporary: 516, 517]

Figure 512. Patch. Akro Agate Company. Machine-made. Multi-color Royal Patch. United States. 5/8 in., ca. app. 1925-1935 (left); Multi-color Peerless Patch. Peltier Glass Company; United States. 21/32 in., ca. app. 1925-1935 (right). *Courtesy of Robert Block.*

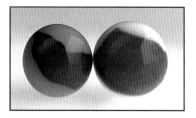

Figure 513. Patch. Vitro Agate Company. Machine-made. Red, blue, white. United States. 21/32 in., ca. app. 1935-1950. *Courtesy of Robert Block.*

Figure 514. Swirl, Patch. Vacor de Mexico. Multi-color. Machine-made. Mexico. 5/8 - 1 in., ca. app. 1990-2003. *Courtesy of Robert Block.*

Figure 515. Rainbow, Patch, Ribbon. Marble King Inc. Multi-color. Machine-made. United States. 5/8 - 3/4 in., ca. app. 1955-1975. *Courtesy of Robert Block.*

Figure 516. Patch. Torchwork. White, green, gold aventurine glass, black base. Mike Edmundson. 7/8 in., ca. 2004. *Courtesy of the author.*

Figure 517. Patch. Torchwork. White, gold aventurine glass, semi-clear blue base. Robert Powers. 3/4 in., ca. 2002. *Courtesy of the artist.*

Transfer Marbles

Transfer marbles, more commonly referred to as "picture marbles" or "comics," were manufactured by the Peltier Glass Company from the late 1920s through the 1930s. Most commonly Patch marbles with a black screened transfer of one of twelve King Syndicate comic characters fired on the marbles surface and then re-fired with an over glaze of clear glass. While unique at the time of manufacture, picture marbles and marbles with encased transfers are popular today, being used as promotional and advertising items for many different subjects and products.

The original comic marble twelve characters in alphabetical order of rarity are Andy, Annie, Emma, Koko, Betty, Bimbo, Herbie, Kayo, Moon, Sandy, Skeezix, and Smitty. There are also known machine-made picture marbles with a Tom Mix transfer and another with an advertisement for Cotes Master Loaf. [Machine-made: Figure 518], [Contemporary: Figure 519-532]

Figure 518. Picture Marbles. Peltier Glass Company. Machine-made. Black transfer, various color Patches. Reproduction box. United States. Marbles: 21/32 in., ca. app. 1925-1935. Box: 1995-2000. *Courtesy of Stanley Block.*

Figure 519. Picture Marbles. Machine-made. Black transfer, white base. Mimics, Peltier Glass Company comic transfers. Attributed to Harold Bennett. 1 in., ca. 1990s. *Courtesy of Robert Block.*

Figure 520. Picture Marbles. Machine-made. Black transfer, white base. Mimics, Peltier Glass Company comic transfers. Attributed to Harold Bennett. 1 in., ca. 1990s. *Courtesy of Robert Block.*

Figure 521. Picture Marble. Machine-made. Black transfer, green base. Attributed to Harold Bennett. 1 in., ca. 1990s. *Courtesy of the author.*

Figure 522. Picture Marbles. Machine-made. Color transfer, white base, reproduction Walt Disney Company characters. United States. 1 in., ca. 1990s. *Courtesy of Robert Block.*

Figure 523. Picture Marbles. Machine-made. Black transfer, white, yellow base, comic transfers, marble company transfers, Coca-Cola Company transfer. United States. 1 in., ca. 1990s. *Courtesy of Robert Block.*

Figure 524. Picture Marbles.
Machine-made. Black transfer,
yellow base, smilie face. United
States. 5/8 in., ca. 1990s.
Courtesy of Robert Block.

Figure 525. Picture
Marbles. Machine-
made. Color transfer,
white base, specialty
logos. United States. 1
in., ca. 1990s. *Courtesy
of Robert Block.*

Figure 526. Picture
Marble. Machine-
made. Color
transfer, red base,
specialty logo.
United States. 1 in.,
ca. 2002. *Courtesy
of Robert Block.*

Figure 527. Picture Marble.
Machine-made. Color
transfer, blue base,
specialty logo. United
States. 1 in., ca. 2002.
Courtesy of Robert Block.

Figure 529. Picture Marbles. Machine-made. Color transfer, centered,
clear base, plastic. China. 1 in., ca. 1990s. *Courtesy of Robert Block.*

Figure 528. Picture Marble. Mineral. Color transfer,
dog, cat, onyx mineral base. Attributed to Larry
Castle, Marlow Peterson. 2-1/8 in., ca. 1980s.
Courtesy of Robert Block.

Figure 531. Picture Marbles. Machine-made. Color
transfer, centered, clear base, plastic; New Kids on the
Block. China. 1 in., ca. 1990s. *Courtesy of Robert Block.*

Figure 530. Picture Marbles. Machine-made. Color transfer, color base;
Pokemon. China. 1 in., ca. 1990s. *Courtesy of Robert Block.*

Figure 532. Golden Rule.
Machine-made. Metal ring
surrounding marble; Do Unto
Others As You Would Have Them
Do Unto You. United States. 7/8
in., ca. 1960s. *Courtesy of Robert
Block.*

Figure 533. Ribbon Swirl. Christensen Agate Company. Blue, yellow. Machine-made. United States. 23/32 in., ca. app. 1927-1935. *Courtesy of Robert Block.*

Ribbon Marbles (Originally produced: 1920-present): One of the most prolific of all machine-made marbles are ribbons. Most ribbon marbles are manufactured with a colored opaque base and multiple ribbons appearing on the marble's surface. Ribbons can appear to be either translucent or opaque depending on the type and company that manufactured the pieces. These small marbles have inspired various names ranging from Superman and Christmas Tree, to Flaming Dragon and Ketchup and Mustard. It doesn't take much imagination to figure which colors were used in the marbles. The cup in the manufacturing machine as described earlier had to be spinning when marble production occurred to achieve this style. [Machine-made: Figure 533-536], [Contemporary: Figure 537-542]

Figure 534. Ribbon Swirl. Champion Agate Company. Orange, green, yellow, black. Machine-made. United States. 23/32 in., ca. app. 1927-1935. *Courtesy of Robert Block.*

Figure 535. Ribbon Swirl. Akro Agate Company. Yellow, red. Machine-made. United States. 5/8 - 7/8 in., ca. app. 1925-1940. *Courtesy of Robert Block.*

Figure 536. Ribbon Swirl. Akro Agate Company. Orange, black. Machine-made. United States. 5/8 in., ca. app. 1925-1940. *Courtesy of Robert Block.*

Figure 537. Ribbon Swirl. Torchwork. Red, white, blue, clear glass. Mike Edmundson. 7/8 in., ca. 1999. *Courtesy of the author.*

Figure 538. Ribbon Swirl. Torchwork. Black, white, gold aventurine glass, red, white, black, blue, black, red. Scott Patrick. 3/4 in., ca. app. 1998-2002. *Courtesy of the author.*

Figure 539. Ribbon Swirl. Torchwork. Black, red, white. John Hamon Miller. 1 in., ca. 2002. *Courtesy of the author.*

Figure 540. Ribbon Swirl. Torchwork. Red, yellow, black, blue. Scott Patrick. 5/8 - 3/4 in., ca. app. 1995-2000. *Courtesy of the author.*

Figure 541. Ribbon Swirl. Torchwork. Red, yellow, white. John Hamon Miller. 7/8 in., ca. 2002. *Courtesy of the author.*

Figure 542. Ribbon Swirl. Torchwork. Red, yellow, blue, white. John Hamon Miller. 1 in., ca. 2003. *Courtesy of the author.*

Slag Marbles (Originally produced: 1920-present): These marbles have been produced in an extremely wide variety of colors and combinations. True slag marbles will have a transparent base color that will show an opaque white glass swirling within the marble, sometimes showing in a numeral nine pattern. The pattern must be a transparent color base with opaque white. A marble exhibiting two opaque colors is no longer referred to as a slag, but rather is now considered a swirl (see below). Nearly all of these marbles will show the opaque white glass to be swirled throughout the marble in a random, not patterned, manner. These marbles are also referred to as "onyx." This is due to the veining onyx mineral appearance they exhibit through their random swirling. [Machine-made: Figure 543-545], [Contemporary: Figure 546-574]

Figure 545. Slag. M.F. Christensen & Son Company. Machine-made. United States. 3/4 - 7/8 in., ca. app. 1910-1920. *Courtesy of Stanley Block.*

Figure 543. Slag. Akro Agate Company. Machine-made. United States. 3/4 in., ca. app. 1920-1930. *Courtesy of Robert Block.*

Figure 544. Slag. Akro Agate Company. Machine-made. United States. 3/4 in., ca. app. 1920-1930. *Courtesy of Robert Block.*

Figure 546. Slag. Single gather. Brown, white. Joe St. Clair. 2 in., ca. app. 1983-1986. *Courtesy of the Marble Collectors Society of America.*

Figure 547. Slag. Single gather. Red, blue, green, white. Joe St. Clair. 2 in., ca. app. 1983-1986. *Courtesy of the Marble Collectors Society of America.*

Figure 548. Slag. Single gather. Red, blue, white. Joe St. Clair. 2 in., ca. app. 1983-1986. *Courtesy of the Marble Collectors Society of America.*

Figure 549. Slag. Torchwork. Multi-color. Scott Patrick. 7/8 in., ca. app. 1999-2002. *Courtesy of the author.*

Figure 550. Slag. Torchwork. Purple, white, green, white, green aventurine glass. Rudy Calin. 1-1/2 in., ca. 2001, 2003. *Courtesy of the author.*

Figure 551. Slag. Torchwork.
Purple, white, clear glass.
Mike Edmundson. 1-1/8 in.,
ca. 2002. *Courtesy of the
author.*

Figure 552. Slag. Torchwork. Multi-color, gold aventurine glass. Robert Powers.
1 - 1-1/4 in., ca. 2001. *Courtesy of the artist.*

Figure 553. Slag. Torchwork.
Multi-color, gold aventurine
glass. Brendan Blake. 1 -
1-1/4 in., ca. 2003. *Courtesy
of the artist.*

Figure 554. Slag.
Torchwork. Multi-color,
red, blue, brown. Richard
Clark. 1 - 1-1/4 in., ca.
2003. *Courtesy of the artist.*

Figure 555. Slag. Torchwork. Multi-color, orange,
blue, pink, tan. Richard Clark. 1-1/8 - 1-3/8 in., ca.
2003. *Courtesy of the artist.*

Figure 556. Slag. Torchwork. Multi-color, blue, red,
orange, green. Richard Clark. 1-1/8 - 1-3/8 in., ca.
2003. *Courtesy of the artist.*

Figure 557. Slag. Torchwork. Multi-color, black, brown, green, purple. Richard Clark. 1-1/8 - 1-1/4 in., ca. 2003. *Courtesy of the artist.*

Figure 561. Slag. Torchwork. Brown, white; blue, white; blue, white; red, white; clear glass. Bruce Breslow. 1-1/8 in., 2002. *Courtesy of the artist.*

Figure 558. Slag. Torchwork. Multi-color, green, red, blue, white. Richard Clark. 7/8 - 1-1/8 in., ca. 2003. *Courtesy of the artist.*

Figure 562. Slag. Rod- and cane-cut. Pink, lavender, blue. Virginia Wilson, Anthony Toccalino. 2 in., ca. 2003. *Courtesy of the artist.*

Figure 559. Slag. Torchwork. Blue, white, clear glass. Bruce Breslow. 1-1/8 in., ca. 2003. *Courtesy of the artist.*

Figure 560. Slag. Torchwork. White, white; green, white; yellow, white; red, white; clear glass. Bruce Breslow. 1-1/8 in., 2002. *Courtesy of the artist.*

Figure 563. Slag. Multi-color. Torchwork. Jerry Park. 1-3/8 in., ca. 2003. *Courtesy of the author.*

Figure 564. Slag. Torchwork. Multi-color, brown, blue. Richard Clark. 1-1/8 in., ca. 2003. *Courtesy of the artist.*

Figure 568. Slag. Torchwork. Light blue, blue, dark blue. Jerry Park. 1-1/4 in., ca. 2003. *Courtesy of the author.*

Figure 565. Slag. Torchwork. Brown, amber, lavender, white, clear glass. Brendan Blake. 1-3/8 in., ca. 2003. *Courtesy of the artist.*

Figure 569. Slag. Torchwork. Red, yellow, blue, pink. Jerry Park. 1-1/4 in., ca. 2003. *Courtesy of the author.*

Figure 566. Slag. Torchwork. Brown, black. *To M.B.* Jerry Park. 1-3/4 in., ca. 2003. *Courtesy of the author.*

Figure 570. Slag. Torchwork. Red, blue, yellow. Jerry Park. 1-5/8 in., ca. 2003. *Courtesy of the author.*

Figure 567. Slag. Torchwork. Purple, black; purple, light blue; black, light brown. Jerry Park. 1-1/4 in., ca. 2003. *Courtesy of the author.*

Figure 571. Slag. Torchwork. Chartreuse, blue, orange. Jerry Park. 1-1/8 in., ca. 2003. *Courtesy of the author.*

Figure 572. Slag. Torchwork. Orange, yellow, blue. Jerry Park. 1-1/2 in., ca. 2002. *Courtesy of the author.*

Figure 573. Slag. Torchwork. Red, black. Jerry Park. 1-1/4 in., ca. 2003. *Courtesy of the author.*

Figure 574. Slag. Torchwork. Light blue, white, clear glass; red, yellow; blue, lavender, light blue, black; red, yellow. Jerry Park. 1 - 1-1/4 in., ca. 2003. *Courtesy of the author.*

Swirl Marbles (Originally produced: 1920-present): Nearly all machine-made marble companies made swirl marbles at one time or another. Swirl marbles were produced in tremendous quantities and varieties. Manufacturing the swirl was accomplished by mixing glass of two or more different colors in one furnace. The difference in color density did not enable the colors to combine together, but rather, produced a stratification that remained as the glass was run through the streaming of the machine where the glass was rounded into a marble. [Machine-made: Figure 575-584], [Contemporary: Figure 585-606]

Figure 576. Swirl. Ravenswood Novelty Works. Machine-made. United States. 5/8 in., ca. app. 1935-1960. *Courtesy of Robert Block.*

Figure 575. Swirl. Akro Agate Company. Machine-made. United States. 11/16 in., ca. 1930-1950. *Courtesy of Robert Block.*

Figure 577. German Swirl. Various colors. Machine-made; Germany. 7/8 in., ca. app. 1950-1980. *Courtesy of Robert Block.*

Figure 578. West Virginia Swirls. Red, green; red, white; yellow, blue. Machine-made; United States. 5/8 in., ca. app. 1940-1950. *Courtesy of Robert Block.*

Figure 579. Swirl. Christensen Agate Company. Assorted color. Machine-made; United States. 5/8 in., ca. app. 1927-1929. *Courtesy of Robert Block.*

Figure 580. West Virginia Swirls. Assorted color. Machine-made; United States. 5/8 in., ca. app. 1940-1950. *Courtesy of Robert Block.*

Figure 581. Swirl. Jabo-Vitro Agate Company. Black, tan. Machine-made. United States. 5/8 - 1 in., ca. app. 1990-2003. *Courtesy of Robert Block.*

Figure 582. Swirl. Peltier Glass Company. Tiger. Assorted colors. Machine-made. United States. 5/8 in., ca. app. 1925-1940. *Courtesy of Robert Block.*

Figure 583. Swirl, Patch. Multi-color. Peltier Glass Company. Machine-made. United States. 5/8 - 11/16 in., ca. app. 1925-1940. *Courtesy of Robert Block.*

Figure 584. Striped Opaque. Red, black, white. Machine-made; Czechoslovakia. 7/8 in., ca. app. 1950-1960. *Courtesy of Robert Block.*

Figure 585. Swirl. German swirls. Machine-made. 7/8 in., ca. app. 1950-1975. *Courtesy of Robert Block.*

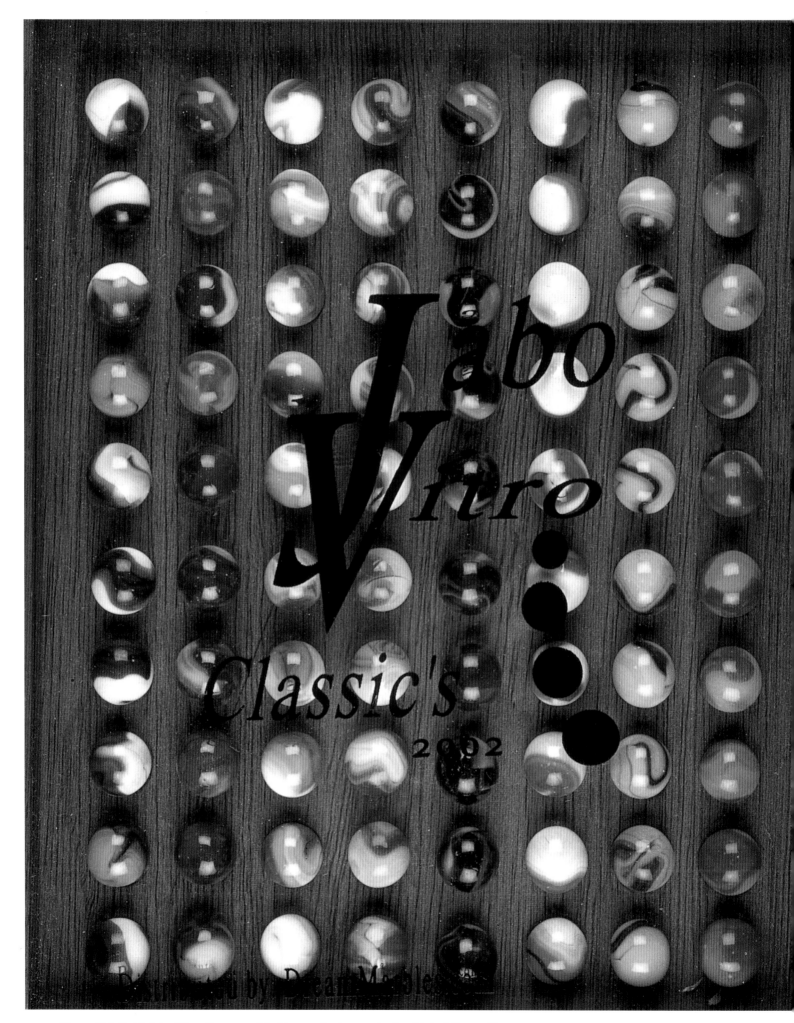

Figure 586. Swirl. Jabo-Vitro Company. Machine-made. Assorted color. United States. *Vitro Swirls. 2002 Fall Classics. No.4/150.* 5/8 in., ca. 2002. *Courtesy of the author.*

Figure 587. Swirl. Single gather. Blue, yellow, orange, clear glass. Robert Lichtman. 1-1/2 in., ca. app. 1985-1989. *Courtesy of the Marble Collectors Society of America.*

Figure 588. Swirl. Torchwork. Blue, white. Attributed to Christopher Robinson. 7/8 - 1-3/8 in., ca. app. 1995-2000. *Courtesy of the author.*

Figure 589. Swirl. Torchwork. Red, orange, blue. Jerry Park. 1-1/4 in., ca. 2003. *Courtesy of the author.*

Figure 591. Swirl. Torchwork. Multi-color. John Hamon Miller. 7/8 - 1-1/8 in., ca. 2002. *Courtesy of the author.*

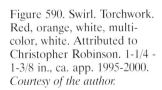

Figure 590. Swirl. Torchwork. Red, orange, white, multi-color, white. Attributed to Christopher Robinson. 1-1/4 - 1-3/8 in., ca. app. 1995-2000. *Courtesy of the author.*

Figure 592. Swirl. Torchwork. Blue, turquoise blue, black. Jerry Park. 1-3/8 in., ca. 2002. *Courtesy of the author.*

Figure 593. Swirl. Torchwork. Silver fume, red base. Tony Parker. 1-1/8 in., ca. 1992. *Courtesy of the author.*

Figure 594. Swirl. Millefiori. Torchwork. Multi-color, including paperweight-style. Greg Hoglin. 1-1/8 - 1-3/8 in., ca. 2002. *Courtesy of the author.*

Figure 595. Swirl. Torchwork. Assorted, including baseball; crafted for interchanging in ring. See Figure 876. Bruce Troeh. 1/2 in., ca. 2002. *Courtesy of the artist.*

Figure 596. Swirl. Torchwork. Multi-color *(left)*; orange, black, white *(center)*; black, white, gold aventurine glass *(right)*; multi-color, gold aventurine glass *(back)*. Mike Edmundson *(left)*, Drew Fritts *(center, right)*, Robert Livesy *(back)*. 5/8 - 1-1/8 in., ca. 1999-2002. *Courtesy of the author.*

Figure 597. Swirl. Torchwork. Multi-color. Bobbie Seese. 3/16 - 3/4 in., ca. 2003. *Courtesy of the author.*

Figure 598. Swirl. Torchwork. Multi-color, including moon and stars, lizard, beachball, gold aventurine glass. Dan Grumbling *(front, center; middle, center)*, Aaron West. 3/4 - 1 in., ca. 2002. *Courtesy of the artists.*

Figure 599. Swirl. Torchwork. Multi-color. Scott Patrick. 1/2 - 3/4 in., ca. app. 2000-2002. *Courtesy of the author.*

Figure 600. Swirl. Torchwork. Multi-color, gold, blue dichroic glass. Phil McGlothlin. 3/4 - 1 in., ca. 2002. *Courtesy of the artist.*

Figure 601. Swirl. Torchwork. Multi-color. Christopher Robinson, Fred Wilganowski. 5/8 - 1 in., ca. 2002. *Courtesy of the author.*

Figure 602. Swirl. Torchwork. Multi-color. Scott Patrick.
1/2 - 3/4 in., ca. app. 2000-2002. *Courtesy of the author.*

Figure 603. Swirl. Rod- and cane-cut. Multi-color, including eyeballs. China. 13/16
in., ca. app. 1995-2002. *Courtesy of Robert Block.*

Figure 604. Opaques. Machine-made. Assorted color opaque marbles, round tin, manufactured for Starbucks Coffee Company. China. 1/2 - 5/8 in., ca. 2002. *Courtesy of the author.*

Figure 605. Assorted. Machine-made. Assorted marbles, tin package, manufactured for NEX Products, Inc. China. 23/32 - 3/4 in., ca. 2002. *Courtesy of the author.*

Figure 606. Cat's-eyes. Machine-made. Assorted, mesh bag. 23/32 in., ca. 2003. *Courtesy of the author.*

Chapter Ten
Mimics, Reproductions, and Repairs

Each of the three topics, mimics, reproductions, and repairs, could have its own chapter filled with complex details and dire admonitions to guide the wary. However, simple direct sentences will provide you with an overview of these crafting and collecting important topics.

The contemporary marble, sphere, and orb field is not much different than any glass, porcelain, painting or other antiques or collectible field. There will always be some who choose to reproduce or mimic what has previously been done.

Keep in mind that there is a difference in mimicking a previously manufactured or crafted piece and actually reproducing such works. To mimic as described in *The American Heritage College Dictionary, Third Edition*, "1. To copy or imitate closely," "3. To resemble closely; simulate," or as also written, "2. A copy or imitation." Whereas, the same dictionary defines the word reproduction as, "1. The act of reproducing or the condition or process of being reproduced." Additionally, it goes on to say of the word reproduce, "1. To produce a counterpart, an image or a copy."

There are those who take advantage of the market and the popularity of an artist's work by reproducing such works. This not only shows a lack of imagination on the reproducers part, it also further deteriorates the long-term benefits brought to bear by the originator of such works. However, mimicking another's works, whether current or older, must be viewed differently. For in fact, mimicry has not only occurred for centuries, but can often times lead to better than original works. The mimics crafted today of antique and machine-made marbles of old not only have a rightful place in the marketplace and collections of those who choose them, they are important historical markers in and of themselves. This dichotomy goes in part to the heart of this book—is there a line to be drawn between a reproduction and a mimic? Readers will have to draw their own conclusion from the information and images provided.

If the work is marked by the artist, and therefore readily available for inspection and identification, should an artist or craftsmen have the artistic license to mimic not just older styles, but more current as well? If, however, the artist or craftsmen intentionally creates a piece that is not just similar, but striking in ALL its similarities, without an artist's mark, without any way for the collector or others interested to place a date or timeframe on the piece, then has the line been crossed? Is the work a true reproduction? Again, readers will have to make that decision for themselves.

Equally important for the collector to be aware of is the unsigned marble that is reminiscent of an antique handmade marble. As in any field where the item becomes a collectible commodity, you will find individuals making efforts to cash in on unsuspecting or uneducated hobbyists. Many of these marbles are extremely high in quality and are difficult for anyone but the most educated collector to identify as reproductions of antique or machine-made marbles. These marbles would of course be valued at a fraction of the authentic marble's worth. It is important to look the glass over very carefully. In the case of a reproduction antique-style marble, a few of the most obvious signs to look for involve the glass itself. Is the glass clean or striated? Does the glass have a crisp, crystal look or is it somewhat less-than-Waterford clear? Are there signs of any damage? Do air-trap bubbles or pinpricks appear in the glass? Remember, the antique handmade marble was made first and foremost as a child's plaything, nothing more than a five-and-dime store toy. The contemporary marbles of today are fashioned with a designer's flair. A high-quality art glass is smooth to the touch all around, with no feel of pontil marks on either the top or bottom pole, and incorporates a palette of vibrant colors not usually associated with those of antique handmade marbles.

Some of the same holds true for reproduction machine-made marbles. The glass of the reproduction will have a very smooth almost oily sheen to it. This glass will show no sign of pitting or color variation. Certain subtleties in the glass expected from a marble that rolled out of a machine would not be seen in the contemporary reproduction produced today. The artist will identify most of these marbles as reproductions of Marble King, Peltier, Akro Agate, Champion, Christensen Agate, and other companies. And the artists who produce them are signing more and more of these torch-worked contemporary marbles. The figures illustrated will enable you to discern a reproduction from an original, but when in doubt, seek advice. If a piece is priced too high or too low, question the authenticity of it. If a work is unsigned, question the authenticity and date it was crafted. You will find your enjoyment of the hobby increase as your awareness of all aspects of marbles, spheres, and orbs increases (e.g., signing is not a style but an aspect). [Figure 607-609]

Repairing contemporary handmade marbles, spheres, and orbs is a much less controversial subject. Just like any piece of fine art, porcelain, glass, pottery, jewelry or other item, there is no good explanation to be offered for not having a piece repaired if damage has been caused. After all, in your collection you want not just the finest pieces you can attain, but also those whose condition is outstanding. This pertains to contemporary marbles, spheres, and orbs only. The debate lingers amongst collectors and others as to whether anything at all should be done to marbles of earlier times.

The best sources of repair for your piece would be the artists themselves, if available and willing. In most cases they will be happy to accommodate you, if practical, so the piece can be returned to its original pristine condition. What is even better is it may be necessary for the piece to be remarked with the artist's mark, something the artist can do when the repair is made. If this is not feasible, there are qualified individuals who are experts in glass repair who can bring your piece back to its original state—or as close as feasible. So go ahead and have your piece repaired if need be, you'll enjoy it that much more.

Figure 607. Swirl, Ribbon. Torchwork. Multi-color, rework, remelt. Scott Patrick. 1/2 - 3/4 in., ca. app. 1998-2002. *Courtesy of the author.*

Figure 608. Swirl, Indian. Torchwork. Multi-color. Christopher Robinson, Fred Wilganowski. 5/8 - 1 in., ca. 1999-2002. *Courtesy of the author.*

Figure 609. Swirl. Torchwork. Multi-color. John Hamon Miller. 3/4 in., ca. 2003. *Courtesy of the author.*

Chapter Eleven
"Novel and Inventive" Contemporary Marbles, Spheres, and Orbs

As was discussed early on in this book, the overriding goal in presenting the research and images of the works illustrated within these pages is to compare and contrast the varied styles, techniques, and designs of contemporary marbles, spheres, and orbs crafted in the studio art setting. Doing so while further exploring the relationship these works have within comparative style, technique, and design to those of their antique handmade and later machine-made fore bearers. It has not been intended, nor expected, that every artist or craftsman working in the field today would have work represented in this volume. The purpose is not to focus on any one or another, but rather the varied breadth of the works themselves. Some names you may recognize as you view the works, others you will not. Many are young and have been working in the field only a short time, others for many years. Works were chosen for illustration because of their interrelationship to those of earlier times, not based on an artist's/craftsman's name or recognition.

Most importantly, this book allows the reader to see through the past to the present. What you'll see will simply amaze you! The use of dichroic glass incorporated as images within spheres; vortex works that beckon you to view them and be drawn down to their very core; glass rods used like paintbrushes to create beautiful garden and undersea themes. What would appear to be the simple use of air to create vibrant twists and purposefully placed bubbles; the use of decades old techniques to replicate the favrille styles of Tiffany, the masking technique developed by Orrefors Crystal in the earlier part of the twentieth century. And today, most importantly, the botanical Orb works of the dean of the Modern American Paperweight Movement, Paul Stankard.

Millefiori and Murrini

(Originally produced: app. 1st century A.D.): Millefiori, from the Italian meaning "thousand flowers," originated as a decorative style in Roman times attributed to the first century A.D. However, it was not until the later Venetian glass workers of the sixteenth and seventeenth century took up the task of crafting intricate cane work that the technique of encasing multicolored pieces of pre-crafted glass to create a design was popularized. Millefiori is most often associated with paperweights and floral design work. Employing this technique the cane sections are intentionally placed in a predetermined pattern. Artists well known for their design and use of murrini or silhouette canes craft the contemporary works of today most often. These cane pieces can be as simple as cut glass colored rod pieces or as complex as figures or scenes. [Contemporary: Figure: 610-658]

Figure 610. Murrini. Rod- and cane-cut. Black, white. Shell Neisler, Dustin Morell. 1/4 in., ca. 2002. *Courtesy of the artist.*

Figure 611. Murrini. Rod- and cane-cut. Assorted. Shane Caswell. 3/8 - 1/2 in., ca. 2002. *Courtesy of the artist.*

Figure 612. Murrini.
Rod- and cane-cut.
Shane Caswell signature
cane. Shane Caswell. 3/8
in., ca. 2002. *Courtesy of
the artist.*

Figure 613. Murrini. Rod- and cane-cut. Assorted. Shane Caswell. 3/8 - 1/2 in., ca. 2002.
Courtesy of the artist.

Figure 614. Murrini. Rod- and cane-cut. Assorted. Shane Caswell. 3/8 -
1/2 in., ca. 2002. *Courtesy of the artist.*

Figure 615. Murrini. Torchwork.
Fish. Jennifer Wilson. 3/4 in.,
ca. 1999. *Courtesy of the author.*

Figure 616. Murrini. Torchwork. Rose, bee, fish,
butterfly. Mike Edmundson, Lewis and Jennifer
Wilson. 3/4 - 1 in., ca. 1999-2001. *Courtesy of the
author.*

Figure 617. Murrini. Torchwork. Heart, peace sign murrini canes, reverse rake pull. MR. Unidentified. 1-1/4 in., ca. 2003. *Courtesy of the author.*

Figure 618. Murrini. Torchwork. Fish, flora, gold aventurine glass. Lewis and Jennifer Wilson. 3/4 - 1-1/8 in., ca. 1997. *Courtesy of the author.*

Figure 619. Murrini. Torchwork. Spiral core, random placed murrini cane. Mike Edmundson. 1 in., ca. 2002. *Courtesy of the author.*

Figure 620. Murrini. Torchwork. Heart. Shane Caswell. 1 in., ca. 2001. *Courtesy of the author.*

Figure 621. Murrini. Torchwork. Star murrini canes. Dinah Hulet. 1-1/8 in., ca. 2001. *Courtesy of the author.*

Figure 622. Murrini. Single gather. Heart murrini canes, paperweight-style. Kathy Young, Christopher Constantin. 1-1/2 in., ca. app. 1983-1989. *Courtesy of the Marble Collectors Society of America.*

Figure 623. Murrini. Torchwork. Packed multi-color murrini canes, paperweight-style, white base, gold aventurine glass, reverse rake-pull. *(Side-view.)* Greg Hoglin. 1-1/4 in., ca. 2004. *Courtesy of the author.*

Figure 624. Murrini. Single gather. Butterfly. Tony Parker. 1-5/8 in., ca. 1992. *Courtesy of the Marble Collectors Society of America.*

Figure 625. Murrini. Torchwork. Cowboy. Kevin O'Grady. 1 in., ca. 2001. *Courtesy of the author.*

Figure 629. Murrini. Torchwork. Man, reverse rake pull. Dinah Hulet. 1-1/8 in., ca. 1998. *Courtesy of the artist.*

Figure 626. Murrini. Torchwork. Willie Nelson, Che Gueverra, flora, reverse rake pull. Chris and Lissa Juedemann. 1-1/4 in., ca. 2003. *Courtesy of the artists.*

Figure 630. Murrini. Torchwork. Woman, reverse rake pull. *(front)* Dinah Hulet. 1-1/2 in., ca. 1999. *Courtesy of the artist.*

Figure 627. Murrini. Torchwork. Dale Chihuly, Lenny Bruce, reverse rake pull. Chris and Lissa Juedemann. 1 - 1-1/8 in., ca. 2003. *Courtesy of the artists.*

Figure 631. Murrini. Torchwork. Woman, reverse rake pull. *(side to back)* Dinah Hulet. 1-1/2 in., ca. 1999. *Courtesy of the artist.*

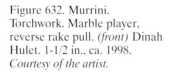

Figure 632. Murrini. Torchwork. Marble player, reverse rake pull. *(front)* Dinah Hulet. 1-1/2 in., ca. 1998. *Courtesy of the artist.*

Figure 628. Murrini. Torchwork. Jimi Hendrix, reverse rake pull. Chris and Lissa Juedemann. 1-3/8 in., ca. 2003. *Courtesy of the artists.*

Figure 633. Murrini. Torchwork. Marble player, reverse rake pull. *(back)* Dinah Hulet. 1-1/2 in., ca. 1998. *Courtesy of the artist.*

Figure 634. Millefiori. Rod- and cane-cut. Packed, multi-color murrini tubes. *(side view)* Douglas Sweet. 2-1/4 in., ca. 2002. *Courtesy of the author.*

Figure 635. Millefiori. Rod- and cane-cut. Packed, multi-color murrini tubes. *(top view)* Douglas Sweet. 2-1/4 in., ca. 2002. *Courtesy of the author.*

Figure 636. Millefiori. Rod- and cane-cut. Packed, multi-color murrini canes. Gentile Glass. John Gentile. 2-3/4 in., ca. app. 2000-2004. *Courtesy of the author.*

Figure 637. Millefiori. Rod- and cane-cut. Packed, multi-color murrini canes. Gentile Glass. John Gentile. 1-1/4 in., ca. app. 2000-2004. *Courtesy of the author.*

Figure 638. Millefiori. Rod- and cane-cut. Packed; multi-color murrini canes. Gentile Glass. John Gentile. 1-1/2 in., ca. app. 1995-2000. *Courtesy of the author.*

Figure 639. Millefiori. Rod- and cane-cut. Date canes, packed, multi-color murrini canes. Gentile Glass. John Gentile. 2-1/8 in., ca. 1998. *Courtesy of the author.*

Figure 640. Millefiori. Rod- and cane-cut. Packed, multi-color murrini canes. Gerry and Pat Colman. 7/8 - 1-1/4 in., ca. 2000. *Courtesy of the author.*

Figure 641. Millefiori. Rod- and cane-cut. Packed, multi-color murrini canes. Gerry and Pat Colman. 1 - 1-1/2 in., ca. 2000. *Courtesy of the author.*

Figure 642. Millefiori. Rod- and cane-cut. Packed, multi-color murrini canes. *(side view)* Gerry and Pat Colman. 1-1/2 in., ca. 2000. *Courtesy of the author.*

Figure 643. Millefiori. Rod- and cane-cut. Packed, multi-color murrini canes. *(top view)* Gerry and Pat Colman. 1-3/8 in., ca. 2000. *Courtesy of the author.*

Figure 644. Millefiori. Rod- and cane-cut. Earrings. Packed checkerboard, multi-color murrini canes. Noble Effort. Richard Marquis, Ro Purser. 1/2 in., ca. 1984. *Courtesy of the author.*

Figure 645. Millefiori. Rod- and cane-cut. Earrings. Packed checkerboard, multi-color murrini canes.
Noble Effort. Richard Marquis, Ro Purser. 1/2 in., ca. 1984. *Courtesy of the author.*

Figure 646. Millefiori. Rod- and cane-cut. Multi-color murrini canes, random. Luke Gilvey. 1-3/4 in., ca. 1998. *Courtesy of the author.*

Figure 647. Millefiori. Torchwork. Multi-color murrini canes, random. Jerry Kelly. 1 in., ca. 2003. *Courtesy of the author.*

Figure 648. Millefiori. Torchwork. Multi-color murrini canes, random. Douglas Ferguson. 1-5/8 in., ca. 2003. *Courtesy of the author.*

Figure 649. Millefiori. Single gather. Multi-color murrini canes, random, black base. Gerry Colman. 1-1/2 in., ca. 1999. *Courtesy of the author.*

Figure 650. Millefiori. Torchwork. Heart murrini canes, random, black base. Gerry Colman. 1-1/4 in., ca. 1997. *Courtesy of the author.*

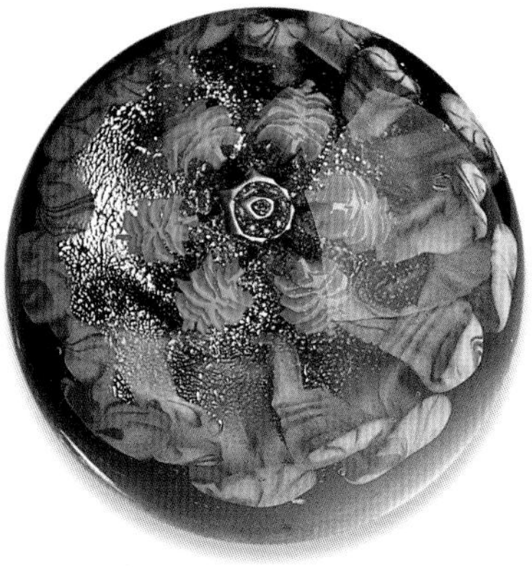

Figure 651. Murrini. Torchwork. Island, palm trees, reverse design, undersea, blue band across equator. *(view one)* Chris and Lissa Juedemann. 1-3/4 in., ca. 2003. *Courtesy of the artists.*

Figure 652. Murrini. Torchwork. Undersea, reverse design, island, palm trees, blue band across equator. *(view two)* Chris and Lissa Juedemann. 1-3/4 in., ca. 2003. *Courtesy of the artists.*

Figure 653. Millefiori. Torchwork. Murrini canes, patterned, rake pull, clear glass. Rajesh Kommineni. 1-3/4 in., ca. 2004. *Courtesy of the author.*

Figure 654. Millefiori. Rod- and cane-cut. Multi-color murrini canes, tubes, random. Douglas Sweet. 2-1/4 in., ca. 2003. *Courtesy of the author.*

Figure 655. Millefiori.
Torchwork. Multi-color
murrini canes, gold
aventurine glass, bands,
random. Greg Hoglin.
1 in., ca. 1997. *Courtesy
of the author.*

Figure 656. Millefiori. Rod- and cane-cut.
Multi-color, four-square murrini canes,
checkerboard, black base. Jody Fine. 1-5/8 in.,
ca. app. 1983-1988. *Courtesy of the Marble
Collectors Society of America.*

Figure 657. Millefiori. Rod- and cane-cut.
Multi-color canes, green aventurine glass,
clear glass. Jody Fine. 1-5/8 in., ca. app.
1992-1996. *Courtesy of the Marble Collectors Society of America.*

Figure 658. Millefiori. Torchwork. Two sided, murrini star canes, circumference ribbon, clear glass. *(side one)* David Strobel. 2-1/8 in., ca. 2004. *Courtesy of the author.*

Figure 659. Millefiori. Torchwork. Two sided, murrini star canes, circumference ribbon, clear glass. *(side two)* David Strobel. 2-1/8 in., ca. 2004. *Courtesy of the author.*

Figure 660. Flora. Torchwork. Pink, yellow flora, green leaves, blue base. Cathy Richardson. 1-1/2 in., ca. 2003. *Courtesy of the author.*

Figure 661. Flora. Torchwork. Multi-color flora, green leaves, light blue base. *(side view)* Cathy Richardson. 1-1/2 in., ca. 2003. *Courtesy of the author.*

Figure 665. Flora. Torchwork. New England tree, mountain scene. *Limited edition 1-1.* Cathy Richardson. 1-3/4 in., ca. 2003. *Courtesy of the author.*

Figure 664. Flora. Torchwork. Yellow flora, green leaves, gold aventurine glass, light blue base. Cathy Richardson. 1 in., ca. 2001. *Courtesy of the author.*

Figure 663. Flora. Torchwork. Pink, yellow flora, green, blue leaves, clear dichroic glass. Cathy Richardson. 1-1/2 in., ca. 2003. *Courtesy of the author.*

Figure 662. Flora. Torchwork. Multi-color flora, green leaves, light blue base. *(bottom view)* Cathy Richardson. 1-1/2 in., ca. 2003. *Courtesy of the author.*

Figure 666. Flora. Torchwork. Desert cactus, mountain scene. Cathy Richardson. 1-5/8 in., ca. 2003. *Courtesy of the author.*

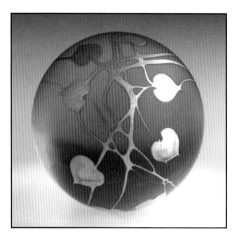

Figure 667. Flora. Rod- and cane-cut. Hearts and vines, Tiffany-style. David Salazar. 1-3/4 in., ca. 2000. *Courtesy of the author.*

Figure 669. Dichroic. Single gather. Torchwork. Dichroic blue/green dragonfly, reeds, translucent blue base. Sara Creekmore. 1-5/8 in., ca. 1998. *Courtesy of the author.*

Figure 668. Patchwork. Single gather. Rod- and cane-cut. Multi-color dichroic glass, green base. Rolf and Genie Wald. 1-3/4 in., ca. 2004. *Courtesy of the author.*

Figure 670. Dichroic. Single gather. Torchwork. Dichroic silver tiger, transparent blue base. David Dunham. 2 in., ca. 2000. *Courtesy of the author.*

Figure 671. Dichroic. Single gather. Torchwork. Dichroic silver tiger, transparent blue base. *(close-up)* David Dunham. 2 in., ca. 2000. *Courtesy of the author.*

Figure 672. Dichroic. Single gather. Torchwork. Multi-color swirl, stars overlay. Sara Creekmore. 2-1/4 in., ca. 1998. *Courtesy of the author.*

Figure 673. Aventurine patch. Single gather. Multi-color aventurine glass, "Wald" signature, gold aventurine glass. Rolf and Genie Wald. 1-3/8 in., ca. 1995. *Courtesy of the author.*

Figure 674. World. Rod- and cane-cut. Multi-layer. Light blue oceans, lakes, red/green dichroic land masses, Graal technique; white swirling cloud cover, clear glass casing. *Artist proof. Signed "For Mark" A.P.* Geoffrey Beetem. 3-1/4 in., ca. 2002. *Courtesy of the author.*

Figure 675. Moon. Rod- and cane-cut. Multi-layer. Dichroic blue/green glass over brown, Graal technique. *Artist proof. Signed "For Mark" A.P.* Geoffrey Beetem. 2-7/8 in., ca. 2002. *Courtesy of the author.*

Figure 676. Man-in-the-Moon. Rod- and cane-cut. Black glass painted face, blue eyes, gold aventurine glass with craters. Rolf and Genie Wald. 2-1/8 in., ca. 2004. *Courtesy of the artists.*

Figure 677. World. Rod- and cane-cut. Multi-layer. Light blue, blue oceans, lakes, brown, green land masses, Graal technique; white swirling cloud cover at pole, clear glass casing. Lundberg Studios. 3-1/8 in., ca. 2003. *Courtesy of Robert Block.*

Figure 678. Dichroic. Rod- and cane-cut. Multi-color dichroic, green aventurine glass, green base. Virginia Wilson and Anthony Toccalino. 2-5/8 in., ca. 2003. *Courtesy of the artists.*

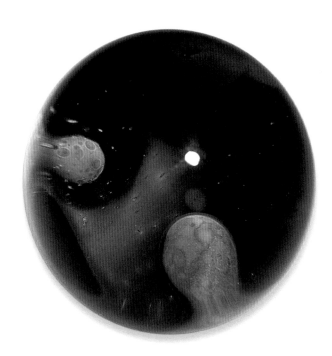

Figure 679. Universe. Torchwork. Multi-color planets, galaxies, fumed glass, black base. Gateson Recko. 3 in., ca. 2004. *Courtesy of the artist.*

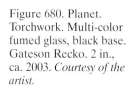

Figure 680. Planet. Torchwork. Multi-color fumed glass, black base. Gateson Recko. 2 in., ca. 2003. *Courtesy of the artist.*

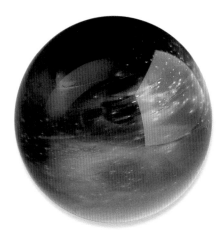

Figure 681. Painted scene. Single gather. New England spring, painted scene, enamel, clear glass. Wendy Besett. 1-7/8 in., ca. 2002. *Courtesy of the artist.*

Figure 682. Painted scene. Single gather. New England summer, painted scene, enamel, clear glass. Wendy Besett. 2 in., ca. 2002. *Courtesy of the artist.*

Figure 683. Painted scene. Single gather. New England autumn, painted scene, enamel, clear glass. Wendy Besett. 2 in., ca. 2002. *Courtesy of the artist.*

Figure 684. Stars and Stripes. Torchwork. Red, white, blue, gold aventurine band. Karen Federici. 1 in., ca. 1998. *Courtesy of the artist.*

Figure 685. Tornado. Rod- and cane-cut. Gold core, blue bands. Tony Parker. 1-5/8 in., ca. 1993. *Courtesy of the Marble Collectors Society of America.*

Figure 686. Conan. Torchwork. Red, black base. Presented to Conan O'Brien, similar piece. Bruce Troeh. 1-1/8 in., ca. 2002. *Courtesy of the artist.*

Figure 687. Clown. Torchwork. Assorted colors, clown face. Bruce Troeh. 1-1/4 in., ca. 2002. *Courtesy of the artist.*

Figure 691. Shamrock. Single gather. Paperweight-style. Green aventurine glass four-leaf clover, glass painted, white, green aventurine glass ground base. David Salazar. 1-3/4 in., ca. 1994. *Courtesy of the author.*

Figure 690. Flora. Single gather. Paperweight-style. Blue flora, green leaves, murrini stars, glass painted, white base. David Salazar. 1-1/2 in., ca. 1986. *Courtesy of the author.*

Figure 689. Flora. Single gather. Paperweight-style. Blue butterfly, red flora, green leaves, glass painted, white base. David Salazar. 1-1/2 in., ca. 1986. *Courtesy of the author.*

Figure 688. White Tiger. Torchwork. White Tiger murrini, murrini cane trees, rake pull. Jesse Taj. 1-1/2 in., ca. 2003. *Courtesy of the author.*

Figure 692. Shamrock. Single gather. Paperweight-style. White, green, gold aventurine glass four-leaf clover, glass painted, green aventurine four-leaf clovers, white, green aventurine pulled glass ground base. *Experimental 1-X.* David Salazar. 1-3/4 in., ca. 2001. *Courtesy of the author.*

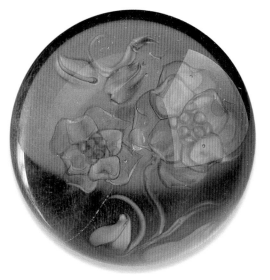

Figure 693. Flora. Single gather. Paperweight-style. Blue, white flora, green leaves, stems, glass painted, transparent pink dichroic glass base. *Experimental 1-X.* David Salazar. 2-1/8 in., ca. 1992. *Courtesy of the author.*

Figure 694. Flora. Single gather. Paperweight-style. Purple, lavender flora, green leaves, brown stems, glass painted, white ribbon glass base. *Experimental 1-X.* David Salazar. 1-7/8 in., ca. 2002. *Courtesy of the author.*

Figure 695. Flora. Single gather. Paperweight-style. Magenta, pink flora, green leaves, stems, glass painted, white ribbon glass base. *Experimental 1-X.* David Salazar. 1-7/8 in., ca. 2002. *Courtesy of the author.*

Figure 696. Flora. Single gather. Paperweight-style. White flora, green leaves, butterfly, glass painted, transparent cranberry red base. David Salazar. 1-7/8 in., ca. 1987. *Courtesy of the author.*

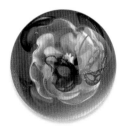

Figure 697. Butterfly. Single gather. Paperweight-style. Monarch butterfly, lavender flora, green leaves, glass painted, blue dichroic glass base. David Salazar. 1 in., ca. 2003. *Courtesy of the author.*

Figure 698. Parrot. Single gather. Paperweight-style. Green parrot, trees, orange harvest moon, glass painted, blue dichroic glass base. Experimental 1-X. David Salazar, Jesse Siegel. 1-3/4 in., ca. 1997. *Courtesy of the author.*

Figure 699. Tree. Single gather. Paper-weight-style. Tree, green aventurine glass ground, multi-color flora, orange harvest moon, glass painted, clear glass base. *Limited edition 1-1.* David Salazar. 1-3/4 in., ca. 2002. *Courtesy of the author.*

Figure 700. Dove. Single gather. Paperweight-style. White dove, light blue swirled clouds, glass painted, dark blue base. David Salazar. 1-3/4 in., ca. 2004. *Courtesy of the author.*

Figure 701. Tree. Torchwork. Paperweight-style. Tree, green, brown, light blue base. George Pavliscak. 1 in., ca. 2003. *Courtesy of the author.*

Figure 702. Frog. Torchwork. Paperweight-style. Green frog, white ground base. Lewis and Jennifer Wilson. 1 in., ca. 2002. *Courtesy of the author.*

Figure 703. Frog. Torchwork. Paper-weight-style. Multi-color brown frog, yellow ground glass, blue base. Lewis and Jennifer Wilson. 1-3/8 in., ca. 1999. *Courtesy of the author.*

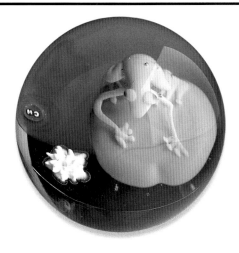

Figure 704. Frog. Torchwork. Paperweight-style. Green frog, green lily pad, white lily, light blue base. Lewis and Jennifer Wilson. 1-7/8 in., ca. 2000. *Courtesy of the author.*

Figure 705. Snake. Torchwork. Paperweight-style. Green snake, brown animal, multi-color ground glass base. Lewis and Jennifer Wilson. 2-3/8 in., ca. 2003. *Courtesy of the author.*

Figure 706. Snake. Torchwork. Paperweight-style. Orange snakes, multi-color, white ground glass base. Lewis and Jennifer Wilson. 2 in., ca. 2002. *Courtesy of the author.*

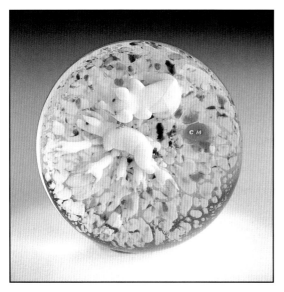

Figure 707. Pigs. Torchwork. Paperweight-style. Pink pigs, piglets, multi-color, green ground glass base, clear glass. Lewis and Jennifer Wilson. 2 in., ca. 2003. *Courtesy of the author.*

Figure 708. Geometric. Torchwork. Multi-color circular designs, light blue, dark blue base. Beth Tomasello. 1-3/8 in., ca. 2003. *Courtesy of the author.*

Figure 709. Rake Pull. Torchwork. Multi-color rake pull design, green, white base. Greg Hoglin. 1-1/8 in., ca. 2004. *Courtesy of the author.*

Figure 710. Rake Pull. Torchwork. Multi-color rake pull design, transparent and opaque base. Greg Hoglin. 1/2 - 1-1/8 in., ca. 2004. *Courtesy of the author.*

Figure 711. Spotted. Torchwork. Red, gray, gold aventurine glass, black base. Tim Waugh. 1 in., ca. 2003. *Courtesy of the artist.*

Figure 712. Spotted. Torchwork. Blue, red, yellow base. Tim Waugh. 7/8 in., ca. 2003. *Courtesy of the artist.*

Figure 713. Spotted. Torchwork. Blue, red, yellow base. Cathy Richardson. 1-1/2 in., ca. 2003. *Courtesy of the artist.*

Figure 714. Flora. Torchwork. Lavender, yellow flora, yellow, green stems, light blue base. George Pavliscak. 1-1/8 in., ca. 2003. *Courtesy of the author.*

Figure 715. Flora. Torchwork. Yellow, white flora, green leaves, stem, blue base. Cathy Richardson. 1-1/2 in., ca. 2001. *Courtesy of the artist.*

Figure 716. Abstract. Torchwork. Green dots, spirals, black base. Victor Gaenzel. 1-1/2 in., ca. 2001. *Courtesy of the author.*

Figure 717. Flora. Torchwork. Multi-color flora, clear glass. KY.
Unidentified. 1-1/4 - 1-1/2 in., ca. 2003. *Courtesy of the author.*

Figure 718. Sea Flora. Torchwork. Multi-color sea flora, clear
glass. Jerry Kelly. 1-1/2 in., ca. 2004. *Courtesy of the author.*

Figure 719. Sea Flora. Torchwork. Multi-color sea flora, clear glass. Jerry
Kelly. 1-1/4 in., ca. 2003. *Courtesy of the author.*

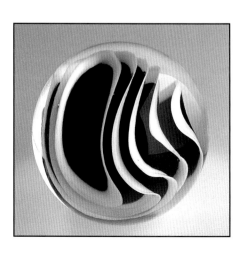

Figure 720. Abstract.
Torchwork. Black, white
parallel flat, curled bands,
clear glass. Drew Fritts. 1-3/4
in., ca. 2002. *Courtesy of the
author.*

Figure 721. Abstract. Torchwork. Red parallel flat, curled bands, black, stretched dots, clear glass. Drew Fritts. 1-3/4 in., ca. 2002. *Courtesy of the author.*

Figure 722. Moon and Stars. Rod- and cane-cut. Yellow crescent moon, white stars, murrini canes, blue base. David Salazar. 7/8 in., ca. 1987. *Courtesy of the author.*

Figure 723. Moon and Stars. Rod- and cane-cut. Yellow crescent Man-in-the-Moon, white stars, murrini canes, blue base. *Limited edition 9/100.* David Salazar. 2-1/4 in., ca. 1998. *Courtesy of the author.*

Figure 724. Abstract. Rod- and cane-cut. Brown, olive, black, swirled, evoking Vincent Van Gogh "Starry Night." David Salazar. 2-1/8 in., ca. 2004. *Courtesy of the author.*

Figure 725. Folded bands. Torchwork. Brown, tan, blue, parallel, raked. Douglas Ferguson. 1-1/4 in., ca. 2000. *Courtesy of the author.*

Figure 726. Sailboats. Torchwork. Multi-color scene, enamel, reverse multi-color rake pull. Gale Morgan. 1-1/2 in., ca. 2004. *Courtesy of the artist.*

Figure 727. Dichroic. Torchwork. Green/blue, black dichroic glass. David Vogt. 1-7/8 in., ca. 1997. *Courtesy of the artist.*

Figure 728. Butterfly. Torchwork. Cobalt blue butterfly, dots, silver/blue dichroic glass *(front)*, dichroic blue butterfly, dots, silver dichroic *(reverse)*, brown band. Teri Conklin. 1-7/8 in., ca. 2002. *Courtesy of the artist.*

Figure 729. Butterfly. Torchwork. Dichroic blue butterfly, dots, silver dichroic *(reverse)*, cobalt blue butterfly, dots, silver/blue dichroic glass *(front)*, brown band. Teri Conklin. 1-7/8 in., ca. 2002. *Courtesy of the artist.*

Figure 730. Abstract. Torchwork. Dichroic blue/green abstract design *(front)*, multi-color rake pull *(reverse)*. Teri Conklin. 1-7/8 in., ca. 2002. *Courtesy of the artist.*

Figure 731. Abstract. Torchwork. Multi-color rake pull *(reverse)*, dichroic blue/green abstract design *(front)*. Teri Conklin. 1-7/8 in., ca. 2002. *Courtesy of the artist.*

Figure 732. Abstract. Rod- and cane-cut. Multi-color canes, swirled, brown, black base. Douglas Sweet. 1-5/8 in., ca. app. 1990-1995. *Courtesy of the Marble Collectors Society of America.*

Figure 733. Abstract. Inhabited Planet. Single gather. Multi-color millefiori canes, air trap, brown, blue, green base. Josh Simpson. 1-3/4 in., ca. app. 1985-1990. *Courtesy of the Marble Collectors Society of America.*

Figure 734. Abstract. Inhabited Planet. Single gather. Multi-color millefiori canes, air trap, silver dichroic glass, white, green base. Josh Simpson. 1-7/8 in., ca. 2002. *Courtesy of the author.*

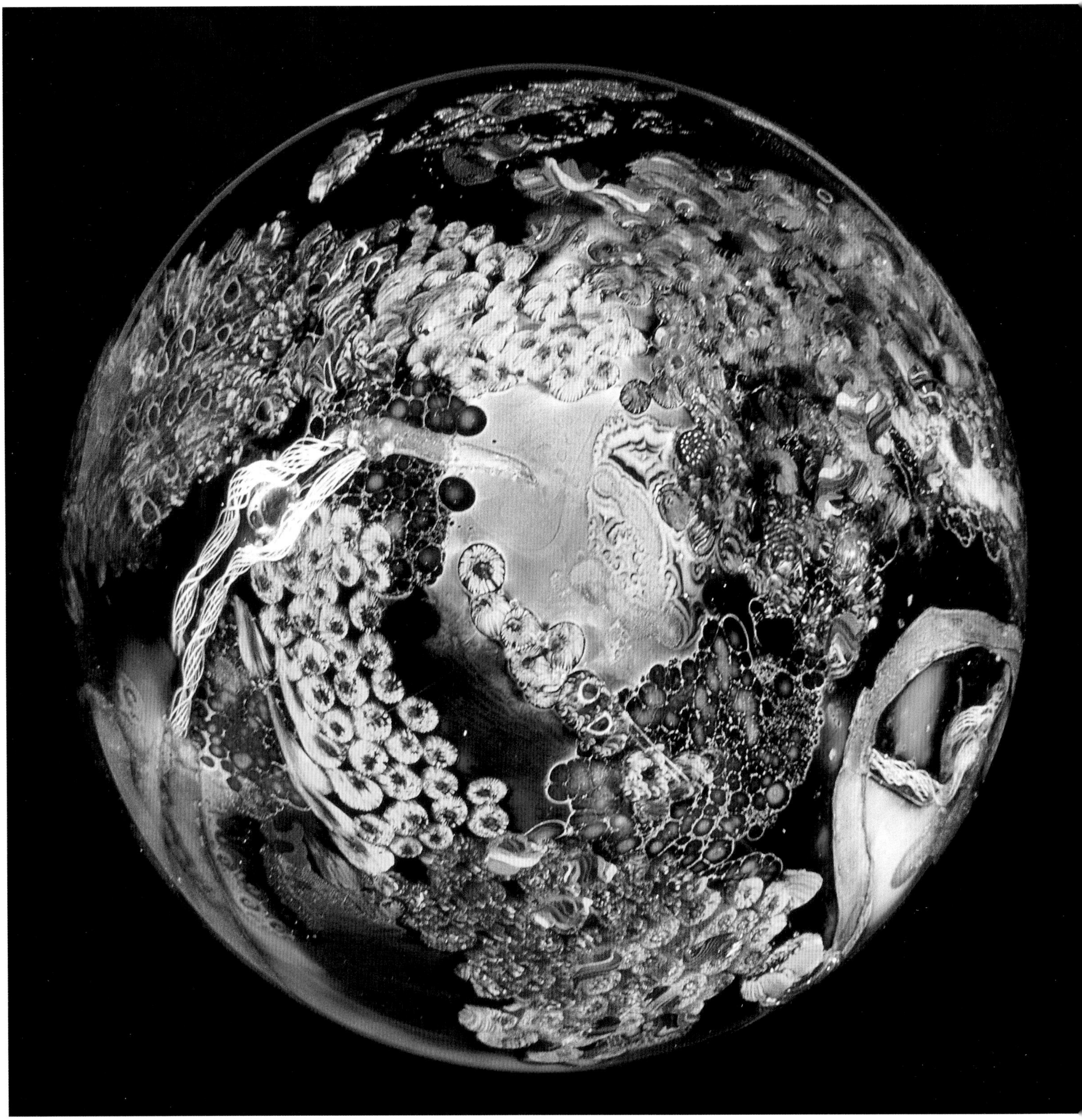

Figure 735. Abstract. MegaPlanet. Single gather. Multi-color millefiori canes, air trap, multi-color base. Josh Simpson. 10 in., ca. 1999. *Photo: Tommy Olof Elder. Courtesy of the artist.*

Opposite page:
Figure 736. Abstract. MegaPlanet. Single gather. Visionary Landscape. Multi-color millefiori canes, air trap, multi-color base. *(close-up)* Josh Simpson. 1990. *Photo: Tommy Olof Elder. Courtesy of the artist.*

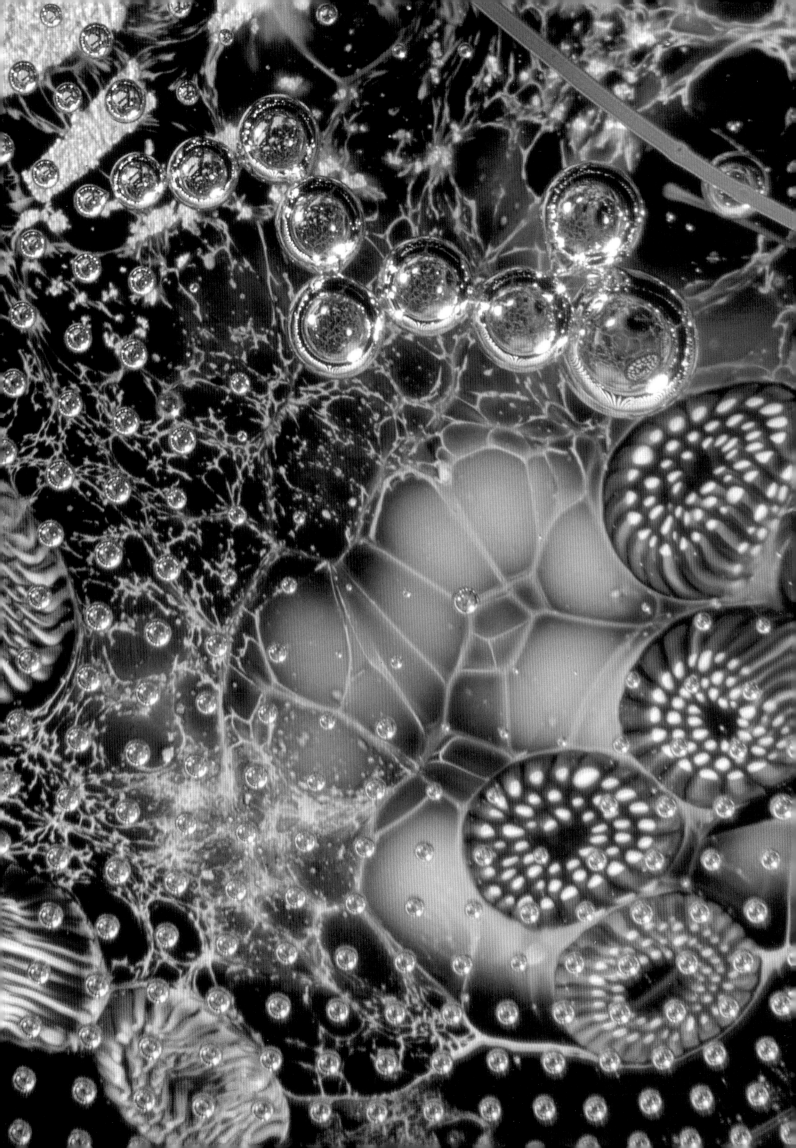

Figure 737. Abstract. MegaPlanet. Single gather. Visionary Landscape. Multi-color millefiori canes, multi-color base. *(close-up)* Josh Simpson. ca. 1998. *Photo: Tommy Olof Elder. Courtesy of the artist.*

Figure 738. Abstract. Inhabited Planet. Single gather. Multi-color millefiori canes, air trap, dichroic glass, multi-color base. Josh Simpson. 1-7/8 in., ca. 2004. *Courtesy of the author.*

Figure 739. Abstract. Rod- and cane-cut. Multi-color swirled, air trap, multi-color base. Douglas Sweet. 1-1/2 in., ca. app. 1990-1995. *Courtesy of the Marble Collectors Society of America.*

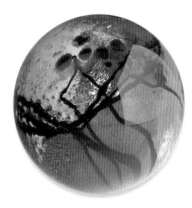

Figure 740. Abstract. Rod- and cane-cut. Multi-color, dichroic glass. Shanti Devi. 1-5/8 in., ca. app. 1983-1986. *Courtesy of the Marble Collectors Society of America.*

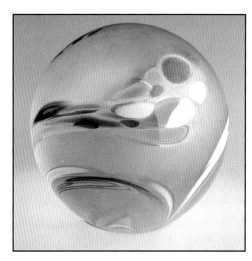

Figure 741. Abstract. Rod- and cane-cut. Multi-color swirled, air trap, iridescent base, Mt. St. Helen's ash glass. North Fork Survivors. 2 in., ca. 2003. *Courtesy of the author.*

Figure 742. Mask. Torchwork. Semi-transparent, iridescent gold mask, blue swirl base, clear glass. Unsigned. Unidentified. 1-1/2 in., ca. 2003. *Courtesy of the artist.*

Figure 743. Mask. Torchwork. Iridescent gold mask, honeycombs encircling, gray, blue base, reverse multi-color rake pull. Unsigned. Unidentified. 1-7/8 in., ca. 2003. *Courtesy of the artist.*

Figure 744. Abstract. Torchwork. Silver dichroic glass, black base. Gateson Recko. 2 in., ca. 2003. *Courtesy of the author.*

Figure 745. Abstract. Torchwork. Gold, green dichroic glass, brown aventurine glass band. Bruce Troeh. 1-1/2 in., ca. 2003. *Courtesy of the artist.*

Figure 746. Abstract. Rod- and cane-cut. Silver fume bands, black base. Phillip Nolley. 1-3/4 in., ca. 2003. *Courtesy of the artist.*

Figure 747. Abstract. Rod- and cane-cut. Multi-color dichroic glass, transparent cranberry red glass. Michael Hansen, Nina Paladino Caron. 1-7/8 in., ca. 2003. *Courtesy of the author.*

Figure 751. Cameo. Rod- and cane-cut. Yellow circle of people, moon, stars, sand blast, matte glass base. Harry and Wendy Besett. 1 1/2 in., ca. 2003. *Courtesy of the author.*

Figure 750. Cameo. Rod- and cane-cut. Blue animals, stars, sand blast, matte glass base. Harry and Wendy Besett. 1-1/2 in., ca. 2003. *Courtesy of the author.*

Figure 749. Outer Space. Rod- and cane-cut. Silver fume comet, yellow sun, silver fume stars, silver fume constellation, blue base. *(view two)* Steven Lundberg. 1-1/2 in., ca. 1999. *Courtesy of the artist.*

Figure 748. Outer Space. Rod- and cane-cut. White, crescent moon, yellow sun, silver fume stars, silver fume constellation, blue base. *(view one)* Steven Lundberg. 1-1/2 in., ca. 1999. *Courtesy of the artist.*

Figure 752. Eye. Torchwork. Blue eye, painted, reverse multi-color rake pull. Beth Tomasello. 1-3/8 in., ca. 2003. *Courtesy of the author.*

Figure 753. Eye. Torchwork. Blue, green, black, various colors, silver, gold dichroic glass. George Pavliscak. 1 in., ca. 2003. *Courtesy of the author.*

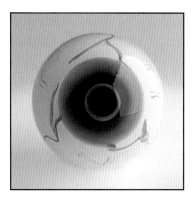

Figure 754. Eye. Torchwork. Green aventurine glass, black, red, white base. Marco Jerman. 1-1/4 in., ca. 1999. *Courtesy of the author.*

Figure 755. Orb. Single gather. H$_2$O Orb. Multi-color glass pieces, hollow glass, liquid filled. David and Deborah Rosenfeldt. 1-1/4 in., ca. 2001. *Courtesy of Robert Block.*

Figure 756. Rake Pull. Torchwork. Butterfly, flower, red, green torsade, blue, tan, rake pull. Christopher Rice. 2-1/8 in., ca. 2004. *Courtesy of author.*

Figure 757. Rake Pull. Torchwork. Yellow, red, black, rake pull. Bruce Troeh. 1-1/8 in., ca. 2003. *Courtesy of the author.*

Figure 758. Rake Pull. Torchwork. Red, yellow, blue, black, rake pull. Dinah Hulet. 1-1/2 in., ca. 2000. *Courtesy of the author.*

Figure 759. Rake Pull. Torchwork.
Lavender, light blue, blue, rake
pull. Cathy Richardson. 1-1/2 in.,
ca. 2003. *Courtesy of the author.*

Figure 760. Rake Pull. Torchwork. Yellow base, red base, orange base,
various color, multi-color rake pull. Greg Hoglin. 1-1/8 in., ca. 2003.
Courtesy of the author.

Figure 761. Rake Pull. Torchwork.
Multi-color, rake pull. *(view one)*
Dinah Hulet. 1-1/2 in., ca. 1996.
Courtesy of the author.

Figure 762. Rake Pull. Torchwork.
Multi-color, rake pull. *(view two)* Dinah
Hulet. 1-1/2 in., ca. 1996. *Courtesy of the
author.*

Figure 763. Rake Pull.
Torchwork. Gray, lavender,
purple, turquoise blue, black,
rake pull. Dinah Hulet. 1-1/8 in.,
ca. 1998. *Courtesy of the author.*

Figure 764. Rake Pull.
Torchwork. Multi-color, rake
pull. Dinah Hulet. 1-1/8 in.,
ca. 1998. *Courtesy of the
author.*

Figure 765. Rake Pull. Torchwork.
Blue, lavender, white, rake pull.
Dinah Hulet. 1-1/2 in., ca. 2003.
Courtesy of the author.

Figure 766. Rake Pull. Torchwork.
Blue, green, black, rake pull.
Dinah Hulet. 1-1/2 in., ca. 2003.
Courtesy of the author.

Figure 767. Rake Pull. Torchwork. Multi-color, rake pull. Dinah Hulet. 1 - 1-1/4 in., ca. 2002-2003. *Courtesy of the author.*

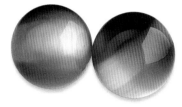

Figure 768. Fiber Optic. Machine-Ground. United States. Green, blue, red, green. 3/4 in., ca. app. 1990-2000. *Courtesy of Stanley Block.*

Figure 769. Fiber Optic. Machine-Ground. United States. Blue, brown, white, blue. 1-1/4 in., ca. app. 1990-2000. *Courtesy of the author.*

Figure 770. Abstract. Rod- and cane-cut. Multi-color dichroic glass, black base. Christopher Rice. 1-1/2 in., ca. 2003. *Courtesy of the author.*

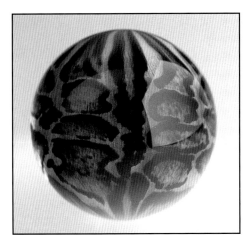

Figure 771. Animal Skin. Rod- and cane-cut. Clouded Leopard. Gray, graal technique, spine. *(view one)* Mark Matthews. 1-3/4 in., ca. 2001. *Courtesy of the author.*

Figure 772. Animal Skin. Rod- and cane-cut. Clouded Leopard. Gray, graal technique, underbelly. *(view two)* Mark Matthews. 1-3/4 in., ca. 2001. *Courtesy of the author.*

Figure 773. Gem. Torchwork. Gemstone heart, emerald green, clear glass. Paul and Dee Snell. 1 in., ca. 2002. *Courtesy of the artists.*

Figure 774. Gem. Torchwork. Gemstone circle, amethyst purple, front and back, white, purple swirl, air trap, clear glass. Paul and Dee Snell. 1 in., ca. 2002. *Courtesy of the artists.*

Figure 775. Gem. Torchwork. Gemstone heart, ruby red, red, yellow ribbon twist, dichroic glass. *(front)* Paul and Dee Snell. 1 in., ca. 2002. *Courtesy of the artists.*

Figure 776. Gem. Torchwork. Gemstone heart, ruby red, red, yellow ribbon twist, dichroic glass. *(back)* Paul and Dee Snell. 1 in., ca. 2002. *Courtesy of the artists.*

Figure 777. Rake Pull. Torchwork. Multi-color lightning design, fire opal, green aventurine glass, rake pull. Josh Sable. 2 in., ca. 2003. *Courtesy of the artist.*

Figure 778. Rake Pull. Torchwork. Honeycomb pattern, fumed glass, rake pull. Douglas Ferguson. 1-1/2 in., ca. 2003. *Courtesy of the author.*

Figure 779. Rake Pull. Torchwork. Turquoise blue, black, blue, air trap, rake pull. Douglas Ferguson. 1-1/8 in., ca. 2000. *Courtesy of the author.*

Figure 780. Rake Pull. Torchwork. Light green, green, air trap, rake pull. George O'Grady. 1-1/2 in., ca. 1999. *Courtesy of the author.*

Figure 781. Abstract. Torchwork. Multi-color dichroic glass, green glass. Unsigned. Unidentified. 1 in., ca. 1999. *Courtesy of the author.*

Figure 782. Rake Pull. Torchwork. Opal, light blue dichroic glass, clear glass, opal, fumed blue, green honeycomb, clear glass. George O'Grady. 1-1/8 - 1-1/4 in., ca. 1999. *Courtesy of the author.*

Figure 783. Vortex. Torchwork. Multi-color dichroic glass, dark blue base. Unsigned. Unidentified. 1-3/8 in., ca. 2000-2003. *Courtesy of the author.*

Figure 784. Vortex. Torchwork. Orange, dichroic glass, blue back, orange flume. Dustin Morell. 2-1/4 in., ca. 2004. *Courtesy of the author.*

Figure 785. Vortex. Torchwork. Orange, dichroic glass, blue back, orange flume. *(close-up interior)* Dustin Morell. 2-1/4 in., ca. 2004. *Courtesy of the author.*

Figure 786. Vortex. Torchwork.
Multi-color, silver aventurine
glass, multi-color back, rake pull.
Shell Neisler. 1-5/8 in., ca. 2003.
Courtesy of the author.

Figure 787. Vortex. Torchwork.
Turquoise blue, orange, outer
aquarium scene, millefiori fish.
2005 error signature cane. Mike
Edmundson. 1-3/8 in., ca. 2003.
Courtesy of the author.

Figure 788. Aquarium scene. Single
gather. Paperweight-style. Orange
murrini fish, barnacles, kelp, coral, green
aventurine glass back; blue murrini fish,
barnacles, kelp, coral, blue swirl back.
David Salazar. 1-1/8 - 1-3/4 in., ca. 2003-
2004. *Courtesy of the author.*

Figure 789. Tidal Pool. Single gather.
Paperweight-style. Orange starfish,
multi-color sea life, ground glass ocean
floor, blue, white swirl back. David
Salazar. 2-3/8 in., ca. 2004. *Courtesy of
the author.*

Figure 790. Undersea. Single gather. Paperweight-style. Brown/orange seahorse, kelp, undersea life, white back. David Salazar. 1-1/2 in., ca. 1987. *Courtesy of the author.*

Figure 791. Undersea. Single gather. Paperweight-style. Black seahorse, kelp, multi-color sea life, ground glass ocean floor, blue, white swirl back. *Experimental 1-X For Mark.* David Salazar. 2-1/4 in., ca. 2002. *Courtesy of the author.*

Figure 792. Heron. Single gather. Paperweight-style. White heron, green, brown cattails, blue lake, white moon, green swirl back. *Experimental 1-X.* David Salazar. 1-7/8 in., ca. 2003. *Courtesy of the author.*

Figure 793. Undersea. Torchwork. Paperweight-style. Murrini fish, undersea life, blue, brown base. Steven Hitt. 1-3/4 in., ca. 2003. *Courtesy of the author.*

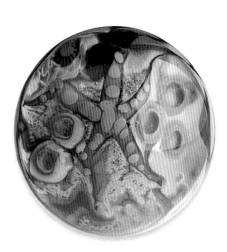

Figure 794. Undersea. Single gather. Paperweight-style. Orange starfish, undersea life, brown base. Cathy Richardson. 2 in., ca. 2004. *Courtesy of the author.*

Figure 795. Undersea. Single gather. Paperweight-style. Orange starfish, undersea life, blue base. Cathy Richardson. 1-3/4 in., ca. 2003. *Courtesy of the author.*

Figure 796. Aquarium. Single gather. Paperweight-style. Orange fish, underwater life, blue base. Cathy Richardson. 1-1/2 in., ca. 2003. *Courtesy of the author.*

Figure 797. Aquarium. Single gather. Paperweight-style. Red fish, underwater life, turquoise blue, blue base. Cathy Richardson. 1-1/2 in., ca. 2003. *Courtesy of the author.*

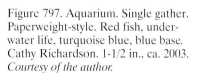

Figure 798. Moon and Stars. Single gather. Paperweight-style. Yellow crescent murrini moon, white murrini stars, blue, white swirl back. *Experimental 1-X For Mark*. David Salazar. 2-1/4 in., ca. 2004. *Courtesy of the author.*

Figure 799. Painted Face. Single gather. Enamel painted stylized face, black, white glass base. Douglas Sweet, Paulette Hall. 3-1/4 in., ca. 1997. *Courtesy of the author.*

Figure 800. Double Face. Single gather. Glass frit two-sided stylized face, red glass base. *Experimental Hair Test.* William Murray. 2 in., ca. 2001. *Courtesy of the author.*

Figure 801. Flora. Single gather. Paperweight-style. Red rose, green aventurine leaf. David Grant Maul. 1-3/4 in., ca. 1995. *Courtesy of Robert Block.*

Figure 802. Flora. Torchwork. Paperweight-style. Red rose, green aventurine leaves. Matthew Reinsch. 1 in., ca. 2003. *Courtesy of the artist.*

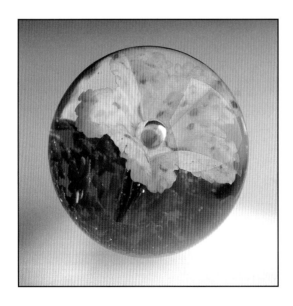

Figure 803. Flora. Single gather. Paperweight-style. Yellow/orange five-petal flora, air trap, green stem, red ground glass base. House of Glass. Joe Rice. 2 in., ca. app. 1990-1995. *Courtesy of the Marble Collectors Society of America.*

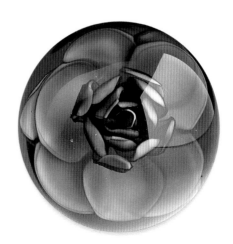

Figure 804. Flora. Single gather. Paperweight-style. Purple flora, green leaves, blue base. To M.B. Steven Lundberg. 2 in., ca. 1999. *Courtesy of the artist.*

Figure 805. Flora. Torchwork. Paperweight-style. Purple flora, orange flora, pink flora bud, green leaves, stems, multi-color ground glass base, reverse multi-color rake pull. *(front)* Beth Tomasello. 1-1/2 in., ca. 2003. *Courtesy of the author.*

Figure 806. Flora. Torchwork. Paperweight-style. Purple flora, orange flora, pink flora bud, green leaves, stems, multi-color ground glass base, reverse multi-color rake pull. *(back)* Beth Tomasello. 1-1/2 in., ca. 2003. *Courtesy of the author.*

Figure 807. Flora. Torchwork. Paperweight-style. Pink flora, green leaves, multi-color snake, multi-color ground glass base. Lewis Wilson. 1-1/8 in., ca. 2002. *Courtesy of the author.*

Figure 808. Flora. Torchwork. Paperweight-style. Orange/yellow flora, yellow/blue flora, white/yellow flora, green aventurine leaves. Matthew Reinsch. 1 - 1-1/4 in., ca. 2003. *Courtesy of the artist.*

Figure 809. Flora. Torchwork. Paperweight-style. Yellow, black, green flora; orange, yellow, green five-petal floras, black base; yellow, brown, gold aventurine glass flora. George Pavliscak. 7/8 - 1-1/8 in., ca. 2003. *Courtesy of the author.*

Figure 810. Flora. Torchwork. Red four-petal flora, dichroic vortex, outer rake pull, green aventurine glass, black base. Christopher Rice. 1-7/8 in., ca. 2003. *Courtesy of the author.*

Figure 811. Flora. Paperweight-style. Three five-petal purple, white petal flowers, green leaves. Harry and Kathleen Boyer. 1-1/4 in., ca. app. 1985-1989. *Courtesy of the author.*

Figure 812. Flora. Paperweight-style. Six-petal lavender, white, red flower, green leaves. David Grant Maul. 2 in., ca. app. 1983-1988. *Courtesy of the Marble Collectors Society of America.*

Figure 813. Flora. Torchwork. White, yellow, green. Cala Lily. Mike Edmundson. 7/8 in., ca. 2000. *Courtesy of the author.*

Figure 814. Flora. Torchwork. Multi-petal, three layer orange/yellow flora. George Pavliscak. 1-1/8 in., ca. 2003. *Courtesy of the author.*

Figure 815. Flora. Torchwork. Multi-petal, three layer lavender/purple flora. George Pavliscak. 1-1/8 in., ca. 2003. *Courtesy of the author.*

Figure 816. Flora. Torchwork. Seven-petal, orange/yellow, green leaves, blue base, clear glass. Mike Edmundson. 1-1/8 in., ca. 2004. *Courtesy of the author.*

Figure 817. Heart. Single gather. Red heart, blue banded swirl, white ghost core, clear glass. David Salazar, Jesse Siegel; red, white, blue heart red, white, blue latticinio bands, clear glass. David Salazar. 1-5/8 - 1-3/4 in., ca. 1998-2002. *Courtesy of the author.*

Figure 818. Patriotic. Torchwork. Blue outline stars, red, white, blue bands; red, white, blue twist, blue murrini stars; red, white blue ribbon core, outline blue stars surround circumference, clear glass. Bruce Troeh. 1-3/8 - 1-1/2 in., ca. 2003. *Courtesy of the artist.*

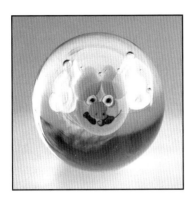

Figure 819. Angel Pig. Single gather. Pink pig, white angel wings, white ghost core, clear glass. *Experimental 1-X.* David Salazar. 1-1/4 in., ca. 2002. *Courtesy of the author.*

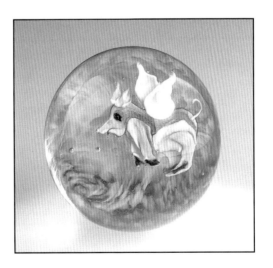

Figure 820. Flying Pig. Single gather. Pink pig, white angel wings, turquoise blue, white swirled base, clear glass. *Experimental 1-1.* David Salazar. 1-3/4 in., ca. 2002. *Courtesy of the author.*

Figure 821. Patterned. Rod- and cane-cut. Multi-color, Indian blanket design, feathered. Gibson Glass. Charles Gibson. 1-1/2 in., ca. 2002. *Courtesy of the author.*

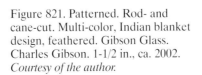

Figure 822. Patterned. Rod- and cane-cut. Brown/green, peacock feather design. Steve Davis. 1-1/2 in., ca. 2003. *Courtesy of the author.*

Figure 823. Patterned. Rod- and cane-cut. Blue/white, snakeskin design. Mike Davis. 1-1/2 in., ca. 2003. *Courtesy of the author.*

Figure 825. Torchwork. Multi-cane pattern. Various color and design cane and pulled glass, blue base. John Kobuki. 1-1/2 in. ca. 2003. *Courtesy of Robert Block.*

Figure 824. Patterned. Rod- and cane-cut. Purple, blue, white, snakeskin design. *To Mark.* Mark Davis. 1-7/8 in., ca. 2003. *Courtesy of the author.*

Figure 826. Abstract. Torchwork.
Brown, white, air trap, reverse twist.
Robert LaGrand. 1-3/8 in., ca. 2002.
Courtesy of the author.

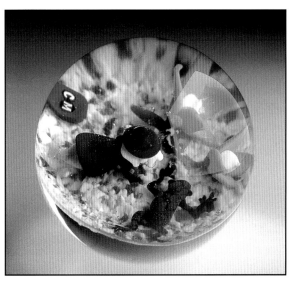

Figure 827. Gnome. Torchwork.
Paperweight-style. Gnome, frog,
flowers, multi-color granulated glass
ground, signature CM murrini cane.
Lewis and Jennifer Wilson. 2-1/4 in.,
ca. 2002. *Courtesy of the artists.*

Figure 828. Flora. Torchwork. Paperweight-style. Purple flora, one partially
opened, one full bloom, green leaves,
stem. *Limited edition 3/12. (view one)*
James Kontes. 1-1/2 in., ca. 2000. *Courtesy
of the author.*

Figure 829. Flora. Torchwork. Paperweight-style. Purple flora, one partially
opened, one full bloom, green leaves,
stem. *Limited edition 3/12. (view two)*
James Kontes. 1-1/2 in., ca. 2000.
Courtesy of the author.

Figure 830. Vortex. Blue, white, back, multi-color rake pull. Rajesh Kommineni. 1-3/8 in., ca. 2003. *Courtesy of the author.*

Figure 831. Rake Pull. Torchwork. Multi-color fumed torsades, green aventurine glass, red base. Rajesh Kommineni. 1-1/2 in., ca. 2004. *Courtesy of the author.*

Figure 832. Rake Pull. Torchwork. Multi-color fumed, black, multi-color dichroic glass core. Rajesh Kommineni. 1-1/2 in., ca. 2004. *Courtesy of the author.*

Figure 833. Rake Pull. Torchwork. Multi-color fumed torsade. Christopher Rice. 1-1/2 in., ca. 2003. *Courtesy of the author.*

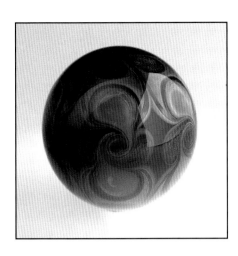

Figure 834. Rake Pull. Torchwork. Red, green, blue torsade, gold aventurine glass, green aventurine glass, tan, blue base. Christopher Rice. 1-1/2 in., ca. 2003. *Courtesy of the author.*

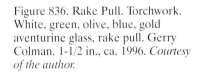

Figure 835. Rake Pull. Torchwork. Multi-color fumed torsade, fire opal, green aventurine glass, rake pull. Josh Sable. 2-1/4 in., ca. 2003. *Courtesy of the artist.*

Figure 836. Rake Pull. Torchwork. White, green, olive, blue, gold aventurine glass, rake pull. Gerry Colman. 1-1/2 in., ca. 1996. *Courtesy of the author.*

Figure 837. Rake Pull. Torchwork. Multi-color, green aventurine glass. Christopher Rice. 1-3/4 in., ca. 2003. *Courtesy of the author.*

Figure 838. Patterned. Rod- and cane-cut. White, purple, snakeskin pattern. Charles Gibson. 1-5/8 in., ca. 1999. *Courtesy of the author.*

Figure 839. Patterned. Rod- and cane-cut. Multi-color, snakeskin pattern. Charles Gibson. 1-3/4 in., ca. 1999. *Courtesy of the author.*

Figure 840. Rake Pull. Torchwork. Blue, red, green aventurine glass torsade, multi-color retticello, blue/green ribbon, rake pull. *(top)* Josh Sable. 1-3/4 in., ca. 2003. *Courtesy of the artist.*

Figure 841. Rake Pull. Torchwork. Blue, red, green aventurine glass torsade, multi-color retticello, blue/green ribbon, rake pull. *(bottom)* Josh Sable. 1-3/4 in., ca. 2003. *Courtesy of the artist.*

Figure 842. Rake Pull. Torchwork. Tan, green, rake pull. Multi-color dichroic, green, blue, rake pull; blue, red, rake pull. Shane Caswell, Frank Oddu. 1 in., ca. 2000-2002. *Courtesy of the author.*

Figure 843. Rake Pull. Torchwork. Multi-color, red, silver dichroic glass tunnel core, rake pull. Unsigned. Unidentified. 1-3/4 in., ca. 2003. *Courtesy of the artist.*

Figure 844. Rake Pull. Torchwork. Red, white, blue, bands, rake pull; red, green, white, rake pull; red, lavender, green aventurine glass, rake pull. Jerry Kelly. 1-1/4 - 1-5/8 in., ca. 2003. *Courtesy of the author.*

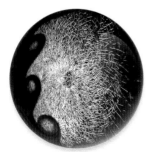

Figure 845. Rake Pull. Infinity. Torchwork. Multi-color dichroic, reverse multi-color rake pull. *(front)* Josh Sable. 1-1/4 in., ca. 2003. *Courtesy of the author.*

Figure 846. Rake Pull. Infinity. Torchwork. Multi-color dichroic, reverse multi-color rake pull. *(reverse)* Josh Sable. 1-1/4 in., ca. 2003. *Courtesy of the author.*

Figure 847. Rake Pull. Torchwork. Black, white rake pull. Unsigned. Unidentified. 1-1/2 in., ca. 2002. *Courtesy of the author.*

Figure 848. Rake Pull. Torchwork. Multi-color rake pull. *Experimental.* Drew Fritts. 1-7/8 in., ca. 2001. *Courtesy of the author.*

Figure 849. Rake Pull. Torchwork. Multi-color rake pull, butterfly series. *Limited edition 27/30.* Drew Fritts. 1-1/4 in., ca. 2000. *Courtesy of the Marble Collectors Society of America.*

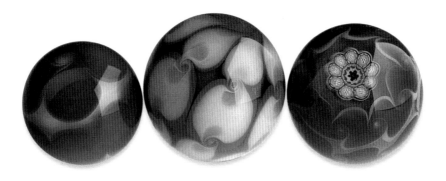

Figure 850. Rake Pull. Torchwork. Multi-color rake pull, murrini cane. Shane Caswell. 1-1/8 - 1-3/8 in., ca. 2002. *Courtesy of the author.*

Figure 851. Rake Pull. Torchwork. Red, white, blue, green aventurine glass, matching base, rake pull, indented lobes. Shane Caswell. Sphere: 1-3/4 in., Base: 1-1/2 in., ca. 2002. *Courtesy of the author.*

Figure 852. Rake Pull. Infinity. Torchwork. Dichroic center window, outer orange, blue, aventurine green, rake pull. Dustin Morell. 2 in., ca. 2003. *Courtesy of the author.*

Figure 853. Rake Pull. Torchwork. Multi-color rake pull, swirl, murrini cane, top, bottom poles. Rajesh Kommineni. 1-3/4 in., ca. 2004. *Courtesy of the author.*

Figure 854. Rake Pull. Torchwork.
Multi-color rake pull, swirl, murrini
canes, top, bottom poles, center.
Rajesh Kommineni. 2 in., ca. 2004.
Courtesy of the author.

Figure 856. Rake Pull. Torchwork.
Multi-color reticello, rake pull.
(back) Josh Sable. 2-1/8 in., ca. 2003.
Courtesy of the author.

Figure 857. Rake Pull.
Torchwork. Multi-color fumed
center, dichroic glass, purple,
reverse multi-color rake pull.
Ben Walsh. 2-1/4 in., ca. 2003.
Courtesy of the artist.

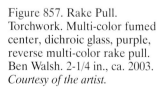

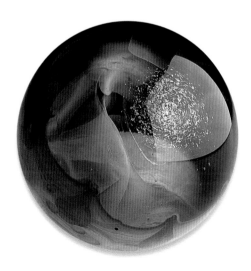

Figure 861. Rake Pull. Torchwork. Light green, green rake pull, black base, light blue, blue outer embellishment. Dinah Hulet. 1-1/8 in., ca. 1998. *Courtesy of the author.*

Figure 860. Rake Pull. Torchwork. Multi-color rake pull, yellow base, orange, black outer embellishment. Dinah Hulet. 1 in., ca. 1998. *Courtesy of the author.*

Figure 859. Rake Pull. Torchwork. Vortex rake pull, multi-color outer embellishment. Daniel Benway. 2-1/8 in., ca. 1999. *Courtesy of the author.*

Figure 858. Vortex. Torchwork. Multi-color dichroic center, reverse blue, green rake pull. Shell Neisler. 2-3/8 in., ca. 2003. *Courtesy of the author.*

Figure 862. Rake Pull. Torchwork. Multi-color rake pull, orange, blue, green, blue outer embellishment. *(side view)* Dinah Hulet. 1-1/2 in., ca. 1998. *Courtesy of the author.*

Figure 863. Rake Pull. Torchwork. Multi-color rake pull, orange, blue, green, blue outer embellishment. *(top view)* Dinah Hulet. 1-1/2 in., ca. 1998. *Courtesy of the author.*

Figure 864. Rake Pull. Torchwork. Multi-color rake pull, multi-color outer embellishment. Dinah Hulet. 1-1/8 in., ca. app. 1996-1998. *Courtesy of the author.*

Figure 865. Abstract. Rod- and cane-cut. Multi-color cane pieces, twist. Steve Davis. 2-1/4 in., ca. 2003. *Courtesy of the artist.*

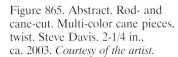

Figure 866. Rake Pull. Torchwork. Multi-color rake pull, black base. Christopher Rice. 2 in., ca. 2003. *Courtesy of the author.*

Figure 867. Dichroic. Torchwork. Multi-color dichroic glass overlay, black base, reverse decoration. Christopher Rice. 1-3/4 in., ca. 2003. *Courtesy of the author.*

Figure 868. Rake Pull. Torchwork. Bob Marley. Dichroic bust, orange rake pull, reverse lion murrini cane, rake pull, circumference ribbon. *(front)* Jerry Kelly. 2-3/4 in., ca. 2004. *Courtesy of the author.*

Figure 869. Rake Pull. Torchwork. Bob Marley. Dichroic bust, orange rake pull, reverse lion murrini cane, rake pull, circumference ribbon. *(back)* Jerry Kelly. 2-3/4 in., ca. 2004. *Courtesy of the author.*

Figure 870. Cameo. Single gather. Clear glass stars, sandblasted matte overlay, multi-color murrini/millefiori base. Douglas Sweet. 2 in., ca. 2002. *Courtesy of the author.*

Figure 872. Eisenglas. Single gather. Stillness of the Dance. Eisenglas (mica) crescent moon, painted enamel figures, black, clear glass. *Limited edition 3/4.* Wendy Besett. 2-1/2 in., ca. 2003. *Courtesy of the artist.*

Figure 871. Cameo. Single gather. Clear glass circles, sandblasted matte overlay, multi-color murrini/millefiori base. Douglas Sweet. 2 in., ca. 2002. *Courtesy of the author.*

Figure 873. Painted. Single gather. Stillness of the Dance. Black painted enamel figures, air trap center. Wendy Besett. 2-1/8 in., ca. 2003. *Courtesy of the artist.*

Figure 874. Air Trap. Single gather. Super Jetson. Pink hour glass air trap, encircled air trap ring. Mark Matthews. 2 in., ca. 2000. *Courtesy of the author.*

Figure 875. Banded Swirl. Rod-and cane-cut. Purple, white bands, orange bands. Artists error. Signed both poles. Top pole: DPSC 10/97; bottom pole: DPSC 11/97 JS. David Salazar, Jesse Siegel. 1-5/8 in., ca. 1997. *Courtesy of the author.*

Figure 876. Geometric. Rod- and cane-cut. Windmill Triangle. Black, white geometric design, graal technique. Mark Matthews. 2-3/4 in., ca. 2002. *Courtesy of the author.*

Figure 877. Abstract. Rod- and cane-cut. Multi-color band, blue base, air trap bubbles. Michael Hansen, Nina Paladino Caron. 2-3/8 in., ca. 1992. *Courtesy of the Marble Collectors Society of America.*

Figure 878. Multi-layer. Torchwork. Millefiori cane base, overlay multi-color butterflies on surface. Christopher Rice. 1-5/8 in., ca. 2005. *Courtesy of the author.*

Figure 879. Painted. Single gather. Sweeny Todd. Double sphere, inside multi-color, enamel paint, clear glass; outside multi-color, enamel paint, clear glass. Harry Besett, Ken Leslie. 3-1/4 in., ca. 2003. *Courtesy of the artists.*

Figure 880. Massager. Rod- and cane-cut. Marbelizer. Hand held neck, shoulder massager. Green, white ribbon, black; green, white nailsea twisted handle. Virginia Wilson, Anthony Toccalino. L. 7 in., D. 2-5/8 in., ca. 2003. *Courtesy of the artist.*

Figure 881. Earth. Precious mineral continents, including turquoise, malachite, rodachrosite and others, lapis lazuli oceans. Separated by gold strand latitude, longitude lines. China. 1 in., ca. app. 1995-2000. *Courtesy of the author.*

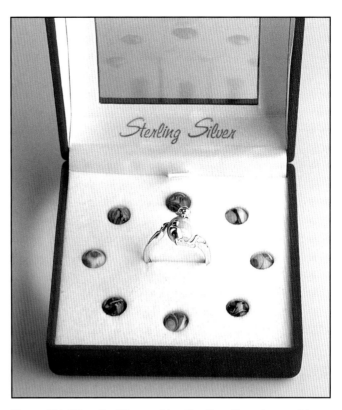

Figure 884. Ring. PeeWee marbles. Sterling silver ring, multi-color, interchangeable peewee marbles. Bobbie Seese. W. 3/4 in., ca. 2003. *Courtesy of the artist.*

Figure 882. Mini Marbles. Bottles. Multi-color, clear glass bottle, cork stopper. Daniel Ambrose. 1-1/2 in., ca. 2002. *Courtesy of the author.*

Figure 885. Gumball Machine. PeeWee marbles. Red, clear plastic gumball machine keychain, multi-color marbles. Bobbie Seese. L. 2-1/2 in., ca. 2003. *Courtesy of the artist.*

Figure 883. Ring. Sterling silver ring for use with interchangeable marbles. See figure 594. Bruce Troeh. W. 3/4 in., ca. 2003. *Courtesy of the artist.*

Figure 886. Marble Rods. Multi-color ribbon, latticinio marble rod. Cuneo Furnace. Steven Maslach. L. 3-1/2 in., ca. app. 1995-2000. *Courtesy of the artist.*

Figure 887. Sculptural Marblies. Painted marbles, clay. Armadillo. Sidney and Debby Oliveira. 5/8 - 1 in., ca. 2004. *Courtesy of the artist.*

Figure 888. Sculptural Marblies. Painted marbles, clay. Chicken. Sidney and Debby Oliveira. 5/8 - 1 in., ca. 2004. *Courtesy of the artist.*

Figure 889. Sculptural Marblies. Painted marbles, clay. Elvis. Sidney and Debby Oliveira. H. 1-5/8 in 2004. *Courtesy of the artist.*

Figure 890. Whitman Botanical Orb. Flamework. Multi-flora, leaves, moss, berries, honeycomb, honeybees, insects; reverse side bouquet, pate de vere mask. *(side one)* Paul J. Stankard. 5-3/8 in., ca. 2004. *Courtesy of private collection.*

Figure 891. Whitman Botanical Orb. Flamework. Multi-flora, leaves, moss, berries, honeycomb, honeybees, insects; reverse side bouquet, pate de vere mask. *(side two)* Paul J. Stankard. 5-3/8 in., ca. 2004. *Courtesy of private collection.*

Figure 892. Apple Blossom Orb. Flamework. Flora, branches, honeybees. Paul J. Stankard. 5-3/8 in., ca. 2004.
Courtesy of private collection.

Figure 893. Floral Botanical Orb. Flamework. Multi-flora, leaves, moss, berries, honeybees, reverse side bouquet, female root figure. *(side one)* Paul J. Stankard. 5-3/8 in., ca. 2004. *Courtesy of private collection.*

Figure 894. Floral Botanical Orb. Flamework. Multi-flora, leaves, moss, berries, honeybees, reverse side bouquet, female root figure. *(side two)* Paul J. Stankard. 5-3/8 in., ca. 2004. *Courtesy of private collection.*

Figure 895. Lilac Bouquet with Honeycomb Swarm Orb. Flamework. Multi-flora, leaves, moss, berries, honeybees. *Commission (side one)* Paul J. Stankard. 5-5/8 in., ca. 2004. *Courtesy of private collection.*

Figure 896. Lilac Bouquet with Honeycomb Swarm Orb. Flamework. Multi-flora, leaves, moss, berries, honeybees. *Commission (side two)* Paul J. Stankard. 5-5/8 in., ca. 2004. *Courtesy of private collection.*

Figure 897. Lilac Bouquet with Honeycomb Swarm Orb. Flamework. Multi-flora, leaves, moss, berries, honeybees; with assorted Orbs. *Commission* Paul J. Stankard. 5-5/8 in., ca. 2004. *Courtesy of private collection.*

Conclusion

Nearly forty years ago the contemporary Studio Glass Movement began in earnest with the breakthrough of Harvey Littleton and Dominic Labino's glass workshops in the northern Midwest United States. At that time it was unthinkable that glass marbles would be a natural, if not later practical outcome of this seismic movement in art history.

Decades and endless experimentation, expense, technical proficiency, and innate talent has allowed the glass artists to do all of the following: Create their own designs, craft their own tools, build their own furnaces and annealing ovens, and be directly involved in the evolutionary process of glass making from beginning to completion—even batching their own glass if desired.

In the introduction to this book I posed the following research questions:

> *Is there a definitive difference in the design, type, and style of contemporary handmade marbles, spheres, and orbs? One that is fundamentally different from the children's marbles of earlier generations? If so, are these works ones that can be considered true glass art, or merely extensions of what has previously been crafted?*

Through the research, images, and text of this book I have concluded that the majority of all marbles, spheres, and orbs have their foundation in the works of earlier times. Additionally, there are those that on occasion directly and more often than not indirectly mimic the styles and designs of others. Though the color palette of today's artist/craftsman is significantly greater, there are many instances when insufficient differences occur in these works. As such, they fail to qualify as "true contemporaries."

However, with time and the increased technical and design evolutions occurring in the studio art field there is an ample body of work by many artists/craftsmen that have no relationship to the work of earlier generations. These works clearly veer from the traditional spherical marble form. Works of this nature take on characteristics more appropriate to comparisons with paperweights, both antique and contemporary and other forms of sculptural glass art. This is not to say that other individuals or studios from those mentioned earlier solely craft these works. In fact, a number of the most well-known as well as youngest contemporary marble, sphere, and orb artists craft paperweights, beads, and other glass art of the finest caliber. What can be seen in the pieces worked, whether by furnace or torch or kiln are numerous overlaps in the Contemporary Marble Movement with other forms of arts and crafts. So much so that a blurring occurs in what would be the traditional boundaries found in other fine arts.

Much like the professionalism of the poet or painter, sculptor or potter, the studio glass artist has achieved a level of success and acceptance in the fine art world that could not have occurred without the hands-on capability achieved by the groundbreaking workshops of the early 1960s.

Throughout much of the text there has been a necessary interrelation in the writing that has focused on the historical summer of 1974 when the founders or "patriarchs" of the Contemporary Marble Movement, Richard Marquis and Ro Purser first put glass rods to fire to create simple 1" swirl marbles from dual glory holes.

The Contemporary Marble Movement continues to owe a debt of gratitude to Harvey Littleton and Dominic Labino, Marquis and Purser, and shortly thereafter to Jody Fine, Jack Wax and Steven Maslach and Josh Simpson. These men had a vision seen through the clear and colors of glass to encourage, experiment, excite and create the marbles referred to as first-generation contemporaries. It wasn't long after that other young men with names like Dane, Giberson, Lonsway, Salazar, St. Clair, Wald, and others began to proliferate a very young and immature market in the beauty of contemporary handmade marbles, spheres and orbs.

With the passing of time, the seriousness with which the public began to look at these spherical objects with more than curiosity began to take hold. And with the twenty-first century a quantum leap has occurred in the artistic beauty, technical craftsmanship, and at times sheer will that has allowed the artists, craftsmen, and studios, both men and women of the Contemporary Marble Movement to break boundaries, push the envelope, and continue to finesse, manipulate, and coax glass in such a way that many of the works being crafted today truly are fine art forms.

Through the representation of well-known galleries across the United States, Europe, and parts of Asia, to the placement of works in major museums' permanent collections, the Contemporary Marble Movement has earned and achieved a rightful place alongside other accepted worldwide glass movements.

So be dazzled.
You'll Be Amazed At What You See!™

In Their Own Words

Artists/Craftsmen of the Contemporary Marble Movement

The following words are observations on the crafting experience by a few artists and craftsmen of the new generation, as well as some of the Contemporary Marble Movement's long-time members. Each was asked to share their thoughts on a unique and very personal approach to a wonderful art form.

Brendan Blake

The relationship between our shared world and our own unique inner world has always fascinated me. Through my artwork I seek to illustrate and capture that dynamic relationship. My creative goal is to maintain a focused effort and continued appreciation, to be able to crystallize my vision into a holistic body of art.

Rudy Calin

I have always been artistic, having spent nearly twenty-five years as a commercial photographer. I collect antique marbles and enjoy the hobby very much. In 1998 I bought some equipment and just started creating without any formal training. I started emulating the early handmade and machine-made marbles I have come to know. I enjoy using bright, vibrant colors as those are the most sought after antique marbles.

Richard Clark

I love what I'm doing! Besides spending time at shows where you meet some terrific people, I have an opportunity to experiment and play with glass and colors. My first marbles were pretty crude, but I practiced, listened to others, and absorbed as much information as I could. Today, I enjoy marble making even more. I look forward to spending time in front of my torch every chance I get, and plan to continue refining my skills and making even better and better marbles as time goes by.

Steven Davis and Davis Handmade Marbles

Following in our Dad, Jim Davis', footsteps, my brothers and I continue crafting contemporary handmade cane-cut marbles. The passion for creating these magic balls of glass grows daily as we entangle, swirl, twist, manipulate, and sometimes control the ingredients that make up the heart of the marble. Each cut of glass tells a unique and interesting story of how and why it came about and should be "round forever."

Mike Edmundson

After years of drawing, painting, and making the occasional photograph, my long-time interest in antique marbles and newer interest in lampworking led to my first marble. My first successful piece came after a year of making broken, cracked, and ugly beads. In developing my abilities as a lamp work artist, I studied both videos and demonstrations by other lamp workers. The rest of my skill and knowledge came through experience at the torch and being inspired by ideas I bring to life in glass.

Chris and Lissa Juedemann

Marbles are an ideal showcase for the miniature portraits and scenes in glass we create using the ancient murrine technique. The sphere adds depth and dimensionality to the work. The marble becomes the playground for the image. It creates a little world that draws the viewer into it, to interact with the murrine.

Ray Laubs

I have been crafting sulphides for five years and the angel was one of the first ones I have done. Having worked with numerous sulphide figures and glass I try to mimic the antique appearance yet still be able to identify it as a contemporary marble without much difficulty.

Nadine Macdonald

I was raised in a family of artists and musicians who shared their love of antique collecting with my sister and I. Marbles took over my collecting bug well into adulthood. I began to pursue making my own ceramic marbles in the mid-1990s, inspired by the ones I never found or could afford. Since childhood I have been fascinated by small treasures I could hold in the palm of my hand, that something so small could command my attention and bring me such pleasure. I love being able to keep that joy alive.

Phillip Nolley

My work does not evolve through meticulous planning, but rather by intuitive, free spirited play. I am striving to combine color, figure, and form by improvising on the simplest possible outline. This practice of free play lends itself to many surprises and disappointments that help maintain excitement within the structured framework needed to attain craftsmanship and technical excellence.

George Pavliscak

Marbles are very compelling, the ultimate in detail and simplicity. A mere sphere is a basic object, and yet infinite in possibilities. When I look at a marble or other piece of glass I tend to see it in terms of its "hard" and "soft" qualities. When I say hard and soft I am speaking of the design elements and the characteristics of the materials used, not the chemical makeup or the physical hardness. The swirl of one color through another may follow a random trail but look crisp and defined, and thus hard. A straight line could become twisted, or the makeup of the line itself could become soft. Needless to say, I am now an avid collector as well as craftsman.

Gateson Recko

After earning a BA in architecture at Columbia University I discovered furnace formed glass and immersed myself within the studio glass movement. Over time I made the transition to flame working and a decade later focused on contemporary glass spheres. I have taken on the challenge of mastering the illusion of unimaginable space trapped within the interior of the glass sphere. The balance between complex designs within a simple form creates new perspectives into the way people look at glass marbles.

Christopher Rice

I have been working on the torch for five years now and it has been quite a journey into the world of glass. My main focus is now on marbles, goblets, candy dishes, and other more intricate glass sculptures. As I have become more confident in my own abilities and work I have taught a number of classes on marble making, and glass in general. It is enjoyable sharing my knowledge with others in the field. I have also spent time writing for *Glass Line* magazine. These have been primarily technical articles, and the proper use of colors in glass crafting.

Eddie Seese

Since childhood I have occupied myself with drawing and creating things with my hands, so working with glass and hand blowing crystal stemware really didn't seem like work at all when I first started. I've worked at Fenton Art Glass and was exposed to an array of tools, molds, colors, etc. This really gave me a good foundation for experimenting and continuing to perfect my marble making techniques. I am particularly interested in the old Italian cane techniques. After I started attending marble shows and realized that others had an interest and appreciation for glass I was off and running. With my own studio, my wife, daughter, and marbles, I look forward to each day.

Bobbie Seese

After attending marble shows with my husband, Eddie, watching him work, and the enjoyment he got out of the craft, I became interested in marble making too. Since I was sure I could teach myself on the torch I learned the art of flameworking. It has been both fun and exciting to craft marbles and incorporate them into jewelry for both women and men. I also enjoy making many of the settings for these marbles, with the rings' marbles being interchangeable. People really enjoy my gumball marble machine which actually dispenses a real pee wee marble. I am beginning to work at the furnace now and enjoy making marbles of all types and sizes. It is a wonderful way to express my creativity.

Virginia Wilson Toccalino and Anthony Toccalino

I began working with glass in 1982, says Virginia, and have been awarded grants and scholarships to study and practice glass working at a number of internationally recognized institutions. My background in textiles has subliminally molded my work, which is known for its sense of style and fluidity. Tony was introduced to glass around the same time and he became very interested in the glass as art medium. We have both greatly benefited by working closely together, where we specialize in both simple and complex cane work. Both linear and threadlike patterns, and that of the Venetian style filigrana cane work dance and sway on complex shimmering pieces that captivate viewer's imagination and stimulate their curiosity.

Bruce Troeh

Simply put my marbles are all about color and the feelings it invokes. I started splashing as much color into my marbles as I could. I never dreamed of making marbles that could be used in the jewelry market in interchangeable pieces. This took me to the extremes of design and color. The art of personal adornment matches color to accompany fashion trends, and needs a jewelers precision to bring marbles to those otherwise unexposed to the art. I have found satisfaction being able to fine tune the color and designs of my handmade marbles within a couple thousandths of an inch, truly "within a hairs breadth." Then I can really let go when it comes to the bigger pieces!

Ben Walsh

In 1999, an acquaintance of mine told me in passing, "Ben, I want to teach you how to lampwork." I knew nothing about it at the time, but since that evening, glassblowing has been a passion and addiction. In addition to lampworking, I am learning off-hand glassblowing and marvel at the fact that I still have so much to learn about the techniques and beauty glass holds.

Tim Waugh

I began my long journey with glass in 1978 while working the midnight shift at the Louie Glass Factory in Weston, West Virginia. While I got to see some old masters at work and loved glassmaking, I did not really like the redundancy of the German production system of making the same piece "over and over" again. In 1998 I started to represent other marble artists' works through on-line auctions and went ahead and made my first piece in early 2002. I have continued refining my lampworking skills ever since. While I make less than 100 marbles a year, each one is designed and crafted to show off my passion for art.

Aaron West

The beauty of the old German handmade toy marbles with their infinite designs and colors is what inspired me to give torchworking a try. Now it is a passion of mine, making marbles that are always one of a kind.

Glossary of Terms

Acetylene torch: A colorless, flammable gas torch used by craftsmen to produce glasswork in the torchwork method.

Agate: A banded, often times multi-colored variety of Chalcedony, occurring in unique patterns. Agate most often forms in rounded nodules that when opened show the internal pattern hidden in the stone.

Aggie: A marble player or collector's term for any type or style of marble; originally from the word Agate.

Akro Agate Company: Decorative glass company founded in 1910 in Akron, Ohio, moved to West Virginia in 1914 until going bankrupt in 1954. Producer of single stream and variegated stream machine-made marbles.

Allies: A marble player or collector's term for a shooter marble.

Alkali: Essential ingredient in making glass, added to the batch in the form of potash to reduce the temperature at which the silica in the form of sand and flint will fuse.

Annealing: The process of subjecting glass to a slow process of heating and cooling to reduce brittleness once cold.

Antique: United States customs laws describe as an item, usually a work of art, furniture, or decorative object made at least one hundred years ago.

Antique handmade marble: Round sphere manufactured prior to 1920 as child's plaything for use in games.

Art nouveau: A design style of decoration of the late nineteenth, early twentieth century, well-known for the depiction of leaves and flowers in flowing lines.

Artist: Individual who creates imaginative works of aesthetic value, usually in the fine arts, showing great creativity and skill.

Artist mark: Form of identification on individual artwork. Can take the form of signature, stamp or other identifying mark.

Aventurine: One of several varieties of the natural mineral quartz or feldspar, including small flakes of mica, hematite or other materials. Also, an opaque or semi-translucent form of glass flecked with small metallic particles, often of chromium oxide.

Banded: Stripes of contrasting color curving from pole to pole. Bands can be on, in or near the surface.

Batch: Mixture of raw materials, generally alkali, lime, potash, and silica, which are melted and fused together to make glass.

Batch room: Area in a glass manufacturing plant where glass colors and recipes are weighed and mixed.

Blocking: The forming of a gather of glass into a spherical form by twisting in a semi-circular concave block of wood, metal or graphite mold.

Blown: Swollen or inflated or, in the case of blown glass, formed by blowing.

Blowpipe: A long narrow pipe with a mouthpiece at one end and a thin ring at the other end that helps retain the gather of molten glass.

Body: The basic part of a marble, upon or into which the design glass is placed. The basic framework or non-design portion of the marble.

Borosilicate glass: A strong heat-resistant glass that contains a minimum of five percent boric oxide.

Brilliant Cut Glass: Fine cut glass with an extremely high glistening finish. Much like a lapidary cutting fine gemstones, this glass will exhibit cuts and facets that produce a "brilliant" appearance.

Brilliant Period, American: Time period from approximately 1880-1915 when numerous American glass companies produced the finest brilliant cut pieces.

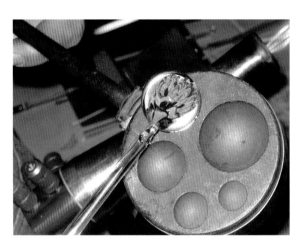

Figure 898. Clowns. Torchwork. Three clown faces surround sphere, various colors, yellow base. Greg Hoglin. 1-1/4 in., ca. 2004. *Courtesy of the author.*

Cage: A type of marble with well-separated veins at the middle tending toward the outside, forming a cage-like network.

Cane: Slender, sometimes patterned rod formed by fusing together groups of colored rods, which, while still molten, are pulled out to reduce their diameter and produce an internal design.

Cane-cut: Glass cut from the host cane.

Carnival glass: Iridescent glassware manufactured in the United States from approximately 1910 to 1930. Most often pressed patterns of gold, orange, and purple iridescence.

Cat's-eye: Machine-made marble type introduced into the United States in the early 1950s from Japan mimicking a cat's eye.

Chair: Bench with arms that support the punty of the gatherer. One hand rolls the shaft while the other shapes the glass by blocking.

Champion Agate Company: Machine-made marble production company that began operations in West Virginia in 1938.

Charge: The process of loading the furnace or melting pot with a batch of glass.

Christensen Agate Company: Single-stream machine-made marble company founded in 1925 in Ohio.

Clambroth: A type of handmade marble. The body is one color with evenly spaced, narrow color bands running from top to bottom pole in the surface glass. These marbles may have sequences of two or more colored glass bands. Originally comes from the milky white base glass color.

Collectible: One of a group of objects prized by fanciers.

Collector: One who collects for the purpose of study, enjoyment or investment.

Commercial: Sphere manufactured for commercial or industrial use.

Conchoidal: Have, relating to, or being a surface characterized by smooth shell-like convexities and concavities.

Condition: To give a grade of condition to.

Craftsman: Individual who practices a craft with great skill.

Crystal: A high quality clear colorless glass.

Cullet: Fragments of raw or broken glass melted down with new ingredients of batch to act as a flux to reduce the time required to produce glass.

Decorative glass house: One that produces decorative or ornamental glass objects in large quantities.

Delft: China manufactured in the Netherlands and glass developed by the Mount Washington Glass Works Company to imitate hand-painted china. Usually white base with blue painted and glazed scenery. Most often windmills, canals, boats.

Dichroic glass: That which reveals different colors at different concentrations having a distinctly different color in reflected or transmitted light. Having been made with a thin layer of metal.

Ding: A small dent or nick.

Divided core: Type of handmade swirl marble having a core of two or more varicolored ribbons from pole to pole. Transparent glass at the marble's center is visible.

End-of-Day: A type of handmade marble or style of glass usually made from left over glass.

English swirl: Vibrant, brightly colored marbles wherein the origin is close to the surface. Refers to both swirls and end-of-day marbles wherein red, orange, yellow, and green are predominate.

Experimental: Relating to or based on experiment.

Facet: A flat often times polished cut on the exterior surface, as in agate marbles.

Feathering: Decorative style first attributed to ancient Egyptians. Achieved through zigzag patterns of trailing glass of one or more colors. May be done by hand or mold.

Filigrana: Italian for "threaded," "grained." Type of glass originally made in Murano, Italy, in the second quarter of the sixteenth century. All styles of decoration in which threads of glass are embedded in clear glass to form a fine network pattern.

Fire polish: The polish resulting from subjecting preheated glass to direct flame or radiant heat.

Flamework: Term often used to refer to the technique of torchwork with glass.

Flux: Alkaline substance and essential ingredient in the batch, aiding the fusion of the silica, added as potash or soda.

Fracture: The act or condition of having been broken, cracked or ruptured.

Frit: Term referring to some of the ingredients of glass that are pre-heated until they are red-hot but not fused; these are then cooled and ground into a fine powder and added to the other ingredients of the batch.

Fulbright scholar: A student or educator studying under an exchange program established by William J. Fulbright, an American politician who proposed the Fulbright Act in 1946.

Fuming: The process of vaporizing precious metal and transmitting the metal vapor to the glass surface. Usually using gold or silver.

Functional glass house: One that produces glass objects for everyday use in mass quantities.

Furnace: Any of various ovens used for melting glass batch.

Gaffer: Head glassmaker, sometimes called a master glasser or blower, who does the most skillful work.

Gather: Blob of molten glass attached to the end of a pontil or blowpipe before an object is formed.

German swirl: Handmade glass marble made in Germany from the mid-1800s to the early 1900s.

Glass: Any of a large class of material of homogenous materials that are typically made by silicates fusing with boric oxide, aluminum oxide, or phosphorous-pent oxide. That which has a random, liquid-like, non-crystalline molecular structure and is either transparent or translucent.

Glass art: Highly executed and designed works, may be both for utilitarian and/or decorative purposes.

Glassman: Term associated with an employee of a glass house or glass factory.

Glass rod: Individual length of transparent or colored glass. Used individually in the torchwork method or combined to produce a glass cane.

Glaze: Liquid mixture applied to the outside of a clay object which, when heated or fired, results in a high glass-like finish.

Glory hole: An opening into the furnace or kiln. Used for reheating the gather of glass when making a piece on a punty.

Gob: A mass of molten glass.

Goldstone: Man-made mineral of glass aventurine with gold-colored inclusions.

Graal glass: Trade name for colored mosaic-like glass developed by Orrefors in Sweden in 1916.

Handmade: Made or prepared by hand without the use of machines.

Helix: A spiral form or structure.

Indian swirl: Handmade marble of dark base glass with colorful bands applied to the surface. Base glass may be transparent, semi-opaque or opaque. Usually does not have a casing layer of glass.

Iridescent: Producing a display of lustrous and brilliant rainbow-like colors.

Joseph's Coat: An end-of-day or swirl-type marble having colorful bands all around. Usually found with one to four dark blue to black bands mixed in. Name is an allusion to the robe of many colors belonging to Joseph of the Old Testament.

Kiln: Any of various ovens for hardening, burning, or drying substances. A brick- lined oven used to bake or fire ceramics.

Lampworking: The process of sculpting glass by twirling thin rods of glass over an oil lamp. Historical term often associated with the technique of torchwork with glass.

Lapidary: One who cuts, polishes or engraves.

Latticinio: Filigree glass of Venetian invention. Appears to have spiraling, crossing or interlacing fine opaque threads in crystal base. A type of hand-made swirl marble with filigree core.

Lehr: The heated metal annealing holder at the end of the production process.

Limited edition: A group identified and limited to a specified quantity of numbered pieces. Not to be reproduced at a later time.

Lobed: One of a type of marble core. Occurs in solid core swirls and end-of-day marbles.

Lutz: Reference to Nicholas Lutz, noted glassmaker of the Sandwich Glass Works. Term used by many marble collectors for aventurine glass marbles.

Machine-made marble: Those marbles commercially produced by machine.

Marble: Small hard balls, usually of glass, used in children's games. Any of various games played with marbles.

Marble King, Inc.: Machine-made marble company begun in 1949 by Berry Pink and Sellers Peltier in West Virginia. Pink marbles sold since the 1920s under the trade name "Berry Pink, Inc."

Marble shear: The tool used to hold, form, and cut a handmade marble as it is being made from the heated cane. Similar to tongs or sheep shears, but usually having a cup on one side and a blade on the other.

Marvering: Pre-shaping of a gather of glass. By rolling the glass on a marvering table or plate a square or cylindrical shape is achieved.

Master Marble Company: Machine-made marble company founded in 1930 by four former employees of the Akro Agate Company. Master Marble closed in 1941 and former owner, Clinton F. Israel, went on to establish The Master Marble Glass Company that closed in 1973, purchased its machinery.

Mica: Any of a group of chemically and physically related aluminum silicate minerals, characteristically splitting into flexible sheets.

Millefiori: Italian for "a thousand flowers." Term used to describe mosaic glass used in three types of glass, ancient, Venetian, and contemporary glass.

Mimic: Appearing similar to another. To copy or imitate closely.

Moon: A surface or subsurface fracture caused by a blow or hit that produces a moon or crescent-shaped feature.

Moretti: Regarded today as the oldest and most prestigious glassmaking family in Italy. A soft glass commonly referred to by artists/craftsmen.

Murrini: Silhouette cane often used in the process to create millefiori.

Nailsea: Style of glass originated in England in the late 1700s. Easily identified by long loops or swirls. Usually white on color, occasionally with flecks or wide ribbons.

Onionskin: A type of end-of-day handmade glass marble. A thin layer of colored glass covers a large transparent center.

Opaque: Impenetrable by light, neither transparent nor translucent. Does not reflect light and has no luster.

Open Stock: Those pieces that are produced and available on a regular basis.

Orb: A sphere or spherical object.

Oven-glazed china: Any form of clay material glazed and heated to a hard substance in an oven or kiln.

Oxygen torch: Used in the torchwork method to provide direct or radiant heat by which to work.

Paperweight: A small, generally heavy, often decorative object placed on papers to hold them down. Originally made by Baccarat, Clichy, and St. Louis during the "classic" period of paperweight manufacture from 1845-1855. Beneath a magnifying dome of clear glass, an orderly millefiori or torchwork design is set low, near the base. The dome can be faceted or cased with one or more colors and showing through which windows were cut.

Pate de vere: French for glass paste. Ancient technique of melting ground glass in a mold and adding a fluxing medium and coloring agent that was either powdered, colored glass or metallic oxide. Revived in France during the second half of the nineteenth century.

Peltier Glass Company: Glass company founded in Illinois in 1886. Recognized as the oldest continuously producing glass company in the United States, having manufactured machine-made marbles since 1920. Peltier is known for making comic or picture marbles.

Peppermint swirl: A type of handmade glass marble easily identified by its red, white, and blue peppermint candy appearance. Believed to have been made first for the United States centennial commemoration.

Pole: Referring to the two opposite points on a handmade marble where the decorations terminate.

Pontil: A long, solid steel rod. A device used to make the gather, to turn the gather while forming a marble. To finish and fire polish. Also called a "punty."

Pontil mark: A rough mark left on one or both poles of a handmade marble where the marble was sheared off the rod or the end of the punty. A cutoff mark left on the marble.

Porcelain: A hard white translucent ceramic made by firing pure clay and then glazing it with fusible materials.

Pot: Used in a glass worker's furnace to hold a glass batch in its molten state for use.

Potash glass: Type of hard glass containing potash, potassium carbonate derived from plant ash.

Prototype: An original type, form or instance serving as a basis for later standards or stages. An early typical example.

Provenance: Proof of authenticity or past ownership.

Punty: An iron or steel rod on which molten glass is handled when being shaped and worked.

Pyrex: "Hard" glass primarily used for heat-resistant glassware in cooking and chemistry. A borosilicate glass with low expansion coefficient used in the torchwork method of glass crafting.

Rake Pull: Design method similar to Nailsea. Achieved by using various tools to pull one or more color of glass over or through another creating a range of designs.

Regular stock: Those pieces that are produced and available on a regular basis.

Reproduction: The act of reproducing or the condition or process of being reproduced.

Retail: The sale of goods or commodities in small quantities directly to consumers.

Reticello: Glass decorated with a mesh of usually opaque white threads beneath the surface. Also referred to as "vetro di trina" or lace glass.

Ribbon core: A type of handmade swirl having one flat ribbon that spirals through the center from pole to pole.

Scribe: Tool used by artist/craftsman to identify through marking their work. Usually metal.

Signature cane: Identifying glass cane chip embedded in host glass. Often designed and crafted by an artist using their initials, date or other specific identifying trait.

Silica: Silicon dioxide occurring as quartz and as the principal constituent of sand used in the making of glass.

Single gather: Produced one at a time by pulling molten glass from a furnace or through building glass on the end of a punty.

Single pontil: Handmade marble having only one cutoff mark.

Single ribbon: A variety of handmade swirl with a flat ribbon-shaped core.

Slump work: The procedure by which glass is heated and conforms to the shape of a mold.

Soda ash: Glass in which the alkali in the batch is obtained from soda, sodium carbonate, rather than potash.

Solid core: A type of handmade glass swirl marble having a center decoration that appears to be a solid geometric shape extending from pole to pole. The core is typically white, sometimes yellow, rarely other colors, and commonly decorated with colored bands or ribbons. Outer decorative lines of color are usually present near the surface.

Sphere: A three-dimensional surface, all points of which are equidistant from a fixed point.

Spiral: A curve on a plane that winds around a fixed center point at a continuously increasing or decreasing distance from the point.

Stria: Elongated imperfections in glass. May be air bubbles caused by unequal density of glasses used. Can cause variation in intensity of hues.

Sulphide: Ceramic objects cast or molded of clay and super silicate of potash for inclusion in glass.

Sulphide marble: A type of handmade marble produced of transparent glass, containing one or more clay figures of persons, animals, toys, numerals, or other objects.

Swirl: To move with a twisting or whirling motion. Something that coils. A type of handmade marble with ribbons or bands of colored glass twisting around inside the axis.

Torchwork: Method by which glass is worked in a gas-oxygen torch. Drawing with glass.

Torsade: A decorative trimming of twisted ribbon or cord.

Translucent: That which transmits light but diffuses to such an extent to prevent distinct images.

Transparent: Capable of transmitting light so that object or images can be seen as if there were no intervening material.

Vintage: Of or relating to a particular time period.

Wholesale: The sale of goods or commodities in large quantities, as for resale by a retailer.

Associated Value Guide

Figure 899. Assorted. Confetti Swirl. Assorted colored rod pieces. Random. Cole Herder. 1-1/2 in., ca. 2004. Flora. Red, yellow flora. Green stem, gray leaves. John Kobuki. 1-1/4 in. ca. 2004. Cameo. Blue stars, sandblasted base. Harry Bessett. 1-1/8 in., ca. 2004. *All courtesy of the author.*

The following Associated Value Guide is provided to the reader as an aid to the figures illustrated in this book. In some instances the range of value for a particular figure will differ from the price the work may be found available for on the primary or secondary market. The values listed have been arrived at through a combination of artist's suggested retail prices; dealer offered prices; realized auction prices, both catalog and Internet; and expert collectors' estimations. The final value range assigned for each figure is merely an estimate of market values at the time of publication, no investment estimation of current or future value should be derived from any of this information. It is provided solely as a guide to conditions at the time of printing.

As with any collectible, prices and values fluctuate based on availability, rarity, and current market conditions and considerations.

The author makes no recommendations, either explicit or implied, as to potential future value of any works illustrated in this book or those of like kind.

On some occasions no assigned value has been applied to a particular work. This is due to either the rarity or unique historical nature of a piece. This is not to say that no value can be assigned, simply the author has chosen not to assign one for the purposes of this publication.

Flypage

Figure 1a. James Alloway. Latticinio. Contemporary	$150-300
Michael Hansen, Nina Paladino Caron. Ribbon Swirl.	
Contemporary	$75-125
Douglas Sweet. Painted Face. Contemporary	$125-225

Foreword

Figure 1. Jody Fine at work. Not applicable	(N/A)*
Figure 2. Canyon School	N/A
Figure 3. Jody Fine portrait	N/A
Figure 4. H.O.T.M.I.R.E.	N/A
Figure 5. Marquis Deluxe postcard. No value assigned	(N/V/A)**
Figure 6. Jim Holmes and Jody Fine	N/A
Figure 7. Marbles and marble stock	N/V/A

On the Cover

Figure 8-10. Paul J. Stankard. Lilac Botanical Honey Bee Swarm Orb. Contemporary	$15,000-30,000
Figure 11. Stankard sketch and notes	N/V/A
Figure 12. Paul Stankard at work	N/A
Figure 13. Paul Stankard at work	N/A

Chapter One

Figure 14. The Morgan Cup. The Corning Museum	N/V/A
Figure 15. The Corning Ewer. The Corning Museum	N/V/A
Figure 16. Covered Goblet w/filigree. The Corning Museum	N/V/A
Figure 17. Bowl and Pitcher. The Corning Museum	N/V/A
Figure 18. Brilliant Cut Glass. The Corning Museum	N/V/A
Figure 19. Pressed Glass. The Corning Museum	N/V/A
Figure 20. Steuben Gazelle Bowl. The Corning Museum	N/V/A
Figure 21. Littleton Vessel. The Corning Museum	N/V/A
Figure 22. Labino Emergence 4-Stage. The Corning Museum	N/V/A
Figure 23. Chihuly Fern Green Tower. The Corning Museum	N/V/A
Figure 24. Marquis Marquiscarpa. The Corning Museum	N/V/A
Figure 25. Johns Manville #475. Industrial marbles	N/V/A
Figure 26. Josh Simpson and Tepee	N/A
Figure 27. Josh Simpson Studio	N/A
Figure 28. Josh Simpson MegaPlanet. Contemporary	$3,000-5,000

Chapter Two

Figure 29. Renaissance Faire. Marin County, California	N/A
Figure 30. Richard Marquis, Ro Purser. Contemporary	$50-100
Figure 31. Richard Marquis, Ro Purser. Contemporary	$400-800
Figure 32. Ro Purser. Contemporary	$400-800
Figure 33. Jody Fine, Richard Marquis, Jack Wax	N/A
Figure 34. Harry and Kathleen Boyer. Contemporary	$45-65
Figure 35. Kris Parke. Contemporary	$20-40
Figure 36. Drew Fritts. Contemporary	$60-120
Figure 37. Jesse Taj. Contemporary	$75-150
Figure 38. James Daschbach. Contemporary	$75-150
Figure 39. Gateson Recko. Contemporary	$500-1000

Chapter Three

Figure 40. Divided Core Swirl. Antique handmade	$100-200
Figure 41. Paneled Onionskin. Antique handmade	$100-225
Figure 42. Micas. Antique handmade	$10-20
Figure 43. Marble Rod Stock. Antique handmade	$15-30
Figure 44. Marble Rod Stock. Antique handmade	$15-30
Figure 45. Agates. Antique and contemporary	$10-100
Figure 46. Corkscrew. Machine-made	$5-10
Figure 47. Swirl. Antique handmade	$20-30
Figure 48. Cat's-eye. Machine-made	>$1
Figure 49. Confetti. Machine-made	$1-3

Chapter Four

Figure 50. Dustin Morell. Contemporary	$100-200
Figure 51. Rudy Calin. Contemporary	$45-65
Figure 52. Lewis and Jennifer Wilson. Contemporary	$150-300
Figure 53. Jody Fine. Contemporary	$25-75

Chapter Five

Figure 54. Geoffrey Beetem. Contemporary	$45-65
Figure 55. David Salazar. Contemporary	$200-300
Figure 56. Rolf and Genie Wald. Contemporary	$45-65
Figure 57. Rolf and Genie Wald. Contemporary	$25-35
Figure 58. Fritz Lauenstein. Contemporary	$25-35
Figure 59. Jody Fine. Contemporary	$15-30
Figure 60. Geoffrey Beetem. Contemporary	$175-350
Figure 61. Laser Crystal. Contemporary	$200-300
Figure 62. Steve, Rick, Mike, John, Mark, and Joe Davis. Contemporary	$200-250
Figure 63. David Salazar. Contemporary	$150-300
Figure 64. David Salazar. Contemporary	$250-350
Figure 65. Mark Matthews. Contemporary	N/V/A

Chapter Seven

Figure 66. Michael Hansen, Nina Paladino Caron. Contemporary	$50-75
Figure 67. Dustin Morell. Contemporary	$60-90
Figure 68. Geoffrey Beetem. Contemporary	$65-95
Figure 69. Charles Gibson. Contemporary	$35-55
Figure 70. Joe St. Clair. Contemporary	$75-150

Figure 71. Joe Rice. Contemporary	$40-60
Figure 72-86. Jody Fine. Contemporary	N/A
Figure 87-98. Jerry Kelly. Contemporary	N/A
Figure 99. Bruce Breslow. Contemporary	N/V/A

Chapter Nine

Figure 100. Clay. Antique handmade	>$1
Figure 101. Steve Parent. Contemporary	$8-15
Figure 102. Steve Parent. Contemporary	$20-40
Figure 103. Steve Parent. Contemporary	$8-40
Figure 104. Steve Parent. Contemporary	$40-60
Figure 105. Emily Block, Kevin Block. Contemporary	$>1-2
Figure 106. James Kirkland. Contemporary	$>1-2
Figure 107. Crockery. Antique handmade	$3-5
Figure 108. Crockery. Antique handmade	$3-8
Figure 109. Stoneware. Antique handmade	$40-60
Figure 110. Dinah Hulet. Contemporary	$85-175
Figure 111. Bennington. Antique handmade	$15-30
Figure 112. Bennington. Antique handmade	$40-50
Figure 113. Bennington. Antique handmade	$1-25
Figure 114. China. Antique handmade	$15-30
Figure 115. China. Antique handmade	$800-1200
Figure 116. China. Antique handmade	$15-30
Figure 117. China. Antique handmade	$10-200
Figure 118. Gregg Pessman. Contemporary	$30-50
Figure 119. Nadine Macdonald. Contemporary	$10-40
Figure 120. Nadine Macdonald. Contemporary	$35-75
Figure 121. Robert Brown. Contemporary	$25-50
Figure 122. Tom Thornburgh. Contemporary	$10-20
Figure 123. Nadine Macdonald. Contemporary	$8-16
Figure 124. Nadine Macdonald. Contemporary	$12-17
Figure 125. Tom Thornburgh. Contemporary	$10-20
Figure 126. Nadine Macdonald. Contemporary	$25-50
Figure 127. Nadine Macdonald. Contemporary	$5-15
Figure 128. Nadine Macdonald. Contemporary	$25-50
Figure 129. Nadine Macdonald. Contemporary	$40-80
Figure 130. Nadine Macdonald. Contemporary	$15-30
Figure 131. Nadine Macdonald. Contemporary	$20-40
Figure 132. Gregg Pessman. Contemporary	$30-60
Figure 133. Nadine Macdonald. Contemporary	$25-450
Figure 134-135. Nadine Macdonald. Contemporary	$8-15
Figure 136. Gregg Pessman. Contemporary	$30-60
Figure 137. Gregg Pessman. Contemporary	$30-60
Figure 138. Tom Thornburgh. Contemporary	$10-20
Figure 139. Nadine Macdonald. Contemporary	$75-125
Figure 140. Nadine Macdonald. Contemporary	$25-45
Figure 141. Nadine Macdonald. Contemporary	$75-150
Figure 142. Nadine Macdonald. Contemporary	$20-30
Figure 143. Nadine Macdonald. Contemporary	$25-50
Figure 144. Gregg Pessman. Contemporary	$75-150
Figure 145. Gregg Pessman. Contemporary	$35-55
Figure 146. Gregg Pessman. Contemporary	$25-35
Figure 147. Nadine Macdonald. Contemporary	$8-15
Figure 148. Gregg Pessman. Contemporary	$35-65
Figure 149. Gregg Pessman. Contemporary	$30-60
Figure 150. Gregg Pessman. Contemporary	$30-60
Figure 151. Robert Brown. Contemporary	$40-70
Figure 152. Robert Brown. Contemporary	$25-50
Figure 153. Robert Brown. Contemporary	$18-35
Figure 154. Robert Brown. Contemporary	$15-40
Figure 155. Gregg Pessman. Contemporary	$35-60
Figure 156. Gregg Pessman. Contemporary	$40-60
Figure 157. Gregg Pessman. Contemporary	$40-60
Figure 158. Gregg Pessman. Contemporary	$40-60
Figure 159. Gregg Pessman. Contemporary	$50-100
Figure 160. Gregg Pessman. Contemporary	$40-60
Figure 161. Gregg Pessman. Contemporary	$40-60
Figure 162. Nadine Macdonald. Contemporary	$15-30
Figure 163. Nadine Macdonald. Contemporary	N/V/A
Figure 164-165. Nadine Macdonald. Contemporary	N/V/A
Figure 166. Nadine Macdonald. Contemporary	$15-30
Figure 167. Nadine Macdonald. Contemporary	$10-20
Figure 168-169. Robert Brown. Contemporary	$75-150
Figure 170-171. Tom Thornburgh. Contemporary	$25-50
Figure 172. Nadine Macdonald. Contemporary	$15-40
Figure 173. Robert Brown. Contemporary	$20-40

Figure 174. Tom Thornburgh. Contemporary	$25-50
Figure 175. Tom Thornburgh. Contemporary	$30-60
Figure 176-177. Gregg Pessman. Contemporary	N/V/A
Figure 178. Gregg Pessman. Contemporary	$45-65
Figure 179. Gregg Pessman. Contemporary	$40-60
Figure 180-181. Nadine Macdonald. Contemporary	$40-80
Figure 182. Coralee Smith. Contemporary	$35-65
Figure 183. Coralee Smith. Contemporary	$30-60
Figure 184. Carpet Ball. Antique handmade	$100-125
Figure 185. Carpet Ball. Antique handmade	$100-125
Figure 186. Carpet Ball. Contemporary	$1-3
Figure 187. Carpet Ball. Contemporary	$1-3
Figure 188. Agate. Antique, Contemporary	$10-100
Figure 189. Agate. Antique, Contemporary	$10-100
Figure 190. Agate. Antique, Contemporary	$10-50
Figure 191. Mineral. Dry Head Agate	$35-50
Figure 192. Mineral. Petrified Wood	$45-65
Figure 193. Mineral. Crazy Lace Agate	$50-75
Figure 194. Mineral. Fluorite in Limestone; Tigereye	$20-35
	$12-20
Figure 195. Mineral. Sodalite	$25-50
Figure 196. Mineral. Rutilated Quartz	$50-75
Figure 197. Banded Swirl. Antique handmade	$125-175
Figure 198. Banded Swirl. Antique handmade	$125-175
Figure 199. Banded Swirl. Antique handmade	$100-150
Figure 200. Banded Swirl. Antique handmade	$125-175
Figure 201. Banded Swirl. Antique handmade	$175-300
Figure 202. Bruce Troeh. Contemporary	$15-30
Figure 203. Dudley Giberson. Contemporary	$65-90
Figure 204. Bruce Troeh. Contemporary	$15-20
Figure 205. William Murray. Contemporary	$15-30
Figure 206. Steve Davis. Contemporary	$30-50
Figure 207. Unidentified. Contemporary	$20-40
Figure 208. Steve Davis. Contemporary	$15-25
Figure 209. Eddie Seese. Contemporary	$30-45
Figure 210. Eddie Seese. Contemporary	$25-35
Figure 211. Steve Davis. Contemporary	$15-25
Figure 212. Shell Neisler. Contemporary	$35-65
Figure 213. Dale Danowski, Matthew Potter. Contemporary	$10-20
Figure 214. Unidentified. Contemporary	$15-25
Figure 215. Drew Fritts. Contemporary	$60-100
Figure 216. Drew Fritts. Contemporary	$60-100
Figure 217. Rolf and Genie Wald. Contemporary	$20-35
Figure 218. Jody Fine. Contemporary	$15-20
Figure 219. Eddie Seese. Contemporary	$45-65
Figure 220. Eddie Seese. Contemporary	$25-45
Figure 221. Robert Lichtman. Contemporary	$25-35
Figure 222. Bermuda Glass Blowing Studio. Contemporary	$30-60
Figure 223. Unidentified. Contemporary	$20-40
Figure 224. Harry Besett. Contemporary	$20-35
Figure 225. Phillip Nolley. Contemporary	$20-35
Figure 226. David Salazar. Contemporary	$15-30
Figure 227. Robert Dane. Contemporary	$45-65
Figure 228. Rolf and Genie Wald. Contemporary	$60-100
Figure 229. David Salazar, Christopher Robinson. Contemporary	$10-25
Figure 230. Clambroth. Antique handmade	$75-100
Figure 231. Clambroth. Antique handmade	$75-100
Figure 232. Clambroth. Antique handmade	$150-200
Figure 233. Drew Fritts. Contemporary	$35-55
Figure 234. Drew Fritts. Contemporary	$50-75
Figure 235. Geoffrey Beetem. Contemporary	$40-60
Figure 236. Mike Edmundson. Contemporary	$35-65
Figure 237. Dale Danowski. Contemporary	$15-30
Figure 238. Divided Core Swirl. Antique handmade	$85-150
Figure 239. Divided Core Swirl. Antique handmade	$75-125
Figure 240. Divided Core Swirl. Antique handmade	$75-125
Figure 241. Unidentified. Contemporary	$15-20
Figure 242. Phillip Nolley. Contemporary	$30-50
Figure 243. Steven Maslach. Contemporary	$25-40
Figure 244. Bruce Troeh. Contemporary	$25-35
Figure 245. Phillip Nolley. Contemporary	$30-50
Figure 246. Unidentified. Contemporary	$30-50
Figure 247. Bruce Troeh. Contemporary	$25-35
Figure 248. Fritz Lauenstein. Contemporary	$30-60
Figure 249. Indian Swirl. Antique handmade	$75-150

Figure 250. Indian Swirl. Antique handmade	$60-120
Figure 251. Indian Swirl. Antique handmade	$150-300
Figure 252. Christopher Robinson. Contemporary	$15-30
Figure 253. Christopher Robinson. Contemporary	$15-30
Figure 254. Christopher Robinson. Contemporary	$15-30
Figure 255. Latticinio Core Swirl. Antique handmade	$100-150
Figure 256. Latticinio Core Swirl. Antique handmade	$10-25
Figure 257. Latticinio Core Swirl. Antique handmade	$40-80
Figure 258. Jody Fine. Contemporary	$50-100
Figure 259. Jody Fine. Contemporary	$12-20
Figure 260. Jody Fine, Douglas Sweet. Contemporary	$25-75
Figure 261. Dudley Giberson. Contemporary	$60-90
Figure 262. Gibson Glass. Charles Gibson. Contemporary	$35-65
Figure 263. Unidentified. Contemporary	$25-50
Figure 264. Ken Rosenfeld. Contemporary	$25-50
Figure 265. Ken Rosenfeld. Contemporary	$25-50
Figure 266. Robert Dane. Contemporary	$50-100
Figure 267. Teign Valley Glass. Contemporary	$25-50
Figure 268. Robert Lichtman. Contemporary	$50-100
Figure 269. Eddie Seese. Contemporary	$25-50
Figure 270. Rolf Greiner-Adams. Contemporary	$20-35
Figure 271. Steven Maslach. Contemporary	$60-110
Figure 272. James Alloway. Contemporary	$150-300
Figure 273. Peppermint Swirl. Antique handmade	$40-80
Figure 274. Gibson Glass. Charles Gibson. Contemporary	$25-40
Figure 275. Mark Matthews. Contemporary	$150-250
Figure 276. Kris Parke. Contemporary	$20-40
Figure 277. Ribbon Swirl. Antique handmade	$65-95
Figure 278. Ribbon Swirl. Antique handmade	$70-100
Figure 279. Ribbon Swirl. Antique handmade	$300-600
Figure 280. Robert Dane. Contemporary	$50-100
Figure 281. Rolf and Genie Wald. Contemporary	$65-120
Figure 282. Dudley Giberson. Contemporary	$90-180
Figure 283. Bruce Troeh. Contemporary	$10-20
Figure 284. Jody Fine. Contemporary	$25-50
Figure 285. Dudley Giberson. Contemporary	$60-120
Figure 286. Rudy Calin. Contemporary	$30-50
Figure 287. William Murray. Contemporary	$25-50
Figure 288. Harry and Kathleen Boyer. Contemporary	$35-70
Figure 289. Unidentified. Contemporary	$25-40
Figure 290. Chuck Pound. Contemporary	$50-75
Figure 291. Steven Maslach. Contemporary	$18-35
Figure 292. Fred Widner. Contemporary	$25-50
Figure 293. Jody Fine. Contemporary	$30-60
Figure 294. Jerry Kelly. Contemporary	$20-40
Figure 295. Jerry Kelly. Contemporary	$60-120
Figure 296. Rolf and Genie Wald. Contemporary	$25-45
Figure 297. Rolf and Genie Wald. Contemporary	$35-45
Figure 298. Steven Maslach. Contemporary	$12-20
Figure 299. Dudley Giberson, Jody Fine. Contemporary	$20-40
Figure 300. Steven Maslach. Contemporary	$20-40
Figure 301. Steven Maslach. Contemporary	$20-40
Figure 302. Fritz Lauenstein. Contemporary	$25-40
Figure 303. Dan Grumbling. Contemporary	$20-40
Figure 304. Beth Tomasello. Contemporary	$45-65
Figure 305. Dan Grumbling. Contemporary	$10-40
Figure 306. David Grant Maul. Contemporary	$30-60
Figure 307. Unidentified. Contemporary	$15-30
Figure 308. Richard Marquis. Contemporary	$40-80
Figure 309. Francis Coupal. Contemporary	$60-120
Figure 310. Jody Fine. Contemporary	$20-40
Figure 311. Unidentified VWT. Contemporary	$25-50
Figure 312. Greg Hoglin. Contemporary	$25-50
Figure 313. Elizabeth Root. Contemporary	$20-40
Figure 314. Eddie Seese. Contemporary	$75-125
Figure 315. Robert Dane. Contemporary	$35-65
Figure 316. William Burchfield. Contemporary	$75-125
Figure 317. Michael Hansen, Nina Paladino Caron. Contemporary	$45-65
Figure 318. Michael Hansen, Nina Paladino Caron. Contemporary	$45-65
Figure 319. Michael Hansen, Nina Paladino Caron. Contemporary	$45-65
Figure 320. David Salazar. Contemporary	$15-30
Figure 321. Robert LaGrand. Contemporary	$10-20
Figure 322. William Burchfield. Contemporary	$60-120
Figure 323. William Burchfield. Contemporary	$60-120
Figure 324-325. William Burchfield. Contemporary	$100-150

Figure 326. William Burchfield. Contemporary $50-75
Figure 327. Dudley Giberson. Contemporary $50-100
Figure 328. Michael Hansen, Nina Paladino Caron. Contemporary $75-125
Figure 329. Dudley Giberson. Contemporary $50-100
Figure 330. Dudley Giberson. Contemporary $50-100
Figure 331. Fritz Lauenstein. Contemporary $40-60
Figure 332. Solid Core Swirl. Antique handmade $125-175
Figure 333. Solid Core Swirl. Antique handmade $50-70
Figure 334. Solid Core Swirl. Antique handmade $50-100
Figure 335. Robert Lichtman. Contemporary $25-50
Figure 336. William Burchfield. Contemporary $40-60
Figure 337. Frank Oddu. Contemporary $15-30
Figure 338. Steven Davis. Contemporary $15-30
Figure 339. Steven Davis. Contemporary $15-30
Figure 340. Christopher Robinson. Contemporary $12-25
Figure 341. David Salazar. Contemporary $15-30
Figure 342. Eddie Seese. Contemporary $50-100
Figure 343. Rolf Greiner-Adams. Contemporary $15-30
Figure 344. Eddie Seese. Contemporary $18-36
Figure 345. Jerry Park. Contemporary $20-40
Figure 346. Steven Maslach. Contemporary $20-40
Figure 347. Eddie Seese. Contemporary $35-70
Figure 348. Phillip Nolley. Contemporary $30-50
Figure 349. Douglas Sweet. Contemporary $30-50
Figure 350. Rolf and Genie Wald. Contemporary $75-150
Figure 351. Rolf and Genie Wald. Contemporary $300-500
Figure 352. James Holmes. Contemporary $75-150
Figure 353. Jody Fine. Contemporary $15-25
Figure 354. Rolf Wald. Contemporary $60-120
Figure 355. Joseph's Coat. Antique handmade $150-300
Figure 356. Joseph's Coat. Antique handmade $50-100
Figure 357. Joseph's Coat. Antique handmade $50-100
Figure 358. Fritz Lauenstein. Contemporary $25-35
Figure 359. Fritz Lauenstein. Contemporary $25-35
Figure 360. Fritz Lauenstein. Contemporary $25-35
Figure 361. Fritz Lauenstein. Contemporary $25-35
Figure 362. John K. Talmage. Contemporary $25-35
Figure 363. Douglas Sweet. Contemporary $30-50
Figure 364. Rolf and Genie Wald. Contemporary $25-35
Figure 365. Steven Davis. Contemporary $18-25
Figure 366. Rolf and Genie Wald. Contemporary $30-60
Figure 367. Rolf and Genie Wald. Contemporary   N/V/A
Figure 368. Rolf and Genie Wald. Contemporary $18-36
Figure 369. Drew Fritts. Contemporary $60-100
Figure 370. Drew Fritts. Contemporary $60-100
Figure 371. Drew Fritts. Contemporary $60-100
Figure 372. Eddie Seese. Contemporary $25-35
Figure 373. Mica. Antique handmade $35-65
Figure 374. Mica. Antique handmade $25-50
Figure 375. Bart and Kerry Zimmerman. Contemporary $35-65
Figure 376. William Murray. Contemporary $25-40
Figure 377. Bart and Kerry Zimmerman. Contemporary $35-65
Figure 378. Paperweight. Antique handmade $2500-3500
Figure 379. Greg Hoglin. Contemporary $45-65
Figure 380. Tony Parker. Contemporary $85-175
Figure 381. Tony Parker. Contemporary $75-150
Figure 382. James Hart. Contemporary $50-75
Figure 383. Sulphide. Antique handmade $70-140
Figure 384. Sulphide. Antique handmade $70-140
Figure 385. Sulphide. Antique handmade $45-90
Figure 386. Sulphide. Antique handmade $70-140
Figure 387. Sulphide. Antique handmade $2800-3200
Figure 388. Joe St. Clair. Contemporary $100-200
Figure 389. House of Glass. Joe Rice. Contemporary $50-100
Figure 390. Joe St. Clair. Contemporary $125-225
Figure 391. Joe St. Clair. Contemporary $100-200
Figure 392. Joe St. Clair. Contemporary $100-200
Figure 393. House of Glass. Joe Rice. Contemporary $50-100
Figure 394. Gibson Glass. Contemporary $40-80
Figure 395. Rick Davis. Contemporary $30-50
Figure 396. Boyd Miller, Tom Thornburgh. Contemporary $80-160
Figure 397. Ray Laubs. Contemporary $25-50
Figure 398. Gibson Glass. Contemporary $40-80
Figure 399. Sam Hogue. Contemporary $30-60

Figure 400. Jim Davis. Contemporary $25-50

Figure 401. Sam Hogue. Contemporary $30-60
Figure 402. Tom Thornburgh. Contemporary $25-50
Figure 403. Tom Thornburgh. Contemporary $25-50
Figure 404. Ray Laubs. Contemporary $45-90
Figure 405. Tom Thornburgh. Contemporary $25-50
Figure 406-407. Paul and Dee Snell. Contemporary $25-45
Figure 408-409. Paul and Dee Snell. Contemporary $25-45
Figure 410. Jim Davis. Contemporary $30-60
Figure 411. Harry Besett. Contemporary $45-70
Figure 412. End-of-Day. Cloud. Antique handmade $80-120
Figure 413. End-of-Day. Cloud. Antique handmade $100-200
Figure 414. End-of-Day. Cloud. Antique handmade $100-200
Figure 415. Unidentified. Contemporary $25-35
Figure 416. Jim Davis (Indiana). Contemporary $35-65
Figure 417. Bobbie Seese. Contemporary $30-50
Figure 418. Robert Lichtman. Contemporary $100-200
Figure 419-420. Robert Lichtman. Contemporary $150-250
Figure 421. Jim Davis (Indiana). Contemporary $25-35
Figure 422. Unidentified. Contemporary $30-45
Figure 423. End-of-Day. Onionskin. Antique handmade $65-125
Figure 424. End-of-Day. Onionskin. Antique handmade $60-120
Figure 425. Eddie Seese, Bobbie Seese. Contemporary $50-75
Figure 426. Steve Davis. Contemporary $40-60
Figure 427. David Salazar. Contemporary $15-25
Figure 428. Davis Handmade Marbles. Contemporary $25-40
Figure 429. Jerry Park. Contemporary $20-30
Figure 430. Robert Lichtman. Contemporary $35-55
Figure 431. Jim Davis. Contemporary $15-25
Figure 432. Robert Hamon. Contemporary $25-50
Figure 433. Robert Hamon. Contemporary $25-50
Figure 434. Phillip Nolley. Contemporary $30-50
Figure 435. Robert Livesy, Phillip Nolley, Jim Davis (Indiana).
   Contemporary $20-60
Figure 436. David Salazar. Contemporary $60-90
Figure 437. Robert Lichtman. Contemporary $25-40
Figure 438. Jim Davis. Contemporary $25-40
Figure 439. Harry and Kathleen Boyer. Contemporary $40-70
Figure 440. Mark Capel. Contemporary $18-36
Figure 441. George Pavliscak. Contemporary $20-40
Figure 442. George Pavliscak. Contemporary $20-40
Figure 443. George Pavliscak. Contemporary $25-45
Figure 444. George Pavliscak. Contemporary $25-45
Figure 445. Harry and Kathleen Boyer. Contemporary $25-45
Figure 446. Steven Davis. Contemporary $18-25
Figure 447. Jerry Park. Contemporary $18-30
Figure 448. Jerry Park. Contemporary $20-35
Figure 449. Drew Fritts. Contemporary $75-150
Figure 450. George Pavliscak. Contemporary $25-40
Figure 451. Drew Fritts. Contemporary $60-100
Figure 452. David Salazar. Contemporary $18-30
Figure 453. Eddie Seese. Contemporary $35-55
Figure 454. Boyd Miller. Contemporary $30-50
Figure 455. Boyd Miller. Contemporary $30-50
Figure 456. Robert Lichtman, Phillip Nolley. Contemporary $30-70
Figure 457. Robert Lichtman. Contemporary $40-70
Figure 458. William Burchfield. Contemporary $40-70
Figure 459. Rolf and Genie Wald. Contemporary $30-40
Figure 460. Rolf and Genie Wald. Contemporary $45-65
Figure 461. Rolf and Genie Wald. Contemporary $20-40
Figure 462. Rolf and Genie Wald. Contemporary $60-110
Figure 463. Teri Conklin. Contemporary $35-60
Figure 464. Eddie Seese. Contemporary $30-60
Figure 465. Drew Fritts. Contemporary $75-150
Figure 466. George Pavliscak. Contemporary $20-40
Figure 467. George Pavliscak. Contemporary $25-40
Figure 468. George Pavliscak. Contemporary $25-40
Figure 469. Ben Walsh. Contemporary $60-100
Figure 470. Ben Walsh. Contemporary $60-100
Figure 471. Drew Fritts. Contemporary $25-50
Figure 472. Terry Crider. Contemporary $40-70
Figure 473. Douglas Sweet. Contemporary $45-75
Figure 474. End-of-Day. Paneled Onionskin.
   Antique handmade $125-250
Figure 475. End-of-Day. Paneled Onionskin.
   Antique handmade $45-90

Figure 476-477. End-of-Day. Paneled Onionskin.	
Antique handmade	N/V/A
Figure 478. Russell Stankus. Contemporary	$40-60
Figure 479. Francis Coupal. Contemporary	$80-160
Figure 480. Francis Coupal. Contemporary	$65-100
Figure 481. Francis Coupal. Contemporary	$40-70
Figure 482. Francis Coupal. Contemporary	$40-70
Figure 483. End-of-Day. Lobed Onionskin.	
Antique Handmade	$50-100
Figure 484. End-of-Day. Lobed Onionskin.	
Antique Handmade	$50-100
Figure 485. Jim Davis (Indiana). Contemporary	$35-55
Figure 486. Jim Davis. Contemporary	$25-35
Figure 487. Mike Davis. Contemporary	$35-55
Figure 488. Steven Davis. Contemporary	$35-55
Figure 489. Kris Parke. Contemporary	$25-40
Figure 490. Ribbon Lutz Swirl. Antique handmade	$200-400
Figure 491. Banded Lutz Swirl. Antique handmade	$200-400
Figure 492. Goldstone. Contemporary	$40-100
Figure 493. John Hamon Miller. Contemporary	$25-40
Figure 494. Rolf Greiner-Adams. Contemporary	$20-35
Figure 495. Mark Matthews. Contemporary	$75-100
Figure 496. Rolf and Genie Wald. Contemporary	$20-65
Figure 497. Transitional handmade. United States	$20-30
Figure 498. Transitional handmade. United States	$20-30
Figure 499. Cat's-eye. Machine-made. Japan	>$1
Figure 500. Cat's-eye. Machine-made. Japan	$1-3
Figure 501. Akro Agate Company. Machine-made	$3-6
Figure 502. Akro Agate Company. Machine-made	$3-6
Figure 503. Akro Agate Company. Machine-made	$3-6
Figure 504. Scott Patrick. Contemporary	$15-30
Figure 505. Kristen Shields. Contemporary	$10-20
Figure 506. Christensen Agate Company. Machine-made	$150-300
Figure 507. Robert Livesy. Contemporary	$20-40
Figure 508. Sam Hogue. Contemporary	$25-45
Figure 509. Mike Edmundson. Contemporary	$40-80
Figure 510. Chuck Pound. Contemporary	$25-45
Figure 511. Phillip Nolley. Contemporary	$25-45
Figure 512. Akro Agate Company. Machine-made;	$1-3
Peltier Glass Company. Machine-made	$1-5
Figure 513. Vitro Agate Company. Machine-made	$1-5
Figure 514. Vacor de Mexico. Machine-made	>$1
Figure 515. Marble King Inc. Machine-made	$1-3
Figure 516. Mike Edmundson. Contemporary	$15-30
Figure 517. Robert Powers. Contemporary	$8-15
Figure 518. Peltier Glass Company. Machine-made	$1000-1500, $85-125
Figure 519. Attributed to Harold Bennett. Contemporary	>$1
Figure 520. Attributed to Harold Bennett. Contemporary	>$1
Figure 521. Attributed to Harold Bennett. Contemporary	>$1
Figure 522. United States. Contemporary	>$1
Figure 523. United States. Contemporary	>$1
Figure 524. United States. Contemporary	>$1
Figure 525. United States. Contemporary	>$1
Figure 526. United States. Contemporary	>$1
Figure 527. United States. Contemporary	>$1
Figure 528. Attributed to Larry Castle, Marlow Peterson.	
Contemporary	$15-30
Figure 529. Chinese. Contemporary	>$1
Figure 530. Chinese. Contemporary	>$1
Figure 531. United States. Contemporary	>$1
Figure 532. Golden Rule. Machine-made	>$5-10
Figure 533. Christensen Agate Company. Machine-made	$40-60
Figure 534. Champion Agate Company. Machine-made	$5-10
Figure 535. Akro Agate Company. Machine-made	$5-35
Figure 536. Akro Agate Company. Machine-made	$5-20
Figure 537. Mike Edmundson. Contemporary	$15-30
Figure 538. Scott Patrick. Contemporary	$15-30
Figure 539. John Hamon Miller. Contemporary	$15-30
Figure 540. Scott Patrick. Contemporary	$15-30
Figure 541. John Hamon Miller. Contemporary	$15-30
Figure 542. John Hamon Miller. Contemporary	$15-30
Figure 543. Akro Agate Company. Machine-made	$3-6
Figure 544. Akro Agate Company. Machine-made	$3-6
Figure 545. M.F. Christensen & Son Company. Machine-made	$10-15
Figure 546. Joe St. Clair. Contemporary	$50-100

Figure 547. Joe St. Clair. Contemporary $40-80
Figure 548. Joe St. Clair. Contemporary $40-80
Figure 549. Scott Patrick. Contemporary $15-30
Figure 550. Rudy Calin. Contemporary $25-50
Figure 551. Mike Edmundson. Contemporary $25-50
Figure 552. Robert Powers. Contemporary $15-30
Figure 553. Brendan Blake. Contemporary $18-36
Figure 554. Richard Clark. Contemporary $20-40
Figure 555. Richard Clark. Contemporary $20-40
Figure 556. Richard Clark. Contemporary $20-40
Figure 557. Richard Clark. Contemporary $20-40
Figure 558. Richard Clark. Contemporary $20-40
Figure 559. Bruce Breslow. Contemporary $20-40
Figure 560. Bruce Breslow. Contemporary $20-40
Figure 561. Bruce Breslow. Contemporary $20-40
Figure 562. Virginia Wilson, Anthony Toccalino. Contemporary $80-150
Figure 563. Jerry Park. Contemporary $20-40
Figure 564. Richard Clark. Contemporary $20-40
Figure 565. Brendan Blake. Contemporary $20-40
Figure 566. Jerry Park. Contemporary $35-65
Figure 567. Jerry Park. Contemporary $20-35
Figure 568. Jerry Park. Contemporary $15-30
Figure 569. Jerry Park. Contemporary $25-45
Figure 570. Jerry Park. Contemporary $20-40
Figure 571. Jerry Park. Contemporary $15-30
Figure 572. Jerry Park. Contemporary $18-36
Figure 573. Jerry Park. Contemporary $15-30
Figure 574. Jerry Park. Contemporary $15-30
Figure 575. TNT, WC. Contemporary $12-24
Figure 576. Ravenswood Novelty Works. Machine-made $2-5
Figure 577. German Swirl. Machine-made $1-2
Figure 578. West Virginia Swirls. Machine-made   >$1
Figure 579. Christensen Agate Company. Machine-made $20-30
Figure 580. West Virginia Swirls. Machine-made   >$1
Figure 581. Jabo-Vitro Agate Company. Machine-made   >$1
Figure 582. Peltier Glass Company. Machine-made $35-45
Figure 583. Peltier Glass Company. Machine-made $5-25
Figure 584. Akro Agate Company. Machine-made $70-90
Figure 585. Striped Opaque. Machine-made. Czechoslovakia $70-90
Figure 586. Jabo-Vitro Company. Machine-made $40-80
Figure 587. Robert Lichtman. Contemporary $25-50
Figure 588. Attributed to Christopher Robinson. Contemporary $12-24
Figure 589. Jerry Park. Contemporary $18-36
Figure 590. Attributed to Christopher Robinson. Contemporary $18-36
Figure 591. John Hamon Miller. Contemporary $20-35
Figure 592. Jerry Park. Contemporary $18-36
Figure 593. Tony Parker. Contemporary $25-40.
Figure 594. Greg Hoglin. Contemporary $30-60
Figure 595. Bruce Troeh. Contemporary $10-20
Figure 596. Mike Edmundson, Drew Fritts, Robert Livesy.
    Contemporary $20-60
Figure 597. Bobbie Seese. Contemporary $5-25
Figure 598. Dan Grumbling, Aaron West. Contemporary $15-30
Figure 599. Scott Patrick. Contemporary $10-30

Figure 600. Phil McGlothlin. Contemporary $15-30
Figure 601. Christopher Robinson. Contemporary $15-30
Figure 602. Scott Patrick. Contemporary $10-30
Figure 603. Unidentified, Chinese. Contemporary $>1
Figure 604. Starbucks round tin. Machine-made $12-24
Figure 605. NEX Products tin. Machine-made $12-24
Figure 606. Cat's-eyes. Machine-made $3-10
Figure 607. Scott Patrick. Contemporary $10-30
Figure 608. Christopher Robinson. Contemporary $15-30
Figure 609. John Hamon Miller. Contemporary $15-30
Figure 610. Shell Neisler, Dustin Morell. Contemporary   N/V/A
Figure 611. Shane Caswell. Contemporary   N/V/A
Figure 612. Shane Caswell. Contemporary   N/V/A
Figure 613. Shane Caswell. Contemporary   N/V/A
Figure 614. Shane Caswell. Contemporary   N/V/A
Figure 615. Jennifer Wilson. Contemporary $12-24
Figure 616. Mike Edmundson, Lewis and Jennifer Wilson.
    Contemporary $15-25
Figure 617. MR. Contemporary $20-30
Figure 618. Lewis and Jennifer Wilson. Contemporary $12-24
Figure 619. Mike Edmundson. Contemporary $20-35

Figure 620. Shane Caswell. Contemporary	$20-35
Figure 621. Dinah Hulet. Contemporary	$75-100
Figure 622. Kathy Young, Christopher Constantin. Contemporary	$50-100
Figure 623. Greg Hoglin. Contemporary	
Figure 624. Tony Parker. Contemporary	$60-120
Figure 625. Kevin O'Grady. Contemporary	$50-100
Figure 626. Chris and Lissa Juedemann. Contemporary	$150-250
Figure 627. Chris and Lissa Juedemann. Contemporary	$150-250
Figure 628. Chris and Lissa Juedemann. Contemporary	$150-250
Figure 629. Dinah Hulet. Contemporary	$180-300
Figure 630-631. Dinah Hulet. Contemporary	$180-300
Figure 632-633. Dinah Hulet. Contemporary	$180-300
Figure 634-635. Douglas Sweet. Contemporary	$175-225
Figure 636. Gentile Glass. John Gentile. Contemporary	$125-200
Figure 637. Gentile Glass. John Gentile. Contemporary	$100-175
Figure 638. Gentile Glass. John Gentile. Contemporary	$50-75
Figure 639. Gentile Glass. John Gentile. Contemporary	$175-225
Figure 640. Gerry and Pat Colman. Contemporary	$50-150
Figure 641. Gerry and Pat Colman. Contemporary	$50-175
Figure 642. Gerry and Pat Colman. Contemporary	$150-300
Figure 643. Gerry and Pat Colman. Contemporary	$125-250
Figure 644. Richard Marquis, Ro Purser. Contemporary	N/V/A
Figure 645. Richard Marquis, Ro Purser. Contemporary	N/V/A
Figure 646. Luke Gilvey. Contemporary	$25-35
Figure 647. Jerry Kelly. Contemporary	$15-25
Figure 648. Douglas Ferguson. Contemporary	$40-60
Figure 649. Gerry Colman. Contemporary	$30-50
Figure 650. Gerry Colman. Contemporary	$35-55
Figure 651. Chris and Lissa Juedemann. Contemporary	$150-250
Figure 652. Chris and Lissa Juedemann. Contemporary	$150-250
Figure 653. Rajesh Kommineni. Contemporary	$60-90
Figure 654. Douglas Sweet. Contemporary	$70-100
Figure 655. Greg Hoglin. Contemporary	$25-40
Figure 656. Jody Fine. Contemporary	$80-160
Figure 657. Jody Fine. Contemporary	$60-120
Figure 658-659. David Strobel. Contemporary	$100-200
Figure 660. Cathy Richardson. Contemporary	$60-120
Figure 661-662. Cathy Richardson. Contemporary	$60-120
Figure 663. Cathy Richardson. Contemporary	$60-120
Figure 664. Cathy Richardson. Contemporary	$25-40
Figure 665. Cathy Richardson. Contemporary	$100-200
Figure 666. Cathy Richardson. Contemporary	$75-150
Figure 667. David Salazar. Contemporary	$50-100
Figure 668. Rolf and Genie Wald. Contemporary	$60-120
Figure 669. Sara Creekmore. Contemporary	$60-120
Figure 670. David Dunham. Contemporary	$75-150
Figure 671. David Dunham. Contemporary	$75-150
Figure 672. Sara Creekmore. Contemporary	$75-150
Figure 673. Rolf and Genie Wald. Contemporary	$50-100
Figure 674. Geoffrey Beetem. Contemporary	$500-1000
Figure 675. Geoffrey Beetem. Contemporary	$300-600
Figure 676. Rolf and Genie Wald. Contemporary	$400-800
Figure 677. Lundberg Studios. Contemporary.	$250-350
Figure 678. Virginia Wilson, Anthony Toccalino. Contemporary	$100-200
Figure 679. Gateson Recko. Contemporary	$750-1500
Figure 680. Gateson Recko. Contemporary	$100-150
Figure 681. Wendy Besett. Contemporary	$200-300
Figure 682. Wendy Besett. Contemporary	$200-300
Figure 683. Wendy Besett. Contemporary	$200-300
Figure 684. Karen Federici. Contemporary	$35-50
Figure 685. Tony Parker. Contemporary	$50-75
Figure 686. Bruce Troeh. Contemporary	$40-60
Figure 687. Bruce Troeh. Contemporary	$35-50
Figure 688. Jesse Taj. Contemporary	$150-200
Figure 689. David Salazar. Contemporary	$175-250
Figure 690. David Salazar. Contemporary	$200-350
Figure 691. David Salazar. Contemporary	$120-200
Figure 692. David Salazar. Contemporary	$150-300
Figure 693. David Salazar. Contemporary	$150-300
Figure 694. David Salazar. Contemporary	$150-300
Figure 695. David Salazar. Contemporary	$150-300
Figure 696. David Salazar. Contemporary	$120-200
Figure 697. David Salazar. Contemporary	$50-75
Figure 698. David Salazar, Jesse Siegel. Contemporary	$90-150
Figure 699. David Salazar. Contemporary	$150-300
Figure 700. David Salazar. Contemporary	$80-150

Figure 701. George Pavliscak. Contemporary $30-50
Figure 702. Lewis and Jennifer Wilson. Contemporary $20-40
Figure 703. Lewis and Jennifer Wilson. Contemporary $30-60
Figure 704. Lewis and Jennifer Wilson. Contemporary $45-70
Figure 705. Lewis and Jennifer Wilson. Contemporary $75-150
Figure 706. Lewis and Jennifer Wilson. Contemporary $60-90
Figure 707. Lewis and Jennifer Wilson. Contemporary $60-90
Figure 708. Beth Tomasello. Contemporary $60-90
Figure 709. Greg Hoglin. Contemporary $40-60
Figure 710. Greg Hoglin. Contemporary $10-60
Figure 711. Tim Waugh. Contemporary $15-30
Figure 712. Tim Waugh. Contemporary $15-30
Figure 713. Cathy Richardson. Contemporary $35-60
Figure 714. George Pavliscak. Contemporary $20-40
Figure 715. Cathy Richardson. Contemporary $40-80
Figure 716. Victor Gaenzel. Contemporary $25-40
Figure 717. KY. Contemporary $20-40
Figure 718. Jerry Kelly. Contemporary $45-70
Figure 719. Jerry Kelly. Contemporary $35-60
Figure 720. Drew Fritts. Contemporary $50-100
Figure 721. Drew Fritts. Contemporary $50-100
Figure 722. David Salazar. Contemporary $25-40
Figure 723. David Salazar. Contemporary $200-300
Figure 724. David Salazar. Contemporary $50-100
Figure 725. Douglas Ferguson. Contemporary $25-50
Figure 726. Gale Morgan. Contemporary $30-60
Figure 727. David Vogt. Contemporary $50-100
Figure 728-729. Teri Conklin. Contemporary $60-100
Figure 730-731. Teri Conklin. Contemporary $60-100
Figure 732. Douglas Sweet. Contemporary $60-100
Figure 733. Josh Simpson. Contemporary $60-100
Figure 734. Josh Simpson. Contemporary $60-100
Figure 735. Josh Simpson. Contemporary $3,000-5,000
Figure 736. Josh Simpson. Contemporary   N/V/A
Figure 737. Josh Simpson. Contemporary   N/V/A
Figure 738. Josh Simpson. Contemporary $60-100
Figure 739. Douglas Sweet. Contemporary $50-80
Figure 740. Shanti Devi. Contemporary $45-75
Figure 741. North Fork Survivors. Contemporary $40-80
Figure 742. Unidentified. Contemporary $40-80
Figure 743. Unidentified. Contemporary $75-150
Figure 744. Gateson Recko. Contemporary $50-75
Figure 745. Bruce Troeh. Contemporary $30-60
Figure 746. Phillip Nolley. Contemporary $30-60
Figure 747. Michael Hansen, Nina Paladino Caron. Contemporary $40-80
Figure 748-749. Steven Lundberg. Contemporary $100-200
Figure 750. Harry and Wendy Besett. Contemporary $35-55
Figure 751. Harry and Wendy Besett. Contemporary $35-55
Figure 752. Beth Tomasello. Contemporary $75-120
Figure 753. George Pavliscak. Contemporary $25-50
Figure 754. Marco Jerman. Contemporary $40-80
Figure 755. Debbie and David Rosenfeldt. Contemporary $45-75
Figure 756. Christopher Rice. Contemporary
Figure 757. Dinah Hulet. Contemporary $100-200
Figure 758. Dinah Hulet. Contemporary $125-225
Figure 759. Cathy Richardson. Contemporary $50-100
Figure 760. Greg Hoglin. Contemporary $40-75
Figure 761-762. Dinah Hulet. Contemporary $150-300
Figure 763. Dinah Hulet. Contemporary $100-200
Figure 764. Dinah Hulet. Contemporary $100-200
Figure 765. Dinah Hulet. Contemporary $150-300
Figure 766. Dinah Hulet. Contemporary $150-300
Figure 767. Dinah Hulet. Contemporary $100-225
Figure 768. Fiber Optic. Machine-Ground. United States $2-5
Figure 769. Fiber Optic. Machine-Ground. United States $3-7
Figure 770. Christopher Rice. Contemporary $25-40
Figure 771-772. Mark Matthews. Contemporary $250-400
Figure 773. Paul and Dee Snell. Contemporary $30-45
Figure 774. Paul and Dee Snell. Contemporary $30-45
Figure 775-776. Paul and Dee Snell. Contemporary $30-45
Figure 777. Josh Sable. Contemporary $85-160
Figure 778. Douglas Ferguson. Contemporary $45-70
Figure 779. Douglas Ferguson. Contemporary $30-50
Figure 780. George O'Grady. Contemporary $40-70
Figure 781. "B." 1" Contemporary $15-25
Figure 782. George O'Grady. Contemporary $30-60

Figure 783. Unidentified. Contemporary	$30-60
Figure 784-785. Dustin Morell. Contemporary	$100-200
Figure 786. Shell Neisler. Contemporary	$40-70
Figure 787. Mike Edmundson. Contemporary	$50-80
Figure 788. David Salazar. Contemporary	$50-150
Figure 789. David Salazar. Contemporary	$175-250
Figure 790. David Salazar. Contemporary	$115-175
Figure 791. David Salazar. Contemporary	$200-300
Figure 792. David Salazar. Contemporary	$125-225
Figure 793. Steven Hitt. Contemporary	$150-250
Figure 794. Cathy Richardson. Contemporary	$50-100
Figure 795. Cathy Richardson. Contemporary	$50-100
Figure 796. Cathy Richardson. Contemporary	$50-100
Figure 797. Cathy Richardson. Contemporary	$50-100
Figure 798. David Salazar. Contemporary	$150-200
Figure 799. Douglas Sweet, Paulette Hall. Contemporary	$225-350
Figure 800. William Murray. Contemporary	$100-200
Figure 801. David Grant Maul. Contemporary	$75-150
Figure 802. Matthew Reinsch. Contemporary	$25-45
Figure 803. House of Glass, Joe Rice. Contemporary	$55-100
Figure 804. Steven Lundberg. Contemporary	$175-300
Figure 805-806. Beth Tomasello. Contemporary	$100-200
Figure 807. Lewis Wilson. Contemporary	$25-40
Figure 808. Matthew Reinsch. Contemporary	$25-45
Figure 809. George Pavliscak. Contemporary	$20-45
Figure 810. Chris Rice. Contemporary	$65-110
Figure 811. Harry and Kathleen Boyer. Contemporary	$40-60
Figure 812. David Grant Maul. Contemporary	$75-125
Figure 813. Mike Edmundson. Contemporary	$20-40
Figure 814. George Pavliscak. Contemporary	$35-55
Figure 815. George Pavliscak. Contemporary	$35-55
Figure 816. Mike Edmundson. Contemporary	$20-40
Figure 817. David Salazar, Jesse Siegel. Contemporary	$45-75
Figure 818. Bruce Troeh. Contemporary	$35-50
Figure 819. David Salazar. Contemporary	$75-150
Figure 820. David Salazar. Contemporary	$125-225
Figure 821. Gibson Glass, Charles Gibson.	$25-40
Figure 822. Steven Davis. Contemporary	$15-25
Figure 823. Mike Davis. Contemporary	$15-25
Figure 824. Mark Davis. Contemporary	$25-50
Figure 825. John Kobuki. Contemporary	$50-60
Figure 826. Robert LaGrand. Contemporary	$20-40
Figure 827. Lewis and Jennifer Wilson. Contemporary	$150-300
Figure 828-829. James Kontes. Contemporary	$250-350
Figure 830. Rajesh Kommineni. Contemporary	$50-65
Figure 831. Rajesh Kommineni. Contemporary	$35-55
Figure 832. Rajesh Kommineni. Contemporary	$35-55
Figure 833. Christopher Rice. Contemporary	$45-70
Figure 834. Christopher Rice. Contemporary	$45-70
Figure 835. Josh Sable. Contemporary	$90-180
Figure 836. Gerry Colman. Contemporary	$40-60
Figure 837. Christopher Rice. Contemporary	$60-100
Figure 838. Charles Gibson. Contemporary	$40-60
Figure 839. Charles Gibson. Contemporary	$50-75
Figure 840-841. Josh Sable. Contemporary	$150-250
Figure 842. Shane Caswell, Frank Oddu. Contemporary	$15-35
Figure 843. Unidentified. Contemporary	$60-80
Figure 844. Jerry Kelly. Contemporary	$30-70
Figure 845-846. Josh Sable. Contemporary	$35-70
Figure 847. Unidentified. Contemporary	$30-45
Figure 848. Drew Fritts. Contemporary	$80-175
Figure 849. Drew Fritts. Contemporary	$60-100
Figure 850. Shane Caswell. Contemporary	$30-55
Figure 851. Shane Caswell. Contemporary	$65-135
Figure 852. Dustin Morell. Contemporary	$50-100
Figure 853. Rajesh Kommineni. Contemporary	$50-100
Figure 854. Rajesh Kommineni. Contemporary	$65-125
Figure 855-856. Josh Sable. Contemporary	$150-225
Figure 857. Ben Walsh. Contemporary	$150-225
Figure 858. Shell Neisler. Contemporary	$100-200
Figure 859. Daniel Benway. Contemporary	$175-250
Figure 860. Dinah Hulet. Contemporary	$150-200
Figure 861. Dinah Hulet. Contemporary	$150-200
Figure 862. Dinah Hulet. Contemporary	$225-300
Figure 863. Dinah Hulet. Contemporary	$225-300
Figure 864. Dinah Hulet. Contemporary	$150-200

Figure 865. Steven Davis. Contemporary — $45-65
Figure 866. Christopher Rice. Contemporary — $100-200
Figure 867. Christopher Rice. Contemporary — $40-65
Figure 868-869. Jerry Kelly. Contemporary — $150-250
Figure 870. Douglas Sweet. Contemporary — $75-125
Figure 871. Douglas Sweet. Contemporary — $75-125
Figure 872. Wendy Besett. Contemporary — $225-350
Figure 873. Wendy Besett. Contemporary — $200-400
Figure 874. Mark Matthews. Contemporary — $600-700
Figure 875. David Salazar. Contemporary — $100-200
Figure 876. Mark Matthews. Contemporary — $200-400
Figure 877. Michael Hansen and Nina Paladino Caron.
  Contemporary — $75-125
Figure 878. Christopher Rice. Contemporary — $80-160
Figure 879. Harry Besett, Ken Leslie. Contemporary — $800-1300
Figure 880. Virginia Wilson, Tony Toccalino. Contemporary — $85-150
Figure 881. Earth. Gemstone. Contemporary — $30-60
Figure 882. Daniel Ambrose. Contemporary — $40-70
Figure 883. Bruce Troeh. Contemporary — $50-75
Figure 884. Bobbie Seese. Contemporary — $50-75
Figure 885. Bobbie Seese. Contemporary — $40-60
Figure 886. Steven Maslach. Contemporary — $20-35
Figure 887. Sidney and Debby Oliveira. Contemporary — $10-20
Figure 888. Sidney and Debby Oliveira. Contemporary — $10-20
Figure 889. Sidney and Debby Oliveira. Contemporary — $10-20
Figure 890-891. Paul J. Stankard. Contemporary — $10,000-15,000
Figure 892. Paul J. Stankard. Contemporary — $10,000-15,000
Figure 893-894. Paul J. Stankard. Contemporary — $11,000-15,000
Figure 895-896. Paul J. Stankard. Contemporary — $25,000-30,000
Figure 897. Paul J. Stankard. Contemporary — $15,000-30,000
Figure 898. Greg Hoglin. Clowns. — N/A Not applicable
Figure 899. Cole Herder, John Kobuki, Harry Bassett.
  Confetti Swirl, Flora, Cameo. Contemporary — N/V/A No value assigned

Select Bibliography

Barrett, Marilyn. *Aggies, Immies, Shooters and Swirls: The Magical World of Marbles*. New York: Little, Brown and Company, 1994.

Battie, David and Simon Cottle. *Sotheby's Concise Encyclopedia of Glass*. London: Conran Octopus Limited, 1997.

Baumann, Paul. *Collecting Antique Marbles*. 4th ed. Radnor, Pennsylvania: Wallace Homestead Book Co., 2004.

Bavin, William. *The Pocket Book of Marbles*. London: Outline Press Limited, 1991.

Biser, Benjamin S. *Elements of Glass and Glassmaking*. Pittsburgh, Pennsylvania: Glass and Pottery Publishing, est. 1897.

Block, Mark. *Contemporary Marbles and Related Art Glass*. Atglen, Pennsylvania: Schiffer Publishing Ltd., 2001.

Block, Robert. *Marbles: Identification and Price Guide*. 4th ed. Atglen, Pennsylvania: Schiffer Publishing Ltd., 2002.

_____. *Marbles Illustrated: Prices at Auction*. 2nd ed. Atglen, Pennsylvania: Schiffer Publishing Ltd., 2003.

Block, Stanley A. *Marble Mania*. Atglen, Pennsylvania: Schiffer Publishing Ltd., 1998.

_____. "Marbles—Playing for Fun and For Keeps." *The Encyclopedia of Collectibles*. New York: Time-Life Publications, 1979.

Bosveld, Jennifer, ed. *Glass Works: Art Glass, Windows, Bottles, Marbles, and Jars*. Johnstown, Ohio: Pudding Glass Publications, 2003.

Brooks, John A. *Glass*. New York: Golden Press, 1973.

Burton, John. *Glass: Handblown, Sculptured, Colored: Philosophy and Method*. New York: Bonanza Books, 1967.

Byrd, Joan Falconer. "Harvey Littleton Reflections, 1946-1994," *American Craft*. April/May 1999. New York: American Craft Council, 1999.

Carskadden, Jeff, and Richard Gartley. *Chinas: Hand-Painted Marbles of the Late nineteenth Century*. Parsons, West Virginia: McClain Printing Company, 1990.

Carter, Kate. "Mad About Marbles: For Collectors It's More Than Just A Game," *Cape Cod Antiques and Arts*. Orleans, Massachusetts: Community Newspaper Company, 1999.

Cloak, Evelyn Campbell. *Glass Paperweights of the Bergstrom Art Center*. New York: Crown Publishers, Inc., 1969.

Costello, Robert B. *The American Heritage College Dictionary*. 3rd ed. New York: Houghton Mifflin Company, 1997.

_____. *The American Heritage Dictionary of the English Language, 3rd Edition*. New York: Houghton Mifflin Company, 1993.

Daniels, Mary. "A Small World: Glass Artist Captures a Bit of Outer Space," *Chicago Tribune*. Chicago: Chicago Tribune Publishing Co., 11 August 1996.

Dietz, Ulysses Grant. *Paul J. Stankard: Homage to Nature*. New York: Harvey N. Abrams, Inc., 1996.

Dolez, Albane. *Glass Animals: 3,500 Years of Artistry and Design*. New York: Harry N. Abrams, Inc., 1988.

Drahotovia, Olga. *European Glass*. New York: Excalibur Books, 1983.

Eckes, Jeff. "Making a Dichroic Marble," *Glass Craftsman*. Richboro, Pennsylvania: Arts & Media, Inc., Issue No. 145, December/January 1998.

Ecklund, Rae. "Creativity Rolls Along," *Marble-Mania*. Trumbull, Connecticut: Marble Collectors Society of America, Volume 84, October 1996.Elville, E.M. *Collectors Dictionary of Glass*. London: Country Life Ltd., 1961.

Gardner, Paul V. *The Glass of Frederick Carder.* New York: Crown Publishers, 1971. Reprinted. Atglen, Pennsylvania, Schiffer Publishing, Inc., 2003.

Gartley, Richard and Jeff Carskadden. *Colonial Period and Early Nineteenth-Century Children's Toy Marbles.* Marietta, Ohio: Richardson Printing Corporation, 1998.

Grist, Everett. *Antique and Collectible Marbles. Identification & Values: 3rd ed.* Paducah, Kentucky: Collectors Books, 1992.

Hawley, Chuck. "Molten Passion," *The Arizona Republic.* Phoenix, Arizona: The Arizona Republic, 31 October 1998.

Hodkinand, Cousen. *A Textbook of Glass Technology.* London: Constable and Company Ltd., 1925.

Holm, Matthew. "Marvelous Marbles," *Country Living.* May 1998.

http://www.scouting.org

http://www.spherestoyou.com

http://www.uspto.gov/web/offices/pac/doc/general/whatis.htm

Jones, Robert. "Why Do We Collect?" *Rock & Gem.* Pasadena, California: Rock & Gem, April 1999.

Layton, Peter. *Glass Art.* Seattle, Washington: University of Washington Press, 1996.

Liebenson, Bess. "Craftwork in the American Tradition," *The New York Times.* New York: The New York Times Publishing Company, 3, December 1995.

Loomis, Frank Farmer IV. *Secrets To Affordable Antiques.* Iola, Wisconsin: Krause Publications, 2004.

Mentasti, Rosa Barovier. *Venetian Glass.* Italy: EBS Verona, 1993.

Miller, Judith. *The Illustrated Dictionary of Antiques and Collectibles.* London: Bullfinch Press, 2001.

_____. *Collectibles Price Guide 2005.* New York: DK Publishing, 2004.

_____. *20th Century Glass.* New York: DK Publishing, 2005.

Morrison, Mel, and Carl Terison. *Marbles: Identification & Price Guide.* Falmouth, Maine: Self published, date unknown.

Mortensen, Kristine. "Marvellous Marbles," *Glass.* New York: New York Experimental Glass Workshop, No. 48, Summer 1992.

Newman, Harold. *An Illustrated Dictionary of Glass.* London: Thames and Hudson Ltd., 1977.

Northend, Mary Harrod. *American Glass.* New York: Tudor Publishing Co., 1935.

Papert, Emma. *The Illustrated Guide to American Glass.* New York: Hawthorn Books, Inc., 1972.

Peterson, Marlow and Larry Castle. *Marbles: The Guide to Cat's-eyes Marbles.* Ogden, Utah: Utah Marble Connection, Inc., 1998.

_____. *Marbles: The Guide to Machine-Made Marbles: 2nd ed.* Ogden, Utah: Utah Marble Connection, Inc., 1995.

Phillips, Phoebe. *Encyclopedia of Glass.* New York: Crown Publishers, Inc., 1981.

Randall, Mark. *Marbles As Historical Artifacts.* Trumbull, Connecticut: Marble Collectors Society of America, 1979.

Reilly, Pat. *Paperweights: The Collectors Guide to Identifying, Selecting, and Enjoying New and Vintage Paperweights.* Philadelphia, Pennsylvania: Running Press Book Publishers, 1994.

Revi, Albert C., ed. *Spinning Wheel's Collectible Glass.* Hanover, Pennsylvania: Everbody's Press, Inc., 1974.

_____. *Encyclopedia of American Cut & Engraved Glass.* Atglen, Pennsylvania: Schiffer Publishing Ltd., 2000.

Rice, Jane Ann. *The Story of St Clair Glass*. Ellwood, Indiana: Richard E. Harney, date unknown.

Rogers, Frances, and Alice Beard. *5000 Years of Glass*. New York: Frederick A. Stokes Company, 1937.

Runyan, Cathy C. *Knuckles Down!* Kansas City, Missouri: Right Brain Publishing, 1985.

Schuler, Frederic. *Flame working: Glassmaking for the Craftsman*. Philadelphia: Chilton Book Company, 1968.

Selman, Lawrence, and Linda Pope-Selman. *Paperweights for Collectors*. Santa Cruz, California: Paperweight Press, 1975.

Sturges, Hollister III, curator. *Visionary Landscapes: The Glasswork of Josh Simpson*. Grennwich, Connecticut: Bruce Museum, 1998.

Tait, Hugh. *Glass 5000 Years*. New York: Harry Abrams, Inc., 1991.

Toso, Gianfranco. *Murano: A History of Glass*. Venice: Arsenale Editrice, 2000.

Van Tassel, Valentine. *American Glass*. New York: Gramercy Publishing Co., 1920.

Vose, Ruth Hurst. *Glass*. London: The Connoisseur, 1975.

Voynick, Steve. "The Magic and Mystery of Glass," *Rock & Gem*. Pasadena, California: Rock & Gem, December 1998.

Webb, Dennis. *Greenburg's Guide to Marbles*. 2nd ed. Sykesville, Maryland: Greenburg Publishing Co., 1994.

Wittmann, Otto, director. *American Glass Now*. Toledo, Ohio: The Toledo Museum of Art, 1972.

Yelle, Richard Wilfred. *Glass Art from Urban Glass*. Atglen, Pennsylvania, Schiffer Publishing Ltd., 2000.

_____. *International Glass Art*. Atglen, Pennsylvania, Schiffer Publishing Ltd., 2003.

Photography and Collection Credits

All photographic illustrations provided by any artist or craftsmen has been credited in the caption for the work illustrated. All crafted pieces illustrated have been credited in the caption courtesy of the appropriate individual(s). The author and Schiffer Publishing Ltd. have provided any unlisted photographic figure illustrations.

Index

General Index

1976 Copyright Act, 46
Acknowledgements, 4
Advertising items, 129
Agate, 75
Agate marbles, 74
Aggie, 35
Akro Agate Company, 35, 125, 149
Akro Agate Corkscrew, 125
Akro Agate Popeye, 125
Akron, Ohio, 125
Alloway, James, 37
American and Sandwich Glass Company, 123
American art form, 32
American Brilliant Cut, 38
American craft, 27
American Heritage Dictionary, College Dictionary, The, 3rd edition, 34, 148
Amethyst, 75
Andy, 129
Angelfish, 40
Annealing oven, 49, 52, 51, 53
Annie, 129
Antique German china, 49
Antique handmade, 56, 151
Apprentice, 47
Art glass, 148
Art Nouveau, 25
Artificial mineral, 123
Artist's mark, 19, 40, 44, 45, 149
Artist's proof, 54, 55
Artist's serigraph print, 43
Associated price, 55
Associated Value Guide, 54, 239
Assyrian pattern, 22
Auction, 38
Auction price, 239
Authenticity, 149
Author's Note, 19
Aventurine glass, 123
Baccarat, 39
Banded lutz, 123
Banded swirl marbles, 78
Beachball, 40
Beads, 227
Beer bottle, 31
Beetem, Geoffrey, 11, 40
Before the Common Era (B.C.E.), 20
Bennington, 9, 12
Bennington marbles, 59
Bennington, Vermont, 59
Berkeley, California, 10
Berkshire Hathaway Company, 27
Besett, Harry, 2, 11
Betty, 129
Bibliography, 56, 252
Bimbo, 129
Blake, Brendan, 229
Blizzard mica, 106
Block, Ann, 5
Block, Claire, 4, 12
Block, Emily, 5
Block, Robert, 4, 12
Block, Stanley, 4, 12
Bocce, 73
Borosilicate, 11, 27, 32
Botanical glass sculpture, 17
Botanical Orb, 17, 151
Brazil, 35, 75
Breslow, Bruce, 4
Bull's eyes, 59
Cage, 50
Calin, Rudy, 229
Cambridge, Ohio, 125
Cane- and rod-cut, 11, 49, 52
Captain Marble, 10, 12
Carder, Fredrick, 22
Carnelian, 75
Carpet Balls, 73
Cat's-eye, 36, 126
Cat's-eye marbles, 127
Ceramic figure, 108
Chalcedony, 75
Champion, 149
Chihuly, Dale, 26, 26
Child's plaything, 14, 15, 31, 125, 148
China, 36, 41
China marbles, 59
Chips, 55
Christensen Agate Company, 35, 125, 149
Christensen, Martin, 125
Christmas Tree, 132
Circular lines, 59
Clambroth swirl marbles, 84
Clambroths, 49
Clara S. Peck Endowment, 20
Clark, Richard, 229
Clarksburg, West Virginia, 125

Clark-Thomas, Jill, 4
Classification, 54
Clay marbles, 57, 58, 59
Cloud, 112
Cloudiness, 55
Cohen, Bertram, 12
Cold work, 27
Collectible, 55
Collectible field, 37
Columbia University, 25
Comics, 129
Commemorative coins, 43
Commemorative stamps, 43
Commodity, 55, 148
Concise History of Glass, 20
Confetti, 36
Contemporary Marble Movement, 3, 4, 14, 15, 16, 17, 29, 30, 31, 32, 37, 45, 46, 227, 228, 229
Contemporary Marbles and Related Art Glass, 14, 15, 16
Copper, 123
Copyright, 19, 46
Coreless swirl marbles, 78
Corkscrew marbles, 127
Corning Ewer, The, 20
Corning Glass Works, 22
Corning Museum of Glass, The, 4, 20, 21, 22, 25, 26
Cotes Master Loaf, 129
Cottage industry, 34
Crockery marbles, 58, 59, 73
Crow's feet, 59
Crucible, 47
Crystalline quartz, 75
Cut glass, 23
Damage, 149
Dane, Robert, 228
Daschbach, James, 32
Daum, Nancy, 45
Davis Handmade Marbles, 229
Davis, Steve, 48, 229
Decorative glass house, 47, 48
Decorative objects, 54
Dedication, 3
Diamond-bit setting, 45
Dichroic glass, 151
Dings, 55
Displaying, 38
Divided core swirl marbles, 86
Doherty, Jr., W.E., 22
Driesbach, Fritz, 26
Dyed, 35
Dyed agates, 75
Ebay, 33
Edmundson, Mike, 4, 229
Eisch, Erwin, 25
Emergence Four-Stage, 25
Emma, 129
Encased, 108
Encased transfers, 129
End-of-Day, 12, 34, 48, 49, 112, 114, 121
Engraving, 23
Enhance color, 75
Etching, 23
Europe, 47, 228
Excellent, 54
Experimental, 41, 44, 54, 55
Facet, 75
Feld, Samuel B., Mr. and Mrs., 22
Fenton Glass, 48
Fern Green Tower, 26
Fine art, 149
Fine, Jodene Goldenring, 4, 49, 50, 51
Fine, Jody, 4, 9, 10, 12, 30, 30, 31, 45, 49, 227
Firing, 49
Flamework, 17, 19, 27, 32, 41
Flame-working, 11
Flaming Dragon, 132
Flora, 59, 73
Floral glass paperweights, 17
Foil coated, 57
Foreign manufactured, 125
Foreword, 9
French paperweights, 107
Frieburg, C., 4
Fulbright Scholarship, 26
Fulbright-Hayes fellowship, 26
Functional glass house, 48
Furnace, 47, 49
Galle, 45
Gallery, 55
Gallery shops, 41
Gas, 55
Gas/oxygen torch, 32, 49, 52
Gemstone, 75
German, 125
German cottage industry, 125

German handmade, 15, 19
Germany, 25, 31, 34, 35, 123
Giberson, Dudley, 228
Gibson, Charles, 48
Gibson Glass, 47, 48
Gift shops, 41
Glass art objects, 47
Glass cullet, 27
Glass rods, 32, 49
Glass scissor, 49
Glass shear, 49
Glass stock cane, 49
Glassblowing, 25
Glasses, 47
Glazed, 73
Glazing, 49
Glory hole, 49, 52
Glossary of Terms, 233
Golden age of machine-made marbles, 35, 125
Goldstone, 123
Good, 55
Good Friday, 34
Grading, 54
Graphite blocks, 52
Graphite mold, 32, 51, 52, 53
Great Depression, 36, 125
Greenberg, Daniel, 26
Grinding, 49
Guinea cocks, 128
Guinea marbles, 128
Guinea-Cobra, 128
H.O.T.M.I.R.E., 10, 30
H.P. Sinclaire & Company, 22
Hamon Handcrafted Glass, 47
Hand cut, 75
Hand cut agate, 35
Handcrafted, 56
Hand painted figure, 108
Hand-painted china, 39, 41, 47, 49
Hand-rolling, 49
Hawkes, T.J., 22
Hazy glass, 55
Heat-treated, 75
Heisch, John, 9, 49, 50, 51
Helix, 49
Herbie, 129
Hobbyist, 148
Holmes, James, 11, 12
Hot metal imprinting, 45
Houghton, Arthur, 20
House of Glass, 47, 48
Hula hoop, 36
Hunt Glass Works, 22
Iacovino-Stankard, Pauline, 4
Idar-Oberstein, 35, 75
Identification, 45
Identifying marks, 54
India, 35, 75
Indian lutz, 123
Indian swirl marbles, 88
Indiana, 47
Indians, 49
Industrial Revolution, 23, 35
Internet, 37, 41, 55, 56, 239
Intersecting lines, 73
Investment potential, 37
Islamic, 20
Italian, 151
Italian glass, 31
Italian paperweights, 107
Italian renaissance, 20
J. Hoare & Company, 22
Jabo-Vitro, 126
Jacks, 36
Japan, 15, 36, 126, 127
Jasper, 75
Jewelry, 149
Johns Manville #475 Fiberglass marbles, 25, 27, 27
Joseph's Coat, 34
Joseph's Coat swirl marbles, 104
Josh Simpson Contemporary Glass, 4, 28
Juedemann, Chris and Lissa, 37, 230
Kayo, 129
Keller, Henry, 22
Kelly, Jerry, 4, 32
Ketchup and Mustard, 132
Kiln work, 27
King Syndicate, 129
Knuckling down, 126
Koko, 129
Kommineni, Rajesh, 32
Labino, Dominick, 25, 227
Lapidary process, 49
Latticinio core swirl, 34
Latticinio core swirl marbles, 89
Laubs, Ray, 230
Laucha, Germany, 34

Leslie, Ken, 2
Levin, Deborah, 4
Lilac Honeycomb Bouquet Swarm Orb, 17, 18
Lime, 20
Limited edition, 40, 41, 43, 54, 55
Limited edition decorative plates, 43
Lipofsky, Marvin, 26
Littleton, Harvey, 25, 25, 31, 227
Lobed, 122
Lonsway, Brian, 31, 228
Lundberg, Steven, 31
Lutz, 34, 123
Lutz, Nicholas, 123
M.F. Christensen & Son Company, 125
Macdonald, Nadine, 230
Machine-made, 15, 56, 148, 151
Machine-made marbles, 49, 56, 125
Madison, Wisconsin, 25
Marble collecting, 31
Marble collectors, 31, 32
Marble Collectors Society of America, 4, 12, 30, 31, 54
Marble King, 149
Marble production, 125
Marble set-up, 49, 52
Marble shearing mechanism, 126
Marble stock, 51
Marin County, California, 29, 29
Marin County Renaissance Faire, 29
Market conditions, 41
Market price, 40
Market value, 55, 239
Marquis Deluxe Studios, 11
Marquis, Richard, 10, 11, 26, 26, 29, 30, 30, 31, 227
Marquiscarpa #26, 26
Marver, 49, 52
Maslach, Steven, 31, 38, 45, 227
Mass production, 49
Massachusetts, 123
Master Marble, 35
Master Marble Company, 125
Matthews, Mark, 11
MCSA, 4, 12, 31, 54
Medical field, 126
Medicinal properties, 76
Megaplanet, 28
Metaphysical properties, 76
Mexico, 15, 35, 36, 56, 75, 126, 127
Mica, 49, 123
Mica marbles, 106
Mid-Atlantic, U.S., 47
Mid-western United States, 227
Mid-Western, U.S., 47
Milky-white base, 84
Millefiori, 151
Millefiori canes, 107
Millefiori marble, 107
Mimics, 148
Mineral, 75
Mineral collectors, 75
Mineral marbles, 39, 74, 75
Mineralogist, 75
Mint, 54
Mocha ware, 73
Modern American Paperweight Movement, 151
Moon, 129
Moon Marble Company, 4
Moretti glass, 32
Morgan Cup, The, 20
Mount Pleasant, New York, 22
Murano, 20, 26
Murrini, 151
Murrini sphere, 29, 30
Museum shops, 41
Mythical figure, 108
National Endowment for the Arts, The, 25
Natural gas, 47
Near mint, 54
Neisler, Shell, 4, 32
New York, 25
Nex Products, Inc., 146
Noble Effort, 30, 30
Nolley, Phillip, 230
Non-glass handmade marbles, 56
Novel and Inventive, 15, 56, 151
Numbered, 55
Ohio, 47, 125
Ohio River Valley, 27, 35, 125
Oily sheen, 149
Olof Elder, Tommy, 28
Onionskin, 12, 34, 48, 114
Onionskin lutz, 123
Onyx, 133
Opaque, 78
Opaque marbles, 49

Open edition production stock, 40, 41, 42, 43, 54
Ornamental objects, 54
Ornaments, 41
Orrefors crystal, 151
Ottawa, Illinois, 125
Paneled Cloud, 121
Paperweight marble, 107
Paperweights, 41, 43, 151, 227
Patch, 127, 128, 129
Pate de vere, 17, 27
Pavliscak, George, 230
Peltier, 149
Peltier Glass Company, 35, 125
Peltier National Line Rainbo, 125
Peppermint swirl, 92
Photography and Collection Credits, 254
Picture marbles, 129
Piece(s), 19
Pitting, 54
Planets, 38
Polished pebbles, 75
Polishing, 49
Pontil, 49, 125, 148
Porcelain, 149
Potash, 20
Premium, 55
Pressed glass, 23
Prestige Glass, 47, 48
Primary market, 239
Private sale, 38
Production-style, 48
Promotional items, 129
Prototype, 41, 42, 43, 44, 54, 55
Provenance, 38, 55
Punty, 50, 52, 53
Purser, Ro, 11, 29, 30, 30, 31, 227
Pyrex, 32
Quartz, 75, 123
Raw materials, 55
Recko, Gateson 4, 32, 38, 230
Regular stock, 40, 41, 42, 43, 54
Renaissance Faire, 30
Renaissance festival, 29
Repairs, 148, 149
Reproductions, 148
Research questions, 14, 227
Retail price, 54, 55, 239
Ribbon core swirl marbles, 92
Ribbon lutz, 123
Ribbon marbles, 132
Ribbon swirls, 29
Rice, Christopher, 32, 37, 230
Ring Taw, 125
Ringer, 36
Rockwell, Robert III and the Rockwell Museum, 22
Rod- and cane-cut, 29, 30, 32, 41, 49
Roman empire, 20
Rube Goldberg, 126
Russian pattern, 22
Sable, Josh, 32
Safety eye ware, 49
Salazar, David, 4, 11, 31, 40, 228
Salt glaze, 59
Sand, 20, 47
Sandy, 129
Saratoga (Mountain) Glass Works, 22
Scenic painted, 59
Schiffer, Nancy, 5
Schiffer, Peter, 5
Schiffer Publishing Ltd., 5
Scouts, 36
Scratches, 55
Scribing, 45
Sculptural art glass, 227
Sculptural objects, 41
Seattle, Washington, 26
Secondary market, 239
Seese, Bobbie, 231
Seese, Eddie, 48, 231
Sheared, 125
Signature cane, 45
Signature mark, 45
Signed, 55
Silhouette cane, 151
Simpson, Josh, 11, 27, 27, 28, 31, 38, 227
Single-gather, 52
Skeezix, 129
Slag marbles, 133
Slag style, 126
Slump work, 27
Smitty, 129
Smoky quartz, 75
Snyder, Jeffrey, 5
Soaking oven, 49, 51
Soda, 20
Soda bottles, 31

Soft glass, 27
Solid core swirl marbles, 101
Spherestoyou.com, 77
St. Clair, Joe, 31, 48, 228
Stankard, Paul, 4, 17, 17, 18, 37, 151
Starbucks Coffee Company, 146
Stardust clambroth, 40
Steinhauser, Susan, 26
Steuben, 39, 45
Steuben division, 22
Stone, 74
Striated, 148
Studio art, 56
Studio glass, 47
Studio glass house, 45
Studio Glass Movement, 25, 26, 29, 227
Sulphide, 108
Summers, Ruth T., 26
Superman, 132
Sweet, Douglas, 11
Swirl, 48, 49, 78
Swirl marbles, 137
T.J. Hawkes & Company, 22
Taj, Jesse, 32
Thousand flowers, 151
Tias, 33
Tiffany, 45, 151
Tinsley Green, England, 34
Toccalino, Anthony, 231
Toledo Museum of Art, 25
Tom Mix, 129
Torch, 49
Torchwork, 19, 27, 32, 41
Torchwork method, 32, 47
Trademark, 19, 46
Transfer marbles, 129
Transitional marble, 126
Translucent, 78
Transparent, 78
Troch, Bruce, 231
Trompe l'oeil, 17
Twentieth century, 125
Twenty-first century, 228
U.S. Postal Service, 43
United Kingdom, 73
United States, 15, 35, 47, 228
United States Mint, 43
United States Patent and Trademark Office, 46
Universe Marble, 38
Unmarred, 54
Unsigned, 19, 148, 149
Vacor de Mexico, 36, 126
Values, 54
Venice, 20
Venini glass factory, 26
Very good, 54
Vintage, 55
Vitro Agate, 35
Vitro Agate Company, 125
Vortex, 151
Wald, Rolf and Genie, 3, 4, 11, 31, 40, 228
Walsh, Ben, 232
Waterford, 148
Waters, Bruce, 5
Waugh, Tim, 232
Wax, Jack, 10, 11, 30, 30, 227
Wear, 55
West, Aaron, 232
West Coast, U.S., 47
West Virginia, 47
Wet-mint, 54
Wheaton Village Marble Weekend, 39
Whitman, Walt, 17
Wickham, Ethel F., Miss, 22
Wildwood, New Jersey, 34
Wilson, Virginia, 231
Wooden blocks, 52
Woolworth's, 31
Work(s), 19
World Congress of Craftsmen, 25
World War, 35
World War I, 125
World War II, 36, 47, 125
Written record, 38
Yahoo, 33
Yo-Yo, 36

Illustrations Index
Agate, Germany, 35, 74, 75
Banded swirl, Germany, 78
Bennington, Germany, 59
Carpet Ball, Germany, 73
Cat's-eye, Japan, 126
China, Germany, 59
Clambroth, Germany, 84
Clay, Germany, 57
Crockery, Germany, 58
Divided core swirl, Germany, 34, 86
End-of-Day, Cloud, Germany, 112
End-of-Day, Paneled Onionskin, Germany, 34, 121
Fancy Bennington, Germany, 59
Goldstone, Mexico, 123
Transitional, United States, 126
Indian swirl, Germany, 88
Joseph's Coat swirl, Germany, 104
Latticinio core swirl, Germany, 89
Lobed Onionskin, Germany, 122
Lutz, Germany, 123
Marble rod stock, Germany, 34

Micas, Germany, 34, 106
Onionskin, Germany, 114
Peppermint swirl, Germany, 92
Picture marbles, United States, 129
Ribbon core swirl, Germany, 92
Solid core swirl, Germany, 101
Stoneware, Germany, 58
Sulphide marbles, Germany, 108

Contemporary Heading Illustrations
Clay
Single Gather
Kirkland, James, 58
Parent, Steve, 57

China
Single Gather
Brown, Robert, 60, 67, 70, 71
Macdonald, Nadine, 60, 61, 62, 63, 64, 65, 66, 69, 70, 71, 72
Pessman, Gregg, 59, 63, 64, 65, 66, 67, 68, 69, 71, 72
Smith, Coralee, 72
Thornburgh, Tom, 60, 61, 64, 70, 71

Carpet Ball
Single Gather
Carpet Ball, China, 73

Mineral
Single Ground
Crazy Lace Agate, Mexico, 76
Dry head agate, Utah, 76
Fluorite in Limestone, Canada, 76
Golden Rutilated Quartz, Mexico, 76
Petrified wood, Arizona, 76
Sodalite, Brazil, 76
Tigereye, Brazil, 76

Banded and Coreless Swirl
Bermuda Glass Blowing Studio, 82
Besett, Harry, 82
Dane, Robert, 83
Danowski, Dale, 80
Davis, Steve, 79, 80
Fine, Jody, 81
Giberson, Dudley, 78
Lichtman, Robert, 82
Murray, William, 78
Nolley, Phillip, 83
Potter, Matthew, 80
Salazar, David, 83
Seese, Eddie, 79, 81
Wald, Rolf and Genie, 81, 83

Clambroth Swirl
Beetem, Geoffrey, 85
Danowski, Dale, 85
Edmundson, Mike, 85
Fritts, Drew, 84, 85

Divided Core Swirl
Lauenstein, Fritz, 87
Maslach, Steven, 87
Nolley, Phillip, 86, 87
Troch, Bruce, 87

Indian Swirl
Robinson, Christopher, 88

Latticinio Core Swirl
Alloway, James, 91
Dane, Robert, 90
Fine, Jody, 39, 89
Giberson, Dudley, 90
Gibson Glass, Charles Gibson, 90
Greiner-Adams, Rolf, 91
Lichtman, Robert, 91
Maslach, Steven, 91
Rosenfeld, Ken, 90
Seese, Eddie, 91
Sweet, Douglas, 39
Teign Valley Glass, 91

Peppermint Swirl
Gibson Glass, Charles Gibson, 92
Matthews, Mark, 92

Ribbon Core Swirl
Boyer, Harry and Kathleen, 94
Burchfield, William, 98, 99
Coupal, Francis, 97
Dane, Robert, 93, 98
Fine, Jody, 93, 95, 97
Giberson, Dudley, 93, 95, 100
Grant Maul, David, 97
Hansen, Michael and Nina Paladino Caron, 98, 100
LaGrand, Robert, 99
Lauenstein, Fritz, 96, 100
Marquis, Richard, 97
Maslach, Steven, 94, 95, 96
Salazar, David, 98
Seese, Eddie, 98
Wald, Rolf and Genie, 93, 95
Widner, Fred, 94

Solid Core Swirl
Burchfield, William, 101
Davis, Steve, 102

Fine, Jody, 104
Greiner-Adams, Rolf, 102
Holmes, James, 104
Lichtman, Robert, 101
Maslach, Steven, 103
Nolley, Phillip, 103
Oddu, Frank, 101
Salazar, David, 102
Seese, Eddie, 102, 103
Sweet, Douglas, 103
Wald, Rolf and Genie, 103, 104

Joseph's Coat Swirl
Davis, Steve, 105
Fritts, Drew, 105, 106
Lauenstein, Fritz, 104, 105
Seese, Eddie, 106
Sweet, Douglas, 105
Talmage, John K., 105
Wald, Rolf and Genie, 105

Mica
Murray, William, 106
Zimmerman, Bart and Kerry, 106

Paperweight/Millefiori
Caswell, Shane, 151, 152, 153
Colman, Gerry and Pat, 156, 157, 159
Edmundson, Mike, 152, 153
Ferguson, Douglas, 159
Fine, Jody, 161
Gentile, John, Gentile Glass, 155, 156
Gilvey, Luke, 158
Hart, James, 107
Hoglin, Greg, 107, 153, 161
Hulet, Dinah, 153, 154
Juedemann, Chris and Lissa, 154, 160
Kelly, Jerry, 158
Kommineni, Rajesh, 160
Marquis, Richard, 157, 158
Morell, Dustin, 151
Neisler, Shell, 151
O'Grady, Kevin, 154
Parker, Anthony, 107
Purser, Ro, 157, 158
Strobel, David, 162
Sweet, Douglas, 155, 160
Taj, Jesse, 32
Wilson, Lewis and Jennifer, 152, 153

Sulphide
Besett, Harry, 112
Davis, Jim, 110, 112
Davis, Rick, 110
Gibson, Charles, Gibson Glass, 109, 110
Hogue, Sam, 110, 111
Laubs, Ray, 110, 111
Miller, Boyd, 110
Rice, Joe, House of Glass, 109
Snell, Paul and Dee, 111
St. Clair, Joe, 108, 109
Thornburgh, Tom, 110, 111

End-of-Day, Cloud
Davis, Jim (IN), 112
Lichtman, Robert, 113
Seese, Bobbie, 113

End-of-Day, Onionskin
Boyer, Harry and Kathleen, 116, 117
Burchfield, William, 118
Crider, Terry, 121
Davis, Jim, 115, 116
Davis, Jim (IN), 114, 115
Davis, Steve, 114, 117
Hamon, Robert, 115
Lichtman, Robert, 115, 118, 119
Miller, Boyd, 118
Nolley, Phillip, 115, 116, 118
Salazar, David, 114, 115, 118
Seese, Bobbie, 114
Seese, Eddie, 118, 119
Sweet, Douglas, 121
Wald, Rolf and Genie, 118

End-of-Day, Paneled Cloud or Onionskin
Coupal, Francis, 122
Stankus, Russell, 121

End-of-Day, Lobed Onionskin
Davis, Jim, 123
Davis, Jim (IN), 122
Davis, Mike, 123
Davis, Steve, 123
Parke, Kris, 123

Lutz or Aventurine Glass
Greiner-Adams, Rolf, 124
Matthews, Mark, 124
Miller, John Hamon, 124
Wald, Rolf and Genie, 124

American Machine-made and Foreign Manufactured
Assorted, China, 146
Cat's-eye, Japan, 36, 127, 147

Corkscrew
Corkscrew, 35
Corkscrew, Akro Agate Company, 127

Patrick, Scott, 127
Shields, Kristen, 127

Guinea
Edmundson, Mike, 128
Guinea, Christensen Agate Company, 128
Hogue, Sam, 128
Livesy, Robert, 128
Nolley, Phillip, 128
Pound, Chuck, 128

Opaques, China, 146

Patch
Edmundson, Mike, 129
Marble King Inc., 129
Patch, Akro Agate Company, 128
Patch, Vitro Agate Company, 128
Powers, Robert, 129
Vacor de Mexico, 129

Transfer
Bennett, Harold, 130
Castle, Larry, Peterson, Marlow, 131
Golden Rule, 131
Picture marbles, Peltier Glass Company, 129
Reproduction Picture marbles box, 129

Ribbon and Swirl
Ambrose, Daniel, 112
Calin, Rudy, 38, 93
Capel, Mark, 116
Conklin, Teri, 119
Edmundson, Mike, 132, 143
Foreign, China, 145
Fritts, Drew, 80, 117, 119, 143
Grumbling, Dan, 96, 143
Hoglin, Greg, 97, 142
Kelly, Jerry, 94, 95
Livesy, Robert, 115, 143
Maslach, Steven, 87
McGlothlin, Phil, 137, 143
Miller, John Hamon, 132, 141, 150
Murray, William, 93
Neisler, Shell, 80
Park, Jerry, 102, 114, 117, 141, 142
Parke, Kris, 123
Parker, Anthony, 142
Patrick, Scott, 132, 144, 145, 149
Pavliscak, George, 116, 117, 119
Pound, Chuck, 94
Ribbon, Akro Agate Company, 132
Ribbon, Champion Agate Company, 132
Ribbon, Christensen Agate Company, 132
Robinson, Christopher, 83, 88, 102, 141, 143, 150
Seese, Bobbie, 143
Swirl, 35
Swirl, Christensen Agate Company, 138
Swirl, German swirls, 138, 139
Swirl, Jabo-Vitro Agate Company, 138, 140
Swirl, Patch, Peltier Glass Company, 139
Swirl, Peltier Glass Company, 139
Swirl, Ravenswood Novelty Works, 137
Tomasello, Beth, 96
Troch, Bruce, 78, 87, 93, 142
Turner, Howard, 137
Walsh, Ben, 119
West, Aaron, 143
West Virginia swirls, 138
Wilganowski, Fred, 144, 150

Slags
Blake, Brendan, 134, 136
Breslow, Bruce, 135
Calin, Rudy, 38
Clark, Richard, 134, 135, 136
Edmundson, Mike, 134
Park, Jerry, 135, 136, 137
Patrick, Scott, 133
Powers, Robert, 134
Slag, Akro Agate Company, 133
Slag, M.F. Christensen & Son Company, 133
St. Clair, Joe, 133
Tomasello, Beth, 135
Wilson, Virginia and Anthony Toccalino, 135

Striped opaque, Czechoslovakia, 139

Murrini
Colman, Gerry, 159
Constantin, Christopher, 153
Parker, Anthony, 153
Young, Kathy, 153

Novel and Inventive Contemporary
Ambrose, Daniel, 219
Besett, Harry and Ken Leslie, 218
Besett, Harry and Wendy, 187, 216
Besett, Wendy, 169
Block, Emily and Kevin Block, 58
Boyer, Harry and Kathleen, 32, 201
Calin, Rudy, 38
Earth, China, 219
Gibson, Charles, Gibson Glass, 203
Hitt, Steven, 196
House of Glass, Joe Rice, 48
Image 3 Crystal, Laser crystal, 42
Kontes, James, 205
Lichtman, Robert, 141

Lundberg, Steven, 199
Maslach, Steven, 220
Matthews, Mark, 216
Maul, David Grant, 199, 201
Murray, William, 198
Oliveira, Sidney and Debby, 220
Rice, Joe, House of Glass, 199
Richardson, Cathy, 162, 163, 164, 197
Rosenfeldt, N. David and Debbie, 188
Salazar, David, 171, 172, 173, 174, 179, 195, 196, 198, 202, 203
Seese, Bobbie, 219
Simpson, Josh, 181, 182, 183, 184
Stankard, Paul, 221, 222, 223, 224, 225, 226
Sweet, Douglas, 181, 184, 216
Sweet, Douglas and Paulette Hall, 198
Tomasello, Beth, 200
Troch, Bruce, 219
Wald, Rolf and Genie, 166
Wilson, Lewis, 200
Wilson, Lewis and Jennifer, 38, 205

Rake Pull
Benway, Daniel, 213
Caswell, Shane, 209, 211
Colman, Gerry, 207
Ferguson, Douglas, 193
Fritts, Drew, 32, 210
Hoglin, Greg, 189
Hulet, Dinah, 188, 189, 190, 191, 213, 214
Kelly, Jerry, 209, 215
Kommineni, Rajesh, 206, 211, 212
Morell, Dustin, 211
O'Grady, George, 193, 194
Oddu, Frank, 209
Rice, Christopher, 188, 207, 214, 215
Richardson, Cathy, 189
Sable, Josh, 193, 206, 208, 209, 210, 212
Troch, Bruce, 188
Walsh, Ben, 212

Vortex
Edmundson, Mike, 195
Kommineni, Rajesh, 206
Morell, Dustin, 38, 47, 194
Neisler, Shell, 195, 213

More Rod- and Cane-Cut
Beetem, Geoffrey, 40, 42, 47, 166, 167
Davis Handmade Marbles, Jim Davis Master Marble Maker Family Collection, 43
Davis, Mark, 204
Davis, Mike, 204
Davis, Steve, 204, 214
Devi, Shanti, 184
Fiber Optic, 191
Fine, Jody, 42
Gibson Glass, Charles Gibson, 48, 208
Hansen, Michael and Nina Paladino Caron, 47, 186, 217
Lauenstein, Fritz, 42
Lundberg, Steven, 187
Lundberg Studios, 167
Matthews, Mark, 44, 192, 217
Nolley, Phillip, 186
North Fork Survivors, Mt. St. Helen's Ash, 185
Parker, Anthony, 218
Rice, Christopher, 191
Salazar, David, 40, 44, 164, 217
St. Clair Glass Work, Joe St. Clair, 48
Wald, Rolf and Genie, 40, 42, 164, 167
Wilson, Virginia and Anthony Toccalino, 168, 218

More Torchwork
Conklin, Teri, 180, 181
Creekmore, Sara, 164, 165
Daschbach, James, 32
Dunham, David, 164, 165
Edmundson, Mike, 85, 202
Federici, Karen, 170
Ferguson, Douglas, 180
Fritts, Drew, 84, 85, 178, 179
Gaenzel, Victor, 177
Hoglin, Greg, 176, 233
Hulet, Dinah, 58
Jerman, Marco, 188
Kelly, Jerry, 178
Kobuki, John, 204
LaGrand, Robert, 205
Morgan, Gale, 180
Parke, Kris, 32, 92
Parker, Anthony, 170
Pavliscak, George, 174, 177, 188, 201, 202
Recko, Gateson, 33, 168, 185
Reinsch, Matthew, 199, 200
Rice, Christopher, 201
Richardson, Cathy, 164, 177
Snell, Paul and Dee, 192
Taj, Jesse, 171
Tomasello, Beth, 176, 188
Troch, Bruce, 170, 186, 203
Vogt, David, 180
Waugh, Tim, 177
Wilson, Lewis and Jennifer, 174, 175, 176